CORRESPONDENCE

OF

JAMES FENIMORE-COOPER

OTSEGO HALL

After John Augustus Hows.

CORRESPONDENCE

OF

JAMES FENIMORE-COOPER

EDITED BY HIS GRANDSON

JAMES FENIMORE COOPER

VOLUME TWO

 BOOKS FOR LIBRARIES PRESS

FREEPORT, NEW YORK

First Published 1922
Reprinted 1971

INTERNATIONAL STANDARD BOOK NUMBER:
0-8369-5881-0

LIBRARY OF CONGRESS CATALOG CARD NUMBER:
70-164597

PRINTED IN THE UNITED STATES OF AMERICA

PART THIRD

(CONTINUED)

Lydenham, near Philadelphia, August 21, 1839
Dear Sir:

Though not my good fortune to know you personally,
I can be no stranger to your well-deserved fame, and I
should be ashamed of taking my pen at so late a day as
this to return you my share of the public thanks for your
admirable naval history, the approbation of it at home
having already been universal and abroad too, as far as
I have seen, but that accidental hindrances prevented my
reading it until very lately. Devoted to our navy, I had
myself during the war of 1812, when a young and humble
member of Mr. Madison's administration, collected some
materials for sketches of its brilliant career at that epoch,
which I rejoice to think I never used; for you have
brought to that part of its history, and all other parts,
qualifications so immeasurably in advance of any one else
that all will have been instructed by you, as well as delighted. You have told us all that any other pen could,
and much, much more. You have shown all our naval
glory in its best lights, yet been just to our great opponent
on the ocean; your narratives are distinct and graphic,
often enchanting; and your reflections scattered throughout the work such as add dignity and value to it—merit-
ing in many instances the careful consideration of our
Legislators and Statesmen. You have given to your
country a work greatly wanted; one that from its entire
execution as well as matter must become standard, and
that will be even more valuable ages hence than now, as
you have embalmed much of what would otherwise soon
have perished.

I have not been able to repress the expression to you
of these my feelings on perusing your work, for which

I think the public gratitude as well as thanks is your due; and I beg, dear Sir, to tender to you the assurances of great respect with which I am

your obedient Servt and fellow

Countryman Richard Rush

TO MRS. COOPER, COOPERSTOWN

Head's, Friday evening, Oct. 4, 1839

My dear wife,

We reached Henderson in good time, and found that Cruger had invited three of his neighbors to dinner. We dined at ½ past 6, and broke up at 5 the next morning. Cruger took me down to Herkimer, and I got into the cars. The train was late, and I had just time to get into the boat, reached town in a storm, but it cleared up and I passed the day there until 5, when I came on here. Ogden was at Saratoga, but I did a little business. I saw Worth and a few friends, but came off in due time.

Lea & Blanchard have about 250 copies of first edition on hand, and we begin to print to-morrow. The book has a great name, and is looking down opposition. Attempts are to be made against it however, in Rhode Island and in the *North American*. I am too strong in truth for them. My publishers keep their feet well these hard times, and paid two of their notes to me, $1350, last week. The *History*, first and last, will make me from $10,000. to $15,000.—with the third volume, quite the latter, I think.

I have been to see Mrs. Rush, but did not find her in. Barton is here, and is about to set up housekeeping, permanently. Willing keeps his house, etc., the *meubles* belonging to Madame. As for Tom, he has the prospect of a valuable agency. Miss Hall has changed her mind with regard to Mr. Pope, in consequence of learning that her cousin, the pretty Miss Coleman, had refused him.

The President is expected here in a day or two, and I shall go and see him. The whole court is turning its head south.

I have not yet seen Tom Stevens. Col. Drayton I have seen, and he has asked me to dine with him. Blanchard has given me a handsome copy of Prescott's *Ferdinand and Isabella*. Not many new books.

Elliott comes out of the inquiry well. He is acquitted of every thing originally charged, and only censured for a few light incidental matters. Even Biddle I am told acquits him of the Hunter and the Barton charge. Stewart says that there is no ground for a court, and it is said has given a very able opinion. Biddle and Patterson did not agree in particulars, though they think there ought to be a court. Patterson died of apoplexy.

I wish you could have some of the peaches we feast on here. They are still abundant, and perfectly delicious. I think of you whenever I eat one, and that is thinking of you pretty often. I shall write again in a few days. My love to all, and tenderest regard for yourself.

J. F. C.

Cruger has given up his dinner party for the 4th, *faute de convives*.

TO MRS. COOPER, COOPERSTOWN

Head's, Oct. 5th, 1839

My dearest wife,

Every thing is in motion here, but I cannot return for ten or twelve days yet. Indeed I think all my arrangements ought now to be made for the winter. I wish very much to bring the girls down, and now think Philadelphia must be the place. I am looking for lodgings, but as yet without success. The novel [*The Pathfinder*] and history are both in press. The latter is doing very well, and my publishers told me this morning that it might still be made worth a large sum of money to me. They value it, as a selling book, very high. They have proposed this morning, to print 3000 copies, second edition, instead of 2000, which, if I accept, will be $700 more in my pocket. With this sum, I shall have netted already $6000 for my last winter's work, of which part is invested in the McNamee house and part in the Pomeroy purchase. We shall now begin to accumulate again, as I have nothing to pay except for investments. The *Naval History* is the best hit I have made, and I now give a month's time to rendering it more complete and perfect. Everybody thinks well of it, and the Perry party will, in the end, be silenced.

Mr. Van Buren is carrying everything before him, and, out of question, will be re-elected. Mr. and Mrs. Poinsett are now in the house, but I have not yet seen them.

We had a bad fire last night close to us, and some thirty or forty buildings have been burned. The times are very hard, but my people stand firm.

Mrs. Willing has invited me this evening to meet a Lady C. Harcourt, so she still keeps in the *beau monde*. I see no difference in Tom's appearance.

I have no intention of purchasing Apple Hill at the present price—I once thought of it, as a speculation.

I never distrusted your management of Paul *à l'exception pris de trop de faiblesse*, on the score of his health. Neither of the ladies you mention are authorities for us, both being notoriously feeble as regards their children.

You must write me again to this place. On Monday I

dine with Mr. Rush, and on Tuesday or Wednesday, I think I shall go to Washington. I ought to go, to render the history better, and the time now presses.

I have dined with Ingersoll, and he says that he will come and see us next summer. The young ladies say they are *agreeable* and have been all along.

If any letter comes soon that seems to be large, send it to me, as I expect some materials for the history. Your best way will be to open the letters and judge for yourself.

Adieu, my love, bless you all.

J. F. C.

TO MRS. COOPER, COOPERSTOWN

Head's, Oct. 8th, 1839

My dearest wife,

I am still detained here, for the *History* is of too much importance to be neglected. I am essentially improving it, and trying to make it a standard work. My absence from home, too, just now can do no harm. I shall wait for a summons to return.

Mr. Maitland has been here. He gives a sad account of James, and I am afraid one that is too true. If what he says is correct, the boy is radically vicious. Your brother will probably let you into the whole affair, when you see him. It is much worse, however, than I had supposed. Mrs. De L— has bought Mrs. Maitland's farm near New Windsor for $11,000, and intends to build. It would seem that, in addition to the main fault, there has been a love affair, and a sort of an engagement. I foretold difficulty from the Yankee arrangement, but Jim, himself, must be inherently bad, or Mr. M— is a sad fellow.

I did not like the manner of the lad. As for his keeping the matter secret, I do not believe a word of it. He made good professions of a desire to do so, and just as I ceased to inquire out of delicacy, he blurted out the whole matter. By his own confessions he ferreted out the secret, when both the Bishop and Mrs. De L.—wished to keep it from him. I can now believe most of what we have heard of him.

I dined yesterday with Mrs. Rush. We had a party of six or seven and a handsome dinner. They were exceedingly civil. Indeed, the history seems to have done more than any of my books.

Now what shall I say about the winter? I cannot find lodgings here, and money is so scarce that I am almost afraid to venture. Still, I think it must be done. I have a project, however, and as this letter will not go until after the arrival of the *Liverpool*, you shall know something more decisive by it. At all events, if you cannot come down this winter, you shall see the Falls next Summer, God willing.

Friday.

I am here yet, busy with both books. The Navy Commissioners are here also, and that is a great assistance to me. I cannot get home until next week—the close of it—but am negotiating for a furnished house in this place. I do not think I shall get it, on account of the price, but shall see.

Tristam Burges is out, and a most miserable failure it is, the most absurd stuff I have ever seen. I am invited by Gen. Well, the Senator from New Jersey, to meet the President at dinner, at Burlington, next Sunday, but shall not go. My way is clear for preferment if I wish it, but you know I do not wish it.

I understand there is a review in the *North American*. This was expected to be done by Slidell, and to treat of the Lake Erie affair. I am told that it is favorable to the book, in the main.

Times look very squally. For myself, I think we have seen the worst, but in England matters are serious. The Bank of England will probably suspend, and that will be to our advantage on the whole.

The first volume of *Pathfinder* is nearly printed. *Naval History* gets on slowly, and I am not sorry, as new facts accumulate.

Dr. Hare has just invited me to dine, but I am engaged with the Commissioners, and must close. I am perfectly well, and everybody compliments me on my good looks.

Adieu, my best love—tenderest regards to all.

J. F. C.

TO MRS. COOPER, COOPERSTOWN

Head's, Saturday, Oct. 19th [1839]

Dearest—

Here I am yet, when I ought to be at Albany, but the two books have detained me, and I am determined to make a good job of them. I do not think we shall quit the Hall this autumn, if we do this winter. The times are so fearfully bad, just now, that I am afraid to venture out of my shell, though I expect a quiet winter, as to my own affairs. I have but one new work, and I shall not write the third volume of the history immediately, if I ever write it.

I expect to quit Philadelphia next week, most probably Tuesday, and shall be home in a day or two. The hostile feeling which exists between N. York and Philadelphia, at this moment, amounts almost to war. The pockets of the knaves are touched, on both sides, and that is touching all the principles they have. God protect the country that has nothing but commercial towns for capitals!

Tristam Burges has come out with his monody on Lake Erie—likewise—Mackenzie—Slidell, in the *North American*. The first is bombastical, silly, and absurd. I believe everybody but Charles King laughs at it. You can form an idea of his logic by one specimen. "At one-half past 2, the wind springing up, Capt. Elliott was enabled to bring the *Niagara* gallantly into close action." These are Perry's words. Now, says Tristam, Perry does not say that Elliott *did* bring his vessel, etc., but that he was *enabled* to bring the *Niagara*, etc. What do you think of this for your free logic?

Mackenzie is superficial and jesuitical. He does not meet the question fairly, cavils at the plainest significations, and shows anything but honesty or talent. Neither is personally abusive, though Mackenzie is false. This review alone satisfies me as to the man's character. He wants candor and a sense of right.

The history, notwithstanding, will carry all before it. It is well spoken of in England, I hear, and will maintain its ground. When abridged, it will be worth $500 a year to me, for the next twenty-eight years; and of course for my life—nothing can drive me but new occurrences.

The first volume of *Pathfinder* is printed—the second is not yet written. The first volume of *History* is also nearly done, but I cannot stay to finish either.

I got a letter from *l'administration des Postes—Bureau des Rebuts et Réclamations*, informing me that a letter addressed to Ma'm'selle C. Fenimore Cooper is detained *faute de dix centimes.* So much for matters of state.

Adieu, my best love.

J. F. C.

On the flyleaf of a small pocket memorandum book carried by Cooper about this time is the following entry in his hand, written in pencil and corrected in ink:

"Dr. Swift heard Lawrence's last words, which were—'Go on deck and tell Mr. Budd to fight the ship until she sinks.'"

FROM A. J. BLEECKER AND W. IRVING

New York, 14th Nov., 1839

My dear Sir

I avail myself of the permission afforded me in your kind letter of the 24th inst. to point out the way in which you can assist me in my application for the Marshalship of this District, and I entertain the hope that you will not think me presumptious in arraying my own opinion against yours as to the propriety of the course proposed. As the appointment will probably be made at an earlier period than that at which you visit Washington (the term of office of the Incumbent expiring on the 14th Dec. next), unless I obtain a letter from you to the President I shall be deprived of the benefit of being known to enjoy your good opinion, and in default of that advantage may not be sufficiently strong to succeed against the multitude of competitors who are striving vigorously for the prize. I make due allowance for the sensitiveness of literary gentlemen in matters of this nature and did I not fully appreciate the value of your name and influence I should hesitate in asking your friendly aid after the intimation you have given of your distrust as to the propriety of affording it in the manner suggested. But that I may not

be censored for extreme selfishness in taxing your friendship at the expense of your better judgement I assure you
I have precedent for the favor solicited, sufficient to
satisfy the most fastidious. Gov. Mahlon Dickerson and
Dr. Milledoln of N. Jersey have written me letters, also
Mr. Jewett late member of Congress from Onondaga and
other friends in Utica and Geneva, all out of the district,
and Gov. Van Ness of Vermont has likewise contributed
his good word in my behalf. The views you express of my
claims as a New Yorker are precisely those I should like
to have presented to the President, and you give me the
strongest encouragement to be importunate in asking for
a letter, by the knowledge you have afforded me of your
sentiments on this subject. This is precisely the ground
taken by Washington Irving, Esq., who favored me with
an excellent letter, a copy of which I attach to show you
how exactly your views agree as to the strong points of
my case. Apologising for the trouble I am giving you,
I am dear Sir,

With sincere regard and esteem

Yours truly

Anthony J. Bleecker.

J. Fenimore Cooper, Esq.
    Letter attached.

Greenburgh, Nov. 2, 1839

My dear Sir

The recommendation of Mr. Anthony J. Bleecker for
the office of U. S. Marshall for this district is I believe
already before you backed by many of the weightiest
friends of the administration. To this let me add my good
word in his behalf as a gentleman of high integrity and
much ability and well qualified to discharge the duties of

the office; let me moreover speak of him in a point of view that I confess has great interest with me as one of the *original well-tried stock* of *"Old Yorkers"* who ought to be cherished and taken care of as the real *seed* corn of our population

ever with truest regard
yours
(signed) Washington Irving

Martin Van Buren, President of U. S.

TO MRS. COOPER, COOPERSTOWN

Stevenson's [Albany], Saturday morning,

Dec. 14, 1839

Dearest—

I was alone to Springfield, when a deaf snuffy old woman was added to my delights. The road was not very bad and, though the weather was menacing, the day became mild and soft. It is now like October. I am at Congress Hall, and have passed the morning with the Lt. Governor and Stevenson.

The latter tells me that Watson, Betty's husband, is a notoriously bad character, a long established loafer, though he was once in apparent prosperity. The state prison must correct him. This has been his character a long time.

Bradish is smiling and well. Left us to go somewhere with his wife. We provoked James, as the French say, to marry this or that young lady. He has had the fitting up of a new Senate Chamber, which, with his new wife, makes him perfectly happy. He has shown his usual state in the Chamber; how it is with the wife I do not know, as I have not seen the lady.

The Manor War is over for the present, but the evil lies deeper than the surface. No blood has been shed, and none will be, I think. But no man can hold such an estate as Rensselaer's in this country, unless he is in a situation to be constantly conferring favors. The end will show. It is said that an attempt has been made to set fire to a barn occupied by troops, and that the incendiary was taken in the act.

I have passed the morning looking at new buildings. Black walnut is much used and is very handsome. The new Church, late theatre, is pretty well in some respects, and bad in others. The pews are decidedly inferior to ours in the way of comfort, the seats and backs inclining too much for comfort, and kneeling boards being too narrow. The chancel is a circle with kneeling board all round it, and organ loft low. The general effect is a want of a churchly character. This is Mr. Kip's new building. It is large, having near 200 pews, near the size of ours.

I go down this evening, and shall dine to-morrow at Head's if nothing happens.

Adieu, my love, with kisses to all.

Your J. F. C.

Ladies' hats very small and very pretty.

James Stevenson was a prominent and well-to-do Albanian, an attorney, and mayor of the city for the years 1826 to 1828. He was a bachelor and brought up in his house his three nieces. He died in 1852.

TO MRS. COOPER, COOPERSTOWN

Head's, Thursday morning, Dec. 19, 1839

My dear Wife—

We had a bad time from Albany down the river. There was no ice, but such a snow storm arose that we were compelled to anchor near Newburgh. Next morning we ran ashore in Tappan, and lay several hours. It was dark when we reached New York. I passed the evening with Mrs. Cruger, and listened to lots of anecdotes. Cruger was still at Henderson, where he has passed the autumn. His wife has not seen him these three months, but laughs at his absence. There is an example for you!

I got here on Monday, and we began work on Wednesday. The delay will keep me here until New Year's. I shall not be much longer going back than I was in coming.

The new edition of the history is not yet published, though it is nearly ready. I have been reading over the manuscript of the novel [*The Pathfinder*], and think pretty well of it. The three last chapters must be strong, however, to give it much success.

Philadelphia is gay, by report; Mrs. Charles Ingersoll my informant. Harris' will, I hear, is a curiosity, the ruling passion governing to the last moment. He manages to let the world know that he has represented his country in Russia and France, had received a snuff box from Alexander. He gives Madame Tousard 20,000 francs, a few other similar legacies, and leaves about $70,000. To Lady Adelaide Forbes, a cousin of Lady William Russell, he sends a sealed packet—no doubt containing her letters. He died in consequence of catching cold by going to Russia to attend the wedding of the young princess with the Duc de Leuchtenberg. Peace be to his soul.

My affairs here look pretty well. Elliott is here, and is looking up in fact, though a good deal discouraged in feeling. The English review attracts no attention, and Slidell still less, if possible; Burges is laughed at. The book stands its ground.

The wine is paid for, and gloves and stockings will be

remembered. I know the pretty hands too well to require a memorandum to buy small gloves.

M. de Saligny is here, fresh from France—*chargé d'affaires* to Texas—swears it is a good country, and prefers Austin to Washington. Thinks Dr. Smith passionate, but a man of talents, and *un richard*.

There has been another terrible bank explosion, in this town. The cashier of the Schuylkill bank appears to have issued $1,300,000 of scrip fraudulently, and has decamped. The bank has stopped payment they say, though what that is it is not easy to explain, as all had stopped paying specie!

God bless you all, and rest assured of my tenderest love.

Yours,

J. F. C.

No court martial as yet ordered on Elliott. No Tom Stevens visible.

TO MRS. COOPER, COOPERSTOWN

Philadelphia, Dec. [20 or 21], 1839

Dearest Wife—

Pathfinder, Vol. II, is about a third printed. The weather has been cold here, is now more moderate, and it is snowing famously at this instant.

I have not seen Mrs. Read—no one indeed but Mrs. C. Ingersoll, though I dine to-day with Cadwalader.

Rogers from Paris is here, as are Saligny, young Deacon, and one or two Parisians. The former thinks this country in a most deplorable state, and says Welles has gone back disgusted, with a determination to quit business and cut America. His wife is in the same mood. I do not know that they are wrong, for each hour reveals some scene of fearful roguery.

Barton is here *sans femme*. Mrs. Livingston has dislocated her hip, cannot travel, and her daughter stays with her. He is in his house, *en garçon*.

The Vespucii is in bad odour, though they tell lies of her. She commenced, I suspect, however, by bouncing about herself.

I am invited to a large party at Mrs. Hare's next Monday, but shall make my excuses. There is no temptation to me in going to these evenings. Other invitations would follow, and my time would not be my own.

Adieu, my dearest love, with tenderest affection to you all. Every body says I am a miracle of fat.

                                  J. Fenimore Cooper

TO MRS. COOPER, COOPERSTOWN

                        Philadelphia, Dec. 25th, 1839
My dearest Sue—

A merry Christmas to you, and to all of our dear children. I regret not being able to be with you to-day, but shall think of you all at dinner, and thank you for many good wishes that I feel certain are held in reserve for me. I have not received a single line from home since I left there, though this will make the fourth letter I have written.

About half of the last volume of *Pathfinder* is printed, but this is an unlucky moment to be here, there are so many holidays, and then the printers have their *blue* days after every festival. This Monday, even, is a bad day, not half the printers working. In plain English, they get drunk one day and sober the next. I do not expect to get away from here, until about the 5th or 6th of January;

which will extend my absence to something more than three weeks.

We have a delightful day, and I have been to mass! The music was good, though a little too dramatical, and the genuflexions as usual. It reminded me strongly of Europe, to be again in a catholic church. I went to the chapel which stood *à côté de nous*. It was filled with Irish of a class better than usual.

I am amazed and shocked with the drunkenness that appears in the streets of Philadelphia to-day. I have seen nothing like it, before, since our return home. Most of the drunkards have been young men, too—apprentices apparently—and roaring drunk.

I hear the Rensselaers live here in good style. The young ladies have the reputation of possessing $16,000 per an. each, and all the elegants are on the alert.—$6000 might be nearer the mark, for their property is not productive. Mrs Rush tells me they keep five carriages—two of which, no doubt, belong to the young men, and one to each of the ladies. Mrs. Rush said she thought Miss Euphemia very lady like. I told her yes, but that they did not belong to the New-York school. There is a report that one is attached to John Van Buren, but will not marry him, on account of her mother's opposition. But gossip, gossip—all is gossip.

Most affectionately and tenderly yours,

J. F. C.

TO H. BLEECKER

Hall, Cooperstown, April 22d, 1840

My Dear Sir,

Mrs. Temple Palmer of New York, a daughter of the late Sir John Temple, is desirous of possessing letters to

our Legation at Brussels, and has written to me to pro-
cure one. Now I do not know who the *chargé* is, but one
of my daughters affirms that you have lately been sent
there from the Hague. I have defended you from this
accusation in vain, resolutely maintaining that you would
not go from the pure Doric of Amsterdam to the patois
of Brabant, but I am obliged to yield. At all events you
are somewhere in that quarter of the world, and may give
Mrs. Palmer a letter to the Brussels *chargé*, if you are
not the man. I can only say that she and her daughter are
acquaintances of ours that we made in Europe, and have
continued at home, and that you ought to be thankful for
an opportunity to know them.

I see your old friend Theo. Sedgwick is dead, but
young Theodore promises to fill his place worthily.
Bradish, you probably are aware, is married, and everybody says is more in love than boys are apt to be at sixteen. I am told he kept his eyes riveted on his young wife
during the time consumed in reading the Governor's message, and that must have been something like a week.
Stevenson, who is a little spiteful at any one who gets
married, circulates these stories.

Well, can the Hollanders really speak Dutch? Poor
Coster (whilom of *The Statesman*) used to affirm that
there was no French at Paris, as he could neither understand nor be understood. I wish devoutly I could spend
an hour or two in some of the galleries that are within
your reach, and look once more at the noble churches and
quaint old houses of Antwerp. Can you fancy that the
people who built the old church at the junction of State
and Market Streets, actually reared the towers of Mech-
lin, Antwerp, and the Hotel de Ville of Brussels?

I have just been revolutionizing Christ Church,

Cooperstown, not turning out a vestry, but converting its pine interior into oak—*bona fide* oak—and erecting a screen that I trust, though it may have no influence on my soul, will carry my name down to posterity. It is really a pretty thing—pure gothic, and is the wonder of the country round.

I wish you all happiness, my dear Sir, and consider myself fortunate in having this opportunity of reminding you of my existence.

Yours very sincerely
J. Fenimore Cooper.

The above was written to Harmanus Bleecker of Albany, New York, and the reference is to the old square Dutch Church which for years stood in the centre of State Street, Albany, at the intersection of what is now known as Broadway.

TO MRS. COOPER, COOPERSTOWN

Philadelphia, Thursday, [May] 14th, 1840

Lea has sold near 4000 of *Pathfinder*. It has great success, in the worst of times. Indeed, it is the only thing that does sell. The opposition reviews are laughed at. They have done me no harm, and themselves a great deal.

TO THE EDITORS OF *The Journal of Commerce*, NEW YORK

Cooperstown, June 18th, 1840

Messrs. Editors,

You have published a short notice of my suit against Mr. Weed, directly censuring me for having brought this and other actions for libels against certain editors of newspapers. As no declaration has yet been drawn up in the case of Mr. Weed, it is not possible that you should know the particular wrong of which I complain, and your remarks must have been made on *general* principles, or on no principles at all. As my actions are for what are technically called *torts*, they are no more fit subjects for newspaper comments than any other similar suits; unless, indeed, you wish to support the doctrine that an editor is not to be held responsible for this species of injustice, like another citizen. Under the circumstances, or after having made my private affairs the subject of your public remarks, I trust you will, at least, so far respect a very obvious principle of right as to give currency to my answer, or, perhaps, as it might be better to term this communication, to my questions. A libel suit is brought for any printed, or written matter that has a tendency to bring a man into disrepute with the world. Three essential conditions are indispensable to the success of the suit: viz., the published matter must be *injurious* in its nature; it must be *false;* and it must be *maliciously* uttered. Now, do you wish to claim that an editor of a newspaper has a right to circulate that which is *injurious*, *false*, and *malicious*, of his fellow creatures, with impunity? Or, do you wish to say that I have no right to the remedies that the law accords to other men?

Possibly you may answer that it was your wish to give me *advice*. If so, permit me to say that this advice would have been more gracefully offered had you waited until I had asked for it. What would you have thought had I inserted a paragraph in a book, giving it as an opinion that Messrs. Hale and Halleck would have done better not to have brought a particular action for a private wrong? Has not the author of a book the same right to obtrude on the public his private opinions concerning the private affairs of his fellow citizens, as the editors of newspapers? Or have the latter, in your estimation, acquired rights by the long and gross abuses that they have practiced, in connection with this subject, that are peculiar to themselves?

My libel suits are termed by a portion of the press "a crusade against the press." Agreeably to Johnson, a "crusade" is "an expedition against Infidels." But, putting aside any refinement on significations, on what principle can one who is defending himself be termed the assailant? Can an action for a *tort* be maintained, unless a wrong has been previously done? Does the number of these wrongs give a claim to any extenuation of the injuries? Is it not rather an aggravation? Are not the assaults of many upon one a proof that the many feel the inherent weakness of their cause? Are they not base? Are they not cowardly? Is it a sign of contempt, or a sign of secret respect, that a hundred join in a cry against one? Is contempt a noisy or a silent state of the human mind?

Is it not the law of the land that the editor who publishes any thing, pending a suit, that has a tendency to impair the rights of either of the parties, is guilty of a high misdemeanor, and renders himself liable to an indictment for what is technically called a "Libel on Justice"? Do not the authorities say that the courts have always visited real offences with signal punishments? Do you think the courts would have the same opinion of the privileges and power of editors, in the case of a conviction for such an offense, as the editors entertain themselves? Do you believe that the patience of the public is inexhaustible, or do you discover symptoms that it is beginning to view the press with a disfavor that, in the end, may not only curtail its abuses, but which may even curtail its

power to our good? And did you ever know a grave
moral wrong persevered in, for any material time, that
did not, in the end, recoil on those who committed it and
bring with it its own punishment?

Allow me to proceed a little further. Are the opinions
of the press any more than the opinions of so many men
who have the control of the journals? Are not these
opinions, too often, dishonestly and fraudulently uttered?
Is "the verdict of the press," as some editors compla-
cently term the opinions of certain members of this corps
concerning my libel suits, anything more than the opinion
of those editors in a matter touching their own pride and
interests? Will this verdict be an offset, either in the
judgment of the community, or in the way of money, to
any verdict that I may obtain from twelve sworn jurors?
If not, would you, or would any sensible man, care a
button about this "verdict of the press," or about those
who give it currency? Is it not a common expression in
the mouths of men, that such and such reports are merely
"newspaper lies," and are not these expressions, and the
opinions on which they are based, becoming daily more
frequent? Would not the boy who cried wolf when there
was no wolf, come in time to be disbelieved when there
was a wolf? In a word, would it not be discreet for that
portion of the press that does regard truth, justice, fair
dealing, decency, propriety, and the rights of others, to
attempt to draw a wide distinction between those who do
not regard these considerations and themselves, and can
they make a better commencement than to manifest a
respect for the privileges of individuals, and not only to
exclude from their columns all comments on the private
affairs of their fellow citizens as a usurpation of an odious
power, but, as far as possible, all comments of their own

as an offense against good taste and the respect due their
subscribers?

Yours, etc.,

J. Fenimore Cooper.

Should you decline publishing this letter, I beg you
will send it to the counting room of J. D. P. Ogden and
Co., Wall Street, directed to me, "to be left until called
for."

TO MRS. COOPER, COOPERSTOWN

Head's, Tuesday, [August] 25th, 1840

My dearest wife,

Mercedes is getting on well, but cannot be finished, as
I have not yet finished.

On Sunday I went to Germantown with Ingersoll and
dined with old Mr. Chew. Of course I saw the celebrated
house, which still retains the honorable marks of the
attack. It was, and is, a strong position, and could only be
carried by artillery, and that pretty heavy. We had at
table, Mr., Mrs., Miss and young Mr. Chew, two
Misses Dallas, Ingersoll and myself. On the whole, a
pleasant day.

I shall dine once only with Ingersoll, though asked
oftener, and nowhere else. I have seen the Ervings twice,
and have taken leave of them. Elwyn was enchanting.
The old lady certainly eschews Tilly, scarce ever looked
at her, though the latter tries hard to catch a smile. There
is some extraordinary mystery, and I think the old lady
intimated as much to me.

Four of Elliott's judges were for cashiering him, and
it is said they were Jones, Downes, Warrington and

Kennedy. I doubt the two last. His sentence is generally thought severe.

What a frightful accident at Albany! None but geese, however, would thus crowd a draw.

Mr. Stone has at last answered my repeated calls on him about the two brigs, admitting that his correspondent was in error, and saying that, no doubt, he was misled by *various* newspapers. I have renewed my call for *one* of these newspapers, and otherwise have demolished him. Even the whig papers here have come out on my side.

Politics are running at the full. The election will be fierce and doubtful. You have a letter from Dr. Hare, his sister having brought it on as far as New York.

Adieu, my best love. Kiss our children and believe me tenderly yours

J. F. C.

TO PAUL FENIMORE COOPER, GENEVA, NEW YORK

Home, Cooperstown, Sept. 18th, 1840

My dear boy,

I did not intend to write to you so soon, but your dear mother thinks you will be curious to know what has been done in the cases of Mr. Webb. There have been no trials, both indictments being carried up to the Supreme Court, under the following circumstances.

The false statement of the *New World*, we found, had been sent to every juror, or to all but eight, and these eight confessed they had not been to any post office since the publication. More than thirty had actually received them. Hundreds of others had been sent into the county, and we were told the Whigs were making the question a party question, in order to save their editor. We found moreover that the County Court judges shrunk from the question, and had little confidence in *sentence*, in the event of a conviction. The counsel for the prosecution, therefore, advised an application to the Supreme Court to stay proceedings, with a view to take the trial out of the county. This I opposed, advising Mr. Crippen to bring on the *last* indictment, that which accused me of having smuggled the first bill through the *Grand Jury first*. This would clear the other indictment up, and enable us to ascertain how far the jury was impartial, since that case could admit of no doubt.

Mr. Webb resisted this course, but the court decided we might try the second indictment first. They then asked time to prepare, pretending they had not yet got ready in that case. This was granted them. This morning they came into court with an order from the Chief Justice to carry the second indictment up to the Supreme Court, to ascertain if it were libellous. This gives us an advantage on trial, as it takes the matter entirely out of the hands of the County Court Judges. It will cause a delay of some months, however. Finding ourselves foiled in this case, and satisfied a fair trial could not be had in this village, we made a similar application in the other case, with a view to change the *venue*. I hope Mr. Webb may still be tried on both indictments, in November. This is the *truth*, and you must disregard all other accounts. I ought to have added that the court decided that we ought to try the second indictment, or suffer a *nolle prosequi* to be entered, Judge Gridley differing from the three county court judges. But this was a minor affair, and does not affect the state of the case. I now leave your sisters to finish the letter.————

The state of agitation and excitement we have been in for the last three days is truly pitiable—and all owing to this *nasty* trial—it is however over now for a short time, and we can breathe freely again. You will be sorry to hear, dearest brother, that poor Richard Morris is dead— he died night before last after a fortnight's illness—after all, Mrs. Baker had not exaggerated when she said he was so sick. I was very much shocked to hear of his death and was very, very sorry. Dick was always a favorite of mine. I think he was the nicest of those boys. We are very anxious to hear from you, and know a little about your examination, how it went off, etc., etc. I hope you are not on your way back, but that there is a *long* letter somewhere on the road for us. There has been no explosion as yet with the Duffs, so I hope we shall be able to keep up a cool intercourse, for of all things a *quarrel* is what I hate, for besides being *wrong*, it is so vulgar. Charlotte is a good deal better. She has taken a drive every day since you left us and she attributes her improvement to these drives. Mr. Duff has opened his school with eighteen boys, no Warrens but in their stead two of Dr. Brandreth's sons—these young "pills" are to have a horse apiece to take exercise on every day. I should not be surprised if Mr. Duff insisted upon each of his other scholars having a horse, and it would produce the better effect if his boys went to church on horseback than on foot. Mrs. Duff overheard one of the young Brandreths tell some of the boys that he had once injured his face and hands very badly playing with some powder which had exploded while he was leaning over it, but that his father's pills had cured it all. Joe Foss brought us up some very nice peaches. I am in the act of eating one now. I take it you have plenty. Roy is returned and is now at school. We miss you, dearest Paul, very very much indeed—the house is so quiet we quite long for a little noise. I hope you are not disgracing us by *yelling* at any party; if you should feel the fit coming on, pray retire as fast as possible. Your slippers are nearly finished—you will get them when aunties go on to Geneva. Ned's are a little further advanced than yours. If Tom Rochester is in Geneva we all beg to be remembered to him. The Jones have gone—you have now all the news. Give our love to all at Uncle's. Every member of the family sends you a most affectionate kiss. Believe me, your sincerely attached sister

Cally.

I have a horrid pen, so you must excuse my writing. The next letter you receive shall be more entertaining.

FROM RICHARD H. DANA

Boston, Sept. 23, 1840

My dear Sir,

I have been so little before the public since you and I met some fifteen or sixteen years ago in New York, that upon looking at my signature you may be likely to say to yourself—Dana! Dana!—Who is he?—O, I do now recollect!

My son was desirous that you should receive a copy of his Journal. But being unknown to you, and hardly feeling that this little matter-o'-fact volume entitled him, as an author, to take the liberty of sending you the work directly from himself, he put me in commission to do it. When half through college the measles left his eyes in so bad a condition that, losing all hope of recovery by the usual methods, he made up his mind to try the effect of a voyage before the mast. As I found that he had looked calmly at all the *disagreeables* of such a condition, that, as he said, if it did not cure his eyes, it would, at least, fit him for active life, I yielded to his wishes, considering though he had been delicately brought up, and was not of a robust frame, that he had a firm mind, Falstaff's great reliance—"the spirit." He returned with his eyes cured, entered the Senior Class, has since gone thro' the course of law studies, and has now opened an office here, with good prospects, I trust, of a fair standing in his profession. The little book will tell you the rest.

I have gone through with a great deal of sickness since you and I met, and in my best estate have been feeble. This, together with the entire unprofitableness of literature to me (who so lack the "means whereby *we* live"), took the heart out of me and I have done comparatively nothing. Lately I have been hawking about a few half literary lectures—a work I hate—which has done me *somewhat* better service. Let me, before I stop, thank you for helping to lighten by your writings so many of my solitary and weary hours. Though it is a long time since you have been among us, you have, nevertheless, often contributed your full share in making the time pleasant which my brother, whom you may possibly remember, and Mr Aleston and myself have past together.

With sincere regards,
dear Sir, Y'rs

To   Richd H. Dana
J. Fenimore Cooper, Esq.

I had laid this aside for a moment, when, upon opening the vol. just sent to me, I found in 5th Chap. that Ames's work is spoken of as the only one written by a hand before the mast. I had looked over the MS. some time back; and it is singular that the story of your first going to sea, which I once heard you tell so graphically, did not occur to me, that I might have set my son right. However, the world has been so curious about all that concerns you, that almost every reader of this Journal will correct the error for himself.

You must excuse my oversight in the order or, rather, disorder in the pages of this letter.

Richard Henry Dana was born in 1787 and died in 1879. He was an essayist and poet of some distinction. He also wrote stories and was the first editor of the *North American Review.*

His son, Richard Henry Dana, Jr., was born in 1815 and was also a writer and author of *Two Years before the Mast.* Both were lawyers.

TO MRS. COOPER, COOPERSTOWN

Macedonian, New York, Oct. 10th, 1840

Dearest,

I found the Shubricks at the City Hotel. The ladies left town for Baltimore this morning, and I did expect we should sail to-morrow, but the *Concord* got up only this morning, and cannot be ready before the middle of next week. This destroys my cruise, as I cannot spare the time, so I go to Philadelphia to-morrow and commence work immediately. I regret this change, but cannot help it.

The town is full, but I should think not gay. I have seen no one, with the exception of a few persons in the street. Not a familiar face that I know.

I have come off to-day to make a feast on chowder with Shubrick, but must go ashore again to-night. We own a ship of the line, a frigate, and a sloop of war, and make a figure. This ship is in fine order.

Shubrick did not wish to leave the squadron. The offer

came from the Department, and probably has a political bearing. The election effects are tremendous, and no one knows what will be the result. I shall try to be back in time to vote. Everybody thinks and talks politics. Of course Miss Shubrick is delighted.

Shubrick sends his best regards, and the ladies left their kindest love. Mary is looking pretty, and Mrs. S— as usual, thin.

When you write to Paul, give my love to him. I cannot send him a journal of a cruise, so he must read *Mercedes* to make amends.

The chowder waits, and I am as ever, tenderly yours, and the girls'.

                                        J. F. C.

TO MRS. COOPER, COOPERSTOWN

U. S. S. *Macedonian*, off the Battery,
                    Thursday, Oct. 15th, 1840

My dear Sue,

You will be surprised at the date of this letter. Shubrick urged me so strongly to go round with him that I came on board last Monday, and we have been living together ever since. I have revived my manuscript, and am now finishing the book [*Mercedes of Castile*] afloat. This will not occasion much delay, if any, and I shall get my cruise. We eat, drink, and sleep on board. Our mess is composed of Shubrick, Capt. Rousseau, and myself. Rousseau, however, leaves us to-morrow, being relieved from the command of the ship. All the officers are applying to leave, now that Shubrick gives up the command. Certainly she is a model vessel, and is every way a finer frigate than I had expected to see. I never knew a better regulated, a quieter, or a more united ship's company.

We sail to-morrow, unless the wind gets foul. At present it is fair, and the weather is very fine, and I hope to be in Philadelphia by Tuesday next—Wednesday at farthest—hence to the election, certainly.

Alfred was on board here to-day, under the care of Com. Bill. Shubrick thinks now he can give the last a berth in the yard, and one reason I have for going round is to see what can be done for him, though the desire for a little cruise is strong within me. Capt. Newton, our cousin Capt. Newton, has just been on board here. He commands the *Fulton*, and his wife is with him. We are five men of war, lying together, viz., *North Carolina* 80, *Macedonian* 36, *Concord* 20 and *Washington* 6, besides the *Fulton*. I have seen your sisters twice, and shall try to see them again before I sail. The Doctor must now be in town. I met Mr. Ransom yesterday—he had begged $160, and finds every body poor. My employments here prevent me from being much on shore. The Commodore is gone to what one of our captains calls a *"déjeuner à la fornichette,"* on board a yacht of John Stevens' called the *Ry-kee-wy-ke*, or The Feather that Floats. I have declined being of the party, in order to get on with *Mercedes*.

Bill is waiting for my letter, and I have only time to give tenderest love for all, keeping the largest share for yourself. Adieu.

J. F. C.—

TO MRS. COOPER, COOPERSTOWN

U. S. Ship *Macedonian*, Sandy Hook,
Oct. 17th, 1840

My dearest wife,

Here we are, at last, at anchor about a cable's length from the spot where we anchored on arriving in '33. The wind is light at the Eastward, and it is questionable if we get to sea even to-night. We shall try, nevertheless, and I still hope to be in Philadelphia by the twentieth. I have seen your sisters again—no bishop—and I think it probable they will go up with me. Mrs. Yates is still in the country.

We are very comfortable on board, where I have now been living these six days. I work on *Mercedes* in the morning, take a row with the Commodore afterwards, and have been ashore once every day. Now, we do not expect to land again, the *Ariel*, Shubrick's gig, being in the painter's hands. The ship is quiet and orderly, and we can just hear the band playing on the poop, with the cabin doors shut. Shubrick has a good many books, and the time passes swiftly. The last week has been a very short one—short since I got afloat.

Capt. Rousseau left us night before last, having got relieved as soon as he found Shubrick was to give up the Squadron. The *Concord* is at anchor a cable's length astern. This ship Shubrick calls his tail, and a very nice-looking tail she is.

I have been reading Collingwood's letters. He says that for twenty years he scarcely saw his wife—one year excepted—and I have thought how *you* would stand that. Well, one is better with a wife, certainly, than without one, and I believe, notwithstanding the *talk*, I miss you quite as much as you miss me.

I feel a little the effects of the easterly wind, but not as much as usual. We are looking out for the English steamer, which is expected every moment, when we shall endeavor to get the news out of her. But, as time and tide stop for no man, so it is also with Steam Boats, and we may not succeed.

Sunday morning. We are now just outside the Hook, a little doubtful if we cross the bar this tide. The *President* in sight about ten miles to seaward. The weather is pleasant, and the wind southeast—southerly—or ahead. Adieu, my love, with blessings and tenderest regards—

Yours ever

J. F. C.

TO MRS. COOPER, COOPERSTOWN

Head's, Oct. 28th, 1840

My dearest Sue,

Here I am again, hard at work, in my dressing gown, and once more an author. The Doctor has been here, but has gone to Baltimore. He returns to-day, or to-morrow, when I shall see him, of course. Everyone says that he looks very well. I have seen the Ervings, over mothered as usual, though I did not see the last. The non-pareil was asleep.

But the greatest treat were your two letters. You speak of mine from the Hook, as if you had not got one written on board the ship a few days previously. *Voici l'histoire de mes mouvements.*

Mrs. Shubrick and Mary left New York Saturday morning in charge of Col. Wetherel. On Monday morning the Commodore, Captain Rousseau and myself went on board ship, to remain. The *Concord* could not be got ready until Friday morning. Rousseau left us for New Orleans, being detached at his own request. Shubrick and myself passed our time very pleasantly, having two boats at our command. Sometimes we pulled to one place, and sometimes to another. Every day we dined on board, burgundy being both good and abundant.

On Saturday, at sun rise, we got under way, with the

wind at northeast, and dropped down to the hook. Here
we were met with an easterly wind and a flood tide,
which compelled us to anchor. Early next morning we
got to sea, crossing the bar with a south east wind, which
was dead ahead. Just as the pilot left us, the *President*
Steamship passed us, bound in. At that moment the *Concord* saluted Shubrick's pennant, and we returned the
salute, both of which salvoes it is probable John took to
himself. At sunset it was blowing fresh, still at s. east.
Next day, about noon, we made the coast of New Jersey,
at Barnegat Light—stood off to sea, and lost sight of the
land about 3 P. M. A squally, dirty night, with a good
deal of sea. Next day, Tuesday, made the land again
about 15 miles to the southward of Barnegat, or near
Little Egg Harbor. Hauled off the land, and ran fifty
miles to seaward, Wednesday all day turning to wind-
ward, near south and southwesterly, keeping well at sea.
About midnight on Wednesday the wind came out of the
northwest, and at day light it was blowing heavily. We
hauled in for the land, with the wind abeam, and about
two o'clock made it on the coast of Maryland, or the
eastern shore of Virginia, I don't know which. At four
were up with Smith's Island, and just at sunset were in
the mouth of the Chesapeake, running into Lynn Haven
Bay, and anchored about 7 o'clock, the *Concord* passing
higher up the bay. Next morning, Friday, the wind was
light and ahead. Beat up a few miles and were compelled
to anchor. About noon a man of war steamer, the *Poinsett*, came down and towed us up. We passed Old Point
about 3, and anchored in the harbor of Norfolk a little
after sunset. S. and I went ashore, and took a look round
that night. Next day I visited the Navy Yard, etc., etc.,
and at eight o'clock the Commodore put me on board the

Baltimore steamer. We came up the Bay on Sunday, and I got here on Monday to dinner.

Last night I saw the Ingersolls, all well and kind inquiries, etc. The two Miss Wilcoxes have been to Schooley's Mountains. d'Hautville was there. He is a nicish little man, of pleasing face and manner, rather quiet and reserved. His English is cross-grained, having as much involution as High Dutch. I did not think his physiognomy Calvinistic. Barry case is decided in *his* favor, but there are doubts about this.

The Willings have been compelled to break up, after all. They are all at lodgings, the furniture, which is here, having been sold. They say she behaves admirably, and there is a rumour, but I doubt its truth, that she thinks of giving lessons on the harp. I do not think the pride of the two families would permit this.

Yesterday I saw Barton's house. The drawing room is altogether the richest thing I have seen in America. The chairs are large, arms highly carved in leaves and gilded. The effect is that of a palace. The gilding extends down the sides, etc., etc.

Everyone talks politics. Nothing else is heard. Young Robert Hare, the jilt, is to be married *next* week to Miss de Pestre. The opinion is, there is not time enough for a quarrel. Mary Ingersoll said last night that he had gone up Chestnut Street, cussing himself, and if he missed a house by any chance, he was certain to come back, like the cholera.

I met Mrs. Tucker in the street yesterday, and she was as intellectual and lovely as ever. We have had a little explosion here to-day, in the house. One of the boarders, a respectable and plain man, by the way, has been obliged to quit us, owing the trifling sum of $1600. for board, wine, etc. He appears not to have paid anything for more than a year—nor two years, indeed. I am sorry for him, as he was a quiet sort of person, though his indiscretion is remarkable.

Write me immediately on receiving this and let me know if any letters are at Cooperstown. I shall be home next week, but not in time for election, I fear.

I am glad you like *Mercedes*. Lea has read it and likes it too. You think very much the same about it. Bentley has changed the name to *Christopher Columbus, or, Mercedes of Castile*, a miserable misnomer and a pure catch penny. Lea & B. had done the same thing, but I have put a stop to the proceeding, and told them I shall hold them responsible for the copyright if any mistake occurs. These booksellers have no souls.

Shubrick sends love, etc. He also sends Sue a box made on board the ship. It is not handsome, but he thought she would prize it. She must write when she gets it to thank him.

God bless you all—my loves and my love.

J. F. C.

TO MRS. COOPER, COOPERSTOWN

Saturday, Nov. 7th, 1840

Dearest—

Owing to an unlucky mistake with the manuscript, I cannot quit P. until Monday. I may be home on Tuesday, but I fear not before Wednesday. Then, I think, I shall remain *all* Winter.

I have bought the chintz, 79¾ yards at 14½ cents, 56 yards glazed muslin, 1 doz. gloves—the stockings, binding and three dresses. The price of the last was $1 per yard. They are fine-striped, rather dark, rich and handsome. The whole comes to $69. I shall endeavor to bring on the tea, though my trunk is already filled. There will be very few books. *Mercedes Worden* will be among them. The English title is changed to *Mercedes*, etc., *a romance of the times of Columbus.*

I have seen but little of the Ingersolls, not having broken a crust there since my arrival, though asked. I have dined with the other two—*violà tout.* I have been excused by Mrs. Elwin, and there is an end of it.

Here we eat, drink, and sleep election. Pennsylvania is still doubtful, though the last news is favorable to Van Buren. The Whigs, this morning, are cooling off, and the majority will not be 500. Virginia, I think, will be for Van Buren. New York, I fear, we must lose, and then we lose the election.

I fear Martin must win, but I hope Seward will be beaten.

Young Elwyn is not even *dead:* of course has not been killed. I heard the mother *speak* to the daughter the other day. The latter seemed frightened. The Major goes to Dearborn in a few days, leaving the ladies behind. They winter with the mother.

Rob Hare is married. Harry Ingersoll witnessed the ceremony, and swears to it.

God bless you all, and rest assured of my tenderest love—you and my *Mercedes.*

J. F. C.

TO PAUL FENIMORE COOPER, GENEVA, NEW YORK

Hall, Cooperstown, Nov. 29th, 1840

My dear Boy,

Your mother and sisters have doubtless kept you acquainted with my movements, which will explain the reason of my long silence. Com. Shubrick wrote to me to join him, at the latest, on a Friday morning, as he expected to sail on that or the succeeding day. I was punctual to an hour, but the ship was not ready, as the Commodore expected the *Concord* to join him before he left New York. The *Concord* did get in on Saturday morning, but she had fifty things to do before she could proceed on a West India cruise. On Saturday, therefore, I reluctantly gave up the project, and intended to go on to Philadelphia by land next morning, when the Commodore persuaded me to wait a few days, promising to sail by the following Saturday at the latest. Monday morning we went on board ship, where I stayed the remainder of the time. Early on Saturday the *Macedonian* got under way, and we dropped down to the S. W. Spit, followed by the *Concord*. The wind coming light and ahead, we were obliged to anchor lying inside until daylight on Sunday. When we got under way from the S. W. Spit, the wind was in south east and light, but we crossed the bar, passing out by Gedney's Channel, but as the night left us the *President* Steamship passed us standing in, and the *Concord* at that moment, coming up, passing beyond the command of Com. Renshaw, saluted the broad pennant of Com. Shubrick. This salute we answered, of course, and then our cruise made a brilliant *début* so far as wine, smoke and *raconteur* were concerned.

After we got outside, the wind freshened, and by two o'clock it blew fresh, dead ahead. As this was the first serious head wind they had experienced in the ship, I was pronounced the Jonah, and there was some grave talk, but no very grave intentions, of throwing me overboard. I put the sin on the fleet surgeon, Dr. Morgan, who had just joined, and a strange steward belonging to Capt.

Smoot of the *Levant*, whom we were carrying round, and by these suggestions, or some other causes, escaped the whale's jaws. About 3 P. M. we passed the light ship, which is a very uneasy anchorage about 13 miles to the southward and eastward of the Hook. At sunset we tacked off Long Branch.

It blew fresh in the night, and we had to shorten sail. In the morning we were off Barnegat, and toward evening we again tacked off shore, abroad of Little Egg Harbor. From this time, Monday night, until Thursday morning, we were struggling against a head wind, blowing fresh, and without a sight of the sun, when the wind came out a north west. We were now so far south, and so far off the land, as to make this purely a free wind. We hauled up, of course, and after running near a hundred miles towards the s. west, made Smith's Island, which lies on the eastern shore, a short distance from Cape Charles. We edged away to avoid the mill ground, and passing the light on Cape Henry about seven o'clock, anchored at eight in Lynn Haven Bay. The wind had got to be light at sunset, and it fell nearly calm in the night. You will see we were just five days in getting from the Hook to Cape Henry. The *Concord* kept us company, sometimes so near as to speak us, and never more than a league distant. The two ships sailed very much alike, and I think both good vessels.

Friday morning the wind was light, and, after beating a few miles up the bay, we were compelled to anchor. Luckily, however, a steamer, the *Poinsett*, came down for us and towed us up. We were saluted by, and returned the salute of, the *Poinsett*—always 13 guns from the *saluter*, and seven from the *saluted*. As we drew near Coney Island, and got a sight of the *Delaware's* masts,

Salvo the third took place. At sunset we passed the *Dela-ware*, and anchored off the town. Thus ended my service, after having been twelve days on board the ship. I remained in her until Saturday night, when I left her for a steamboat, and came up the Bay on Sunday. On Monday I reached Philadelphia. The *Macedonian* had a set of very fine young men on board her. The Commodore was much beloved, and he left his ship with regret. Com. Wilkinson took charge of the squadron a few days after I left Norfolk. William goes, or rather has gone, with him, the ship having sailed.

Your aunts will soon leave us for Geneva, but with an expectation of returning in the course of the Winter. The house is entirely finished, and all the rooms are furnished, so that they can probably be more comfortable here than with you. We have seven vacant rooms, after giving them an excellent apartment, while I fancy your uncle has no great excess of space. You see, poetic justice requires them to stay where they are.

Mr. Webb has got his trial postponed on a plea of a want of time to be in readiness. He cannot escape, however, notwithstanding all his manœuvres, but will eventually be punished. I have beaten Messrs. Stone and Benjamin on the demurrers argued at Utica last Summer, and they have let the time the Court gave them to amend pass without doing anything, from which we infer they give the matter up as a bad job. If we are right in our notions of the practice, we now call a jury and assess the damages, without a trial in open court. You will see by this that the other side dare not even attempt a defense. They are such rogues, however, and have recourse to so many tricks and expedients, that it is difficult to determine what their real intentions are. That I shall beat them, one and all, is certain, if law and evidence can avail.

The Duff Greens are Duff Greys, on all days but Sundays. Some of the figures in bayonet belts and car-touch boxes, and have a fearfully bloody look. They occasionally make a noise, very much in the *feu de joie* style. I should think the *éclat* of the school, by all I hear, a more settled thing than its gentility. It appears to be matter of exultation that one of its members has got into a college. I am *told*, artillery is the next step.

I am looking out for a match for Pumpkin, whose name of right should be Molasses, when she shall set up our lumber sleigh and two. The wood choppers are at work at the Chalet, and shortly its trees will be blazing in the chimneys of the Hall.

The Henderson House feud is accommodated, the gentleman having returned quietly to his allegiance crying *peccavi*. This is all right, and we shall get our neighbors back.

We have no news here. The *Colonel* has gone on his Winter's campaign, the Chief Justice is just back from his especial term, and I believe Dick has got in his rents. It snows, and your aunts meditate a flight. I shall be at home to receive you, and you will find a large trunk in waiting, a proof that we do not intend you shall remain always.

Is not the Glentworth affair a most melancholy bit of villainy? and yet a Grand Jury prevents the Judge who would punish it, and lets the rogue go free. Depend on it, my son, we live in bad times, and times that threaten a thousand serious consequences, through the growing corruption of the nation. If public virtue be truly necessary to a republic, we cannot be one, but, unknown to

ourselves, must be something else. The fact is, govern-
ments often profess to be one thing and practice another,
and we are not what we profess to be.

You will not be sorry to hear that there are twenty
young turkeys at this moment feeding under my window,
most of which will be in waiting for your return. The
bass have almost entirely failed us this autumn, while the
lake fish never were more plenty. Dan Boden has taken
eight or ten of the latter in a day, and with the hook. On
the whole we are not starving, and shall be delighted to
see you.

Most affectionately your father
J. Fenimore Cooper.

TO MR. G. ROBERTS

Otsego Hall, Cooperstown, Jan. 2nd, 1841

Dear Sir,

My engagements render a compliance with your request out of the question. The remuneration would be no
inducement, for I never asked or took a dollar in my life
for any personal service, except as an officer in the Navy,
and for full grown books. I do not say this on account
of any feeling, for I think writers ought to be paid, and I
would often have received compensation of this sort on
general principles, though I could not be remunerated for
lost time in writing for any periodical. I only wish to say
that I am not deterred by any pecuniary consideration,
and, at the same time, that I think writers ought to be
remunerated. But I am under engagements that I find
it difficult to execute in time.

Some fifteen or twenty years since my publisher became
embarrassed and I wrote two short tales to aid him. He
printed them, under the title of *Tales for Fifteen*, by

Jane Morgan. One of these stories, rather a feeble one I fear, was called *Heart*, the other *Imagination.* This tale was written one rainy day, half asleep and half awake, but I retain rather a favorable impression of it. If you can find a copy of the book, you might think *Imagination* worth reprinting, and I suppose there can now be no objection to it. It would have the freshness of novelty, and would be American enough, Heaven knows. It would fill three or four of your columns.

The ordinary English hack writers utter a vast deal of nonsense. In the paper you sent me is a very silly article about Murray, whose character is not at all understood. One of the writer's facts is downright nonsense. He says that Mr. Murray never publishes novels. I suppose he has published hundreds. He published *Pioneers* for me, and I had a good deal of difficulty in getting *The Pilot* out of his hands, where it had been placed by a friend. I found him anything but liberal, and he knew that this was my opinion of him, for he sounded Mr. Miller to know whether a visit from him would be agreeable to me. Mr. Murray is a great man only among very little men.

Do you think size as important in a journal as quality? We have so much mediocrity in this country that, excuse me for asking it, I think distinction now might better be sought in excellence. There is a serious physical objection to mammoth sheets; they are difficult to read. I confess I would rather write for a small sheet than for a large one, if I were in the way of writing for either.

Is Mr. Longfellow in this country, and do you ever see him? He did me the favor a few years since to send me some Danish translations. I was under the impression that he was *Chargé d'affaires* in Copenhagen, and wrote him in answer to that country. I could wish him to know this, and, if I recollect right, you did me the favor to forward the books from Boston. If I am not in error, will you explain this affair to Mr. Longfellow?

Your Obe. Ser.
J. Fenimore Cooper.

TO MRS.' COOPER, COOPERSTOWN

Globe, New York, Monday, March 29th, 1841
Dearest,

I got here, by the river, on Saturday. Yesterday I went to the Navy Yard, and after dinner I visited Mrs. Maitland. Found her well established, with a puppet of a daughter, who kissed and hugged me in a very precocious manner. She is half Maitland—half Ellison. Her mother was very amiable—no Mrs. De Lancey, yet. I then saw Mrs. Yates, who expects the Neils in June. She is over head and ears in business, and thinks she cannot reach Cooperstown this summer. Next to Mrs. Banyer's, where I drank tea, and passed two or three hours. Then to Mr. Gay's, for an hour, and next to bed.

Mr. Balmanno is Ogden's clerk. *He* sent me the account of the Hall, which was written by his wife. He owns the house at Geneva, and wishes to sell it for $9000. Will it not suit your sisters? Perhaps it might be got for less money. Of course you will tell them this, and if they like the place, I might obtain the last price.

You will see a letter from me in the *Post*. I think it floors Mr. Mackenzie as far as it goes. Barber is annihilated, and my letter has brushed off that mosquitoe. Everybody says that—everybody but the editors who raised a clamor the other way.

Benjamin is down—away down—character understood, and sinks fast to Webb's level.

I shall go to Philadelphia to-morrow, and be back here this week. Home, I think, by Saturday or Sunday. The Court House may detain me, but I trust not.

I shall make the purchases here, on my return. Every body says I am too fat, and I know I am very well. With love and blessings to all at home,

Yours as ever

J. Fenimore Cooper.

TO MRS. COOPER, COOPERSTOWN

Head's, Friday, April 2nd, 1841

Dearest,

I have seen Mrs. Elwyn and Tilly, but not Mrs. Erving, who has not yet left her room. She has been very seriously ill, but sees her friends at night. I shall call on her this evening or to-morrow. Last evening I passed with the Henrys, and the night before with Com. Read. The last looks old—very old, but says he is not yet religious, though his wife is.

I met the Miss Wilcocks in the street, but have not yet been to Ingersoll's. Met him this morning, and promised to go round this evening, but have entered no houses except those named.

I hear that Tom Stevens has left his family utterly destitute. He speculated largely, and ruined himself. Indeed, I have heard his death attributed to a mishap connected with his losses. Renshaw says a civil process was served on him the night he died, and that he did not get over it. What makes the matter worse is the fact that the last Congress stopped the pensions of officers' widows, those who fell in battle excepted.

John Jay and his wife, with Miss Dubois, came on

with me, and are now here. Dr. Hare and son sail for England to-day. Philadelphia is struck by a paralysis, but things are by no means as bad as I expected to find them. Ogden thinks we have reached the bottom.

I hear nothing of the Court House, and fear it may have been mismanaged since I left. Certainly it was in a fair way before.

Gen. Harrison is very ill, and serious apprehensions are entertained for him. I hear nothing of Mr. Sargent or his mission, but shall learn more when next I see Ingersoll.

Mr. Dallas has given me some papers of Elliott's, and complains that the Commodore has not done the genteel thing in relation to the honorarium. Poor fellow, they have put him *à sec*, I suppose, and he cannot help himself. With kindest love to all, I remain, yours,

tenderly, and in perfect health,

J. F. C.

TO MRS. COOPER, COOPERSTOWN

Head's, Sunday, 13th [June, 1841]

Dearest Sue,

As L. & B. do not desire to publish [*The Deerslayer*] until August, I shall leave Philadelphia the last of this week and go to New York, in order to complete my moneyed arrangements. The first volume is now done, and in four or five days more the second will be so far advanced as to be easily finished through the Post Office, and the other matters must be attended to.

It has been horribly hot here, but the weather is now much cooler. I am perfectly well, and very prudent. I have seen Mrs. Erving, who is better, and about to join her husband near New York. Tilly and the mother were out—gone to lecture, though different ways. I dined with Ingersoll yesterday; part of the ladies in the country. They are all well, and made many kind enquiries. Mary Ingersoll, my favorite, was not there. I have seen no one else but the Henrys.

I have bought the d'Hauteville case, and have been reading the testimony. The fact is two *têtes montées* have run against each other. *She* has been *very* wrong, and he has been *wrong*. You will all read it, and I think the girls will laugh over it. There is a good deal of it, and that is lucky, inasmuch as I shall bring scarcely any other book.

The anti-Biddle feeling is very strong, and quite as ferocious as the pro-Biddle feeling was formerly. Benton is here—wife on the river. He joins her in a few days, however. Willing and Niles are competitors for the chargé d'affaireship at Turin. I have seen none of them. Thom. Francis died after 48 hours of illness.

I have hopes of the President. The Portuguese account comes straight, and is consistent and probable.

Write me at the Globe, New York, in answer to this. I hear nothing of engagements or marriages. John Sargent it is thought will go to England, and Mr. Cass will be Vicar of Bray. The return of the *Brandywine*, I fear, compromises Bolton sadly. *Entre nous*, they say he betrays some of his mother's malady. He quits the ship and Capt. Girsinger takes her.

This house is very thin, and we are only seven at table. As for myself, I am as ever

Most tenderly and truly yours, with love for the babes,

J. F. C.

If you do not write, in what respect are you a good wife? I put it to your conscience, as M. d'Hautville says.

TO MRS. COOPER, COOPERSTOWN

Head's, Tuesday, [June] 22nd, 1841

My dearest wife,

Here I am still, contrary to my expectations. I am detained by a new bargain and a desire to get rid of *Deerslayer* entirely. I am now bargaining for an abridgment of *Naval History*.

Sunday I met our friend the *Rev.* Bartow of Georgia. He was in deep mourning and I find he has lost his wife, the greatest loss that can befall a man, after a few years of marriage. He came here for his health, and is now much better. He wishes to get a chaplaincy and to go out in the *Brandywine*, the Rev. Charles vacating. He called the last a butterfly. I gave him good counsel, which, like all good counsel, will I presume be lost. He is to see me again.

About 80 pages of *Deerslayer* remain to be printed. Of these some 30 will be disposed of to-day. I hardly think it as good as *Pathfinder*, but sufficiently different. It has a strong moral, and some capital scenes. Lea has read half, and likes it exceedingly. Thinks it equal quite to *Pathfinder*.

I have seen the Ingersolls, old and young. The Henrys once, Gurney Smith, Math. Alsop and a few others. The feeling against Biddle is ferocious. I have seen the Ervings three times. The old lady is much subdued in manner, and Tilly appears happier. The boys are but little changed—John is John, and Larry Larry. Mrs. Mac *en congé*.

Barton is still here, but on the wing. Our house is not in favor, though quite as good as ever, but the sons injure it. I think they begin to know it. The old man is reviving.

Extraordinary scenes are enacting at Washington. Whiggery tumbling to pieces, and old Quincy Adams a general tormentor. I presume this congress will finish him. Tom Cooper's daughter is the lady of the White House, and Tom *thinks* Mr. Tyler will veto the Fiscal Agent.

I hope Mann cuts the grass even, this is important. He should keep a sharp scythe.

In the Stewart case (Webb-Stewart) a verdict has been had against Stewart on the ground that the old maid was *non compos*. He was a good rogue, that G—— — adventurer. The property is said to be worth $500,000, but that must mean the whole estate.

Surprisingly few people travel, though things are coming slowly round.

Give my best love to the children, and reserve a little better for yourself. I do not think I am a bad father, and yet I love my wife a little better than any child I have, good as all mine are. Can this be because the wife is so good, or because I am a fool?

Yours tenderly
J. F. C.

TO MRS. COOPER, COOPERSTOWN

Head's, Sunday, August 15, 1841

I got through in New York, in sufficient season to reach this place by midnight Friday. Yesterday I made my bargain, and to-morrow we begin work. I hope to get through by the 25th next month. It is well I have been so prompt, as I hear of a scheme of Mackenzie's to cut me out. We shall see in the end which will prevail. *Deer-*

slayer is just out—no opinions yet of its standing. Of course nothing is yet known of its sale.

I hear a great promotion is to be made in the Navy. It will include Irvine, Shubrick, Ned Byrne, etc., and Bridge will be a captain.

I met the French admiral here, and he tells me Mrs. Shubrick is quite well. Nothing unpleasant occurred as to Schotes.

J. F. C.

TO MRS. COOPER, COOPERSTOWN

Head's, Wednesday, [September] 8th, 1841

Dearest,

I am well, and am getting on well, but it requires time. The book is about half done, and this in eight working days; in ten more it will be out of my hands, though I must still wait a few days to get it bound, etc.

The French Admiral has just left us. He is an amiable man, and one of good sense too, but one of strong prejudices concerning this country. Among other things he has got strange ideas of our religious exaggerations, and more particularly of the Methodists. Last Sunday morning he asked me if I had heard the Methodists the previous night, in one of their religious meetings. *"Ou donc, et quand, Admiral?" "Vers minuit, et dans les rues. Ils ont courus les rues, en priant et criant à haute voix, avec un petit clocher. Bah! quel drôle de religion!"* On inquiry, I found there had been an alarm of fire, and one of the hose companies had passed his windows! Yesterday, he found the "Methodists" again. It was at night, *"au coin de la sixième et Chestnut." "Ils ont criés, bravo, bravo!"* It was a meeting of Irish repealers. Barton has just given me a story of Davicaz' that surpasses this even. A Louisianan, a Creole, was walking among her slaves, and discussing with her friends the best mode of ruling her blacks. "*Il ne faut qu'un système. Mon système, à moi, ce n'est que les récompenses et les punitions. Ecoutez! Je m'adresse à mes nègres, et vous aller voir l'effet. Mes amis, vous savez que les cannes sont mûres. Demain, il faut bien travailler. Vous me connaissez—vous savez mon système. Si vous ne travaillez pas, vous serez fouettés: mais, si vous travaillez, vous ne serez pas fouettés— voilà!*"

There is a strange story about Mrs. Tucker. Some time after the death of her husband, she received a letter from a captain in the Austrian engineers, whom she had known in Europe, where he still was, offering her his hand. She accepted him, and the man is now here, come to fulfil his engagement. But she is dying of an inward cancer. The Doctors declare the case hopeless, and she gives herself up, as she thinks so much happiness could not be in reserve for her. When and where the courtship took place, the legend does not say. The above facts are, however, from her relating.

I see by the late papers that our little acquaintance Camille Borghese, now Prince Aldobrandini Borghese is about to marry Mademoiselle d'Ahremberg, the daughter of the Duc d'Ahremberg, a quasi Frenchman of high rank.

We have a thousand rumours here, mostly false, and among them one that says that affairs look serious again with England. I believe we shall have war before all things are settled, but, so wrong headed are our people, that I fear they will fight on a question in which they are wrong, when we have so many causes of quarrel in which we are right.

Mr. Tyler enjoys the choicest benediction of the Whigs. It is thought he will veto the new bank law, in which case there is to be a Whig manifesto showing him up.

I saw Mrs. Erving and Tilly night before last. I thought Tilly in good spirits. They say the old lady is religious, and that she treats her daughter more kindly. The old lady is in hourly expectation of her hopeful son from New Orleans. He is the delight of her eyes. The Ervings are at Sing Sing. The Major is dreading promotion, as it will take him from his present regiment. The boys are all well. Mrs. Charles Ingersoll tells me she thinks Mrs. Erving consumptive, and in a bad way, but I hope she is mistaken.

This town is sadly cut in the way of fortunes; more so than I had believed. One of the Coxes, who had half a million a few years since, has not one tenth of his means left. Many others, out of business, have suffered in equal proportions.

The Bank of the United States, in one sense, exists no longer. It has assigned its assets, and of course has nothing to do. This was done to escape executions. It was the wisest thing it could do, though not absolutely honest. This affair of the Bank is worse than that of the Great Fire. Is not all this done to rebuke a country that thinks, eats, talks, drinks, and dreams dollars?

I hope the wood comes in fast, this fine weather. In your answer let me know what is doing.

The Willing is absent and in grief. She has lost a fine boy—Arthur—by dysentery. They are at Brighton.

Toni's diplomatic hopes are extinct. The wags say that if his appointment had been a "Soup" he might have suited "Turin." But a Philadelphian must pun. Charlotte shows the blood of the vicinity.

Mr. Miller is here, and I think Caroline is the one, by his manner of speaking, though he does not often introduce their names.

I have not broken bread out of the house, though Ingersoll has asked me. I shall go and see Commodore Biddle in a day or two. Nick seems doomed. I think, however, the law suits will die a natural death. It is mean in men who well knew, at the time when the money went, to make a noise about it now.

Had you not better send the Platonists *apples?* The melons here are now delicious, and I am getting some seed. I eat both, with benefit.

Give my love and blessing to the children, and accept an embrace for yourself.

Yours most tenderly
J. F. C.

FROM AN UNKNOWN ENGLISHMAN

England, September, 1841

Sir

I see with the greatest pleasure that you have published another of your most interesting novels, *The Deerslayer*, and that you have again brought before us an old and favorite character, the Leather-Stocking, in whose adventures I am exceedingly interested, and indeed I take a great interest in every thing relating to the Red Indians. I wrote a letter to you about 4 months ago which I hope you have received, enclosed to Mr. Richard Bently, the

Publisher of your Novels. I am happy to tell you that
you have succeeded in making the Leather-Stocking as
great a Hero as Homer has Achilles, or Virgil, Æneas.
I have not yet read *The Deerslayer*, but I have read a
part of it in Bently's Miscellany, entitled *The Death of
the Red Man*, with which I am greatly delighted, so I
hope and trust you will continue to write novels about
the Indians and Leather Stocking, such as about various
exploits of the Leather Stocking alluded to by him in
The Last of the Mohicans and *The Prairie*, etc., or you
might also write about the deeds of Tecumseh, the
Shawanese, etc., for every one is greatly interested with
your Novels, but they do not get such extensive circulation at first as they do when they are published in the
Standard Novels. As I said before I am greatly interested in the North American Indians, but I hear from
Mr. Catlin (the Man who exhibits all Indian ornaments,
arms, etc., in London) much to my regret, that it is Probable, they will soon be extinct, for that about 170,000
Buffaloes are slaughtered annually in America, for the
sake of their skins, and that in about 10 years they will
be entirely destroyed, and that when that happens
250,000 Indians, now living on a plain of about 3000
miles in extent, must either die of Starvation or attack
the White Settlers, and by them be destroyed, and at
which circumstance I should be very sorry, for I intend
shortly to go to America, and pass some months among
the Indians. I am sorry that I must continue to be
Anonymous, tho I wish it were the contrary. Novels
about the Contests of the Bloody Ground, or about Black
Hawk, or General Wayne's Indian Wars, would be
exceedingly interesting, and would get immense circulation, but any thing about the Leather Stocking would be

better than any others, but I hope you will write no more like *The Heidenmauer*, or *The Monikins*.

I remain, Sir,

yours very truly

P. S. I would like

"*Nunc lustrare viis—et vastos fingere Tauros.*"

TO MRS. COOPER, COOPERSTOWN

Philadelphia, Sept. 17th, 1841

My dearest Sue,

Your letter reached me last night. The verdict is about half what it ought to have been, but is the more likely to be paid. I think I could have doubled it—but Dick says there were impracticable men on the jury. It will cost Benjamin, as it is, some 6 or 800 dollars. You will be glad to hear I am nearly through. I have sold the abridged *Naval History*, and have made a fair bargain. I hope to be in New York on Monday, and home *before* Sunday—perhaps on Wednesday.

Joe Miller is here with his wife. They both look well. I saw Mrs. Erving, Tilly, and the New Orleans son last night. I fear Mrs. Erving is in a decline. The Major must now be promoted into the 3d, which is stationed in Florida, and he may carry his wife there.

I have seen Mad. Elsler, dined in her company at Com. Biddle's, passed a night at Charles Ingersoll's, and dined with Joe. So much for my dissipations.

I am the only person left at Head's. He keeps me out of charity, but the furniture is actually selling to-day. We are scattered to the four winds, and I think my visits

to Philadelphia are ended. My next book will be printed
through the post office.

The letter from Bentley was highly satisfactory—
Deerslayer is doing well, and I hope will still do better.
The press says nothing about it. Mr. Miller tells me
Susan De Lancey *writes him* she cannot go to Coopers-
town. As for the Laights, you will know better in a day
or two. Fifty people have told me that they were at
Sharon.

J. F. C.

FROM JOSEPH RANSOM

Gilbertsville, Oct. 15th, 1841

My dear Sir,

On my journey home, the other day, from New York
I came to the knowledge, in a conversation about you and
your excellent works, that you had beaten your miserable
traducer Park Benjamin; and as your daughter, I heard,
was returning to Cooperstown, I could not but avail myself of the opportunity of thus telling you how greatly
I rejoiced at it; as well as at the same time of expressing
my opinion, that the state of the public mind is, very
obviously I think turning round in your favor. The fact
is, you are accomplishing a most glorious achievement for
your country; and this is beginning to be recognized by
it,—except in those contemptible instances, where the
mind, having become utterly vitiated, by an interesting
connexion with a villainous system, is no longer capable
of entertaining any correct moral perceptions; nor can it
be otherwise, I think, than that all sensible men, and
especially those in publick capacities, will look to you
with gratitude and reverence, as not only the champion
of their liberties, but as the successful defender of every

thing sacred and dear to them. It may not, indeed, be yet, alas! that the country will be *able* to estimate, *fully*, the true nature of the conquest wh. you are making for it;— for such is the confused and disorganized state of things; and such, as a necessary consequence, the perverted medium through wh. the judgement has to operate; that both your fearful position, and the work you are accomplishing, will to a most serious extent, be inevitably overlooked. Yet to me, at least, who am not at all mixed up with the existing state of things, it appears that no mortal could occupy a more perilous station, than that into wh., with so much courage and ability, you have thrown yourself;—for what is it, but to have entered the lists *alone*, against the power by wh. the country has been subjugated; and thus, in defiance of all opposition whatever, to have succeeded, as you have done, in raising it from so degrading a predicament? My dear Sir, I cannot but regard this, as unquestionably the most glorious thing that you have done. By your works, indeed, you have been, and still are, at once the ornament and the light of your country; but in this matter you are truly a *Reformer*, and such a man I consider is, of all others, the greatest and most important to the world; inasmuch as his object is to bring men back again to the truth of things, and consequently his work must be, after a sort at least, *divine*. I pray that God may still grant you success, and make you to triumph over all your enemies; and this, indeed, I am compelled to do the more earnestly, as I feel that, in a most important sense, you are actually fighting *my own*, as well as every body else's battle.

I was very glad to hear from your daughter that you were all well. We are, thank God, quite so, and very comfortably settled in our new Parish. Mrs. Ransom

unites with me in best respects to yourself, Mrs. Cooper,
and the family; and thanking you for all your great kindness to us, I remain
> ever, my dear Sir,
>> your most obedient servant
>>> Joseph Ransom

To J. Fenimore Cooper, Esqr., Cooperstown

TO CAPTAIN CONNER, WASHINGTON

Otsego Hall, Cooperstown, Nov. 7, 1841

Dear Conner,

You will find your berth as Commissioner no sinecure,
if I am to trouble you with my commissions. However,
honour has its penalty as well as dishonour, and, so, here
goes. I have a nephew who is desirous of getting a berth
with some captain, or commodore, as his clerk. He commenced life as a sailor, and has already been seven years
at sea, three of them with Shubrick and Wilkinson, as
their clerk. He left the latter because the surgeon told
him to quit the West Indies. He writes a good hand, and,
without being a genius, he is a steady, diligent, honest
good fellow. Morally there is no cause to complain of
him, for he has not been sent to sea to tame, but because
his mother made a bad second match, and ruined him and
his brothers.

Now all I want to trouble you with is to find out what
ships are likely soon to be put into commission, and who
is to have them. Of course I ask no secrets, but only
early information of what anybody may have for asking.
The Home Squadron *must* be fitted, and I hear Nicholson is to have it. Where is he, and is this known to be
true? Any captain, however, would do as well as a com-

modore. I should like to get the young man with Nicholson, nevertheless, as he must have a big ship, and is good natured. If you can help me in this way, have the goodness to drop me a line.

The secretary refused my offer, two months after I had sold the book on much better terms, to a publisher. I do not know whether the service cares at all about this work or not, but if it is to be bought, 100 copies will now cost it nearly double what I offered it for; since the booksellers take the lion's share of the profits.

You have got one precious fellow in your cabinet— Mr. John C. Spencer. If he does not "breed a riot" I shall be mistaken. At Albany the Whigs publicly exult in his removal. Take a specimen of his character. I offered to sell the new edition of *Naval History* to a bookseller in New York, who agreed to take it, if a *certain person* would do so and so. After a few days I found out that the *certain person* was Mr. Spencer, and that the "so and so" was his consent, as Superintendent of our common schools, to put the work in the district school library—a series of books published by the Harpers, under his Imperial Patronage. I immediately declined selling the work on conditions so humiliating to a freeman, and disposed of it, subsequently, in Philadelphia. Sometime afterwards curiosity induced me to inquire of the New York bookseller if Mr. Spencer had ever answered his application. I was shown his answer, and read it with my own eyes. He declined putting the *Naval History* into the District School Library on the ground that the *book was controversial on the subject of the Battle of Lake Erie, and he had uniformly declined admitting any controversial works.* He then witnessed his rejection of two or three biographies, on the same princi-

ple. Now, in the first place, it is the *want* of controversy
in the *History* that has made the clamor about it—my
abstaining from accusing Elliott, etc. But the d - - - - d
scoundrel had actually put in Mackenzie's life of Perry,
which is *all* controversy, which avows itself to be controversy in its preface, and controversy on the Battle of
Lake Erie, too, several months before he wrote that
letter! I pledge you my honour to these facts. I have
lately been told that the biographies he mentioned as
having been rejected on account of their controversy, he
had officially admitted, but, on receiving a notice from
Gen. Dix, his predecessor in office, informing him that
they contained deliberate attacks on the democratic party,
and that if published in the series, the abuse would be
exposed, he withdrew them. The last I give you on
respectable information—the first I know to be true. I
wonder if there is such a thing as an honest politician?

> Very truly yours
> J. Fenimore Cooper.

If Nicholson is to have the Home Squadron, have the
kindness to let me know where he is to be found. By the
way, what a scrape poor Bolton has got into!

FROM THOMAS BALDWIN

> Phila., Nov. 10 [1841]

Sir

I have long regretted that you did not extend your
Gleanings in Europe to Germany, and having just finished a second perusal of your France and Italy the desire
has increased. I think a book of Travels on Germany,
Prussia and Austria a desideratum, yet every traveller
when he approaches their confines lays down his pen. I

do not presume that the wishes of one man (however high in station) to be sufficient motive for an author to publish a work (my name is a very humble one) but a straw may turn the balance when it is *in equilibrio*. And I thought perchance your mind might be in the same state in regard to a work on those countries, as it was in respect to the Deer Slayer when you received the anonymous letter from Europe.

I hope you may find it both agreeable to yourself (and profitable) to lay the world again under obligations to yourself for the work I desire.

Be that as it may I acknowledge myself already indebted to you for many happy hours in the perusal of your various works. No work of fiction, not even any of Scott's, gave me such thrilling pleasure as your *last of the Mohicans* and the Series of Gleanings are the choicest *morceaux* in the travelling way I ever met with. That you may long live to enjoy the fruits of your labors, is the sincere wish of one of your most humble readers (in point of wealth and station).

I think authors may often not be aware how great the amount of pleasure they give is. There is a very large and quiet under stratum of readers, who are never heard of by the public, and whose criticisms never reach the press, who judge works by their real merits, and enjoy them much more than those who hope to rise to eminence by criticising what they could never equal or amend.

I give my name (it is that of an humble teacher) because I would not shrink from any liability that this probably improper liberty may bring on me.

your very obliged reader
Thos. Baldwin

J. Fenimore Cooper, Cooperstown

Fonda, friday p. m., 19, Nov. 1841

To
Schuyler Crippen Esq.
Dist. Atty. of Otsego Co.

Sir, Having just closed the trial commenced on Wednesday A. M. on the original indictment found against me by the grand jury of Otsego County for a libel on J. Fenimore Cooper in a review of *Home as found*, and the jury not having yet returned a verdict either in my behalf or against me, I am prepared to make an overture for the settlement of the second indictment. The Indictment referred to now pending is based upon an article in the *C. and E.* announcing that the indictment just tried had been found in Otsego County and is as follows:—

(Here insert the article alluded to)

I am now satisfied that I was in error in regard to the manner in which that indictment was procured. The whole article was hastily written, and in speaking of Mr. Cooper as being "the most wholesale libeller of any man living" I had in my mind and intended to be understood as only characterising some of his published works in relation to his Countrymen, and under the peculiar circumstances in which the parties still remain in relation to the first indictment and which are to remain unaffected by this communication, I agree that the publication of this letter in the *C. and E.* shall be considered as cancelling the entire article.

Very respectfully
Your ob^t Sevn^t
J. Watson Webb.

James Watson Webb was born in Clavarack, New York, February 8, 1802, and died in June, 1884. He was educated in Cooperstown, entered the army in 1819, and remained in the service until 1827, when he resigned and became editor of the New York *Courier*, afterwards known as the *Courier and Enquirer*. To expedite the business of reporting, Mr. Webb established a daily horse express between New York and Washington, with relays of horses every six miles of the way. This cost him $7,500.00 a month, but enabled him to obtain news twenty-four hours before his rivals. He was minister to Brazil and author of several books.

TO PAUL FENIMORE COOPER, GENEVA, NEW YORK

Hall, Cooperstown, Nov. 21st, 1841

My dear Boy,

As you and your dear sisters will feel anxious to hear the accounts of the Fonda campaign, I now send the "bulletin."

We found Mr. Webb at Fonda, but no Mr. Weed. All three of the causes were called, within an hour after the opening of the Court. An attorney appeared for Mr. Weed to say that his counsel would certainly arrive in the next car, that Mr. Weed's daughter was very ill, but that he had promised to come up in the next train, etc. Under the circumstances, I consented to wait till next day. Next day no Weed, and no Jordan. Satisfied that all this delay was to allow the friends of Weed and Webb to work out of doors, and being distinctly told that several prominent Whigs were active, and had come to Fonda with no other cause than to help their editors, we insisted on going on. We took an inquest against Weed, which implies that he made no defense. You will judge of the jury, when I tell you that three Whigs on this

jury insisted on finding a verdict for Mr. Weed! Of
course such a verdict would be set aside. Five were for
$1200, and one was for $1500. At length the jury sent
in word to the Judge it could not agree. We sent word
back they must, and shortly after they came in with a
verdict of $400. This was about half what it ought to
have been, but was pretty well for so miserable a jury.

On Wednesday, we got at Mr. Webb. Our jury was
bad as well could be. Nine Whigs, and some of them
extremely ignorant and prejudiced. It was told us there
was but one man on it at all capable of trying such a
cause. This was a Mr. Lansing, and a relative of Mrs.
Sutherland. On the trial we had the best of it, altogether.
They refused to let me speak, and it all fell on Dick.
Your cousin spoke for eight hours, or two days, and annihilated the other side. *He made infinitely* the best argument. The other side did nothing. The moral impression
was altogether in our favor, and Dick swept away a mass
of rubbish, in so clear a manner that we shall have no
more of it. But the Whigs were too much drilled, and
the jury could not agree. After being out nine hours, the
Court discharged them. It is understood that seven of the
Whigs were for acquittal, and the other five for guilty;
that four of these five, after being from eight in the morning to ten at night without food, yielded to the seven, on
the ground that if there were *doubts*, the defendant ought
to be acquitted—a false plea, you will understand, as
these doubts would have been their own—but that Mr.
Lansing told the Court they *never could* agree. It is said,
he never would consent that a man should be acquitted
in so clear a case. Of course, this case will be tried over
again in the Spring.

Before the jury was discharged in the cause just mentioned, Mr. Webb sent us a proposition to retract the charges of the second libel, for which he was indicted. After several hours of consultation, he made his retraction, which is to be published in his paper, and that affair was settled.

Then we got our verdict of $400 against Weed; one retraction from Mr. Webb, and in one case the jury did not agree. I make no doubt the *alleged ground* of the disagreement was the principle of a privileged *communication*, which Judge Sutherland will explain to you, and that the real ground was outdoor corruption.

I have been really delighted with Dick's success. His manner was as good as his matter, and there was but one opinion about the last. He dissected Mr. Webb's article, clause by clause, exposed its contradictions and falsehoods, in the most unanswerable manner. Mr. Jordan made a poor speech, Mr. Spencer a tolerably good one.

I hear the best accounts of you, my son, and your mother and myself feel a gratification in it, that you will never understand until you become a parent yourself. We are also pleased with Doctor Hawk's opinion of Roy.

Everyone sends love, and I think you ought to go often as possible to see your sisters. Send or bring me a catalogue. Be attentive to Platt and Charles and occasionally give them a little treat in the way of good things, or an excursion.

Yours very affectionately
J. Fenimore Cooper

FROM S. F. B. MORSE

New York, Nov. 30, 1841

My Dear Sir,
It is not because I have not thought of you and your

excellent family that I have not long since written you, to know your personal welfare. I hear of you often, it is true, through the papers. They praise you as usual, for it is praise to have the abuse of such as abuse you. In all your libel suits against these degraded wretches, I sympathize entirely with you, and there are thousands who now thank you in their hearts for the moral courage you display in bringing these licentious scamps to a knowledge of their duty. Be assured the good sense, the intelligence, the right feeling of the community at large are with you. The licentiousness of the press needed the rebuke which you have given it, and it feels it too, despite its awkward attempts to brave it out. I will say nothing of your *Home as found;* I will use the frankness to say that I wish you had not written it. But when am I ever to see you? Do call on me if you come to the city. I wished much the last summer to make you a call, but could not without a sacrifice that I could not sustain. When in Paris last I several times passed 59 rue St. Dominique; the gate stood invitingly open and I looked in, but did not see my old friends, although every thing else was present. I felt as one might suppose another to feel on rising from his grave, after a lapse of a century. Remember me kindly to Mrs. Cooper and all your family.

Truly as ever Yr Friend and Ser^vt

Saml F. B. Morse.

James Fenimore Cooper, Esqr, Cooperstown

FROM THOMAS BALDWIN

Phila., Dec. 4 [1841]

Honored Sir

Will you pardon me for again intruding on your privacy, when I promise you this shall be the last time;

but I cannot forbear to express the value I set on the honor you have done me in replying to my note, which was very unexpected but very grateful to me. Do not I beg you Sir accuse me of obsequiousness. I value *myself* with *myself* solely upon what God has given me. Though I trust few men would pay less homage to the "dollar gentry" than myself—yet I never felt any degradation in venerating genius, the stamp of divinity itself. The letter you have sent me shall be handed down to my representative and when the name of Cooper shall have become the property of history, as the first distinguished *original* American writer, I doubt not it will be still more highly valued than at present. A young man of my acquaintance (a student at law) came home the other day with a treasure which his mother has carefully locked up for him. It was the signature of J. Fenimore Cooper given to him by his preceptor. Yes Sir! there is no one (however much the editors may abuse you, not even the editors themselves) but, when he speaks of American literature proudly points to the name of Cooper. I am astonished at the indifference manifested to your *Gleanings in Europe* since my friends read and admire them. I think it must partly be owing to the commercial derangements that have prevailed since you published them, and partly (no doubt) to the offence you have given to the class who plume themselves on their dollars. But you have a very large class of readers that are not of much profit to you, who depend on libraries, and of whom you hear not through your publishers. I am glad to find any man who dares to stem the current of public opinion; and therefore was much pleased to find old John Q. taking a different view of the English attack on China than the public's (though mine in this case is that of the public) because I am glad to see a public man with *some inde-pendence* of opinion. The fact is demagogues have poi-soned the public taste by their fulsome and designing flattery. I cannot recollect any of your strictures on Americans that I thought unjust, but permit me to say I regretted that you did not think it proper to soften the manner a little. Most that I hear give a sentiment on the matter, regret your controversy with the press, as it has the power of misrepresentation. I regret it from a sel-fish motive, from fear that you will cease to write alto-gether or leave the country. I deeply lament on my own account that we are not to have the works referred to, in your letter. But I sincerely thank you, for the amount you have already added to my happiness by your writings.

I have long since ceased to look to newspapers for opinions, and only read them for the passing history of the day. I was so much struck with the justness of your animadversions upon the dependence of opinion in this country upon England, that I made it the subject of a newspaper essay some few months since; in which I re-ferred to your opinions. I have to thank you particularly for giving me a clearer idea of the locale of Rome than I ever before had, and especially for giving me juster views of Italian character. I had been in the habit of looking upon "Italians" with contempt. Not the first time you will say that ignorance has been the source of that feel-ing. In short I do not regret the *matter* of any thing you have written, though it had been better perhaps for your-self had the *manner* been a little softened. The world has never thanked those who reform or reprove it, from Socrates and Jesus to our own day, till it was too late to make amends to the object of their ingratitude. I think you mistake your countrymen somewhat, the papers do

not represent the thinking public—and I suppose the un-
thinking public are easily led every where. You occupy a
higher place than any other American author. Mr. Irving
is a delightful writer, his style is classic, he makes you
laugh or weep, but he does not make *me think* as you do.
And in description of scenes and places to my mind no
man equals you. Irving's genius is quiet and gentle following more in old models. Yours is bold and original.
When we read Irving we think how *sweetly* he writes.
When we read Cooper we are absorbed by his subject, or
our minds have been set to thinking and extending his
views. Will you pardon this second interruption of your
privacy. With desires that our common country may learn
to cherish genius, I am yrs

Thos. Baldwin

There was this paragraph in the paper, which I take,
on Monday last. "So much misrepresentation has been
indulged in towards this gentleman by a *portion* of the
press, that we doubted the statement. The letter of Mr.
Cooper confirms the justness of our doubts. Sueing editors is not the best method of conciliating the press, but
no one can blame a resort to the laws when it is for pro-
tection against a spirit of determined persecution." I hope
my countrymen will soon learn that the most effective
method of promoting their country's glory is by cherish-
ing her men of genius, and more particularly so in the
infant state of literature.

Your country owes you a heavy debt of admiration and
gratitude, and I for one acknowledge the obligation to
the full. And more particularly for your flattering notice
of my letter. After I had written it I felt some fears that
you might publish it as another evidence of the effrontery
of Americans. I had thought myself beyond being influ-

enced by our venal press, but it proved I did not know myself. I shall not intrude upon you again. With deep admiration for your genius and gratitude for the character you have given to American literature, I am your obt. Serv.

Thos. Baldwin

J. Fenimore Cooper, Cooperstown

TO MRS. COOPER, COOPERSTOWN

Philadelphia, Saturday, Feb. 5th, 1842

Dearest,

Soon after my last was written, Kit Hughes came to see me. He had come on from Baltimore with Ingersoll, and was waiting for the funeral. I have seen Dr. Mitchell, accidentally, and from him got the particulars of the poor girl's death. Mrs. Charles Ingersoll also gave me some particulars. It seems she was declining some months, though her father did not seem to be aware of it. They all went to Washington early in January, but Mary Ingersoll became so weak and languid that her father brought her back and left her with her uncle Ben Wilcocks. He then returned to his post. Dr. Mitchell says she complained of indigestion and of an inability to sleep from pain in her back. A little opium quieted the first, and the last was removed from cupping. He and Chapman thought her in no danger. Saturday morning, to his astonishment, he found her with her pulse at the elbow. She had been heated in the night, and taken a little cold in consequence of having had most of the bed clothes removed. He gave her, in wine glasses, quite a pint of medicine before he could bring back the pulse. At the next visit she had relapsed, and brandy would not affect her pulse. He then wrote for her father, and in an hour she died. Her death was easy, and with full consciousness.

She was buried Thursday. I wrote Ingersoll a note, and he sent me a particular invitation. The funeral was large and highly respectable. I never saw stronger manifestations of sympathy. Poor Ingersoll stood it pretty well, but he staggered at the grave. A hundred ladies were there. I saw all the Ingersoll family, dressed so plainly and so differently from what was usual as to make it difficult to recognize them. The Miss Wilcocks looked really of the ordinary height, they were so bowed down. They were not with their cousin when she died. Mrs. Charles Ingersoll was greatly agitated. I walked with Gurney Smith, who is Ingersoll's ex-warden. The Bishop was there, but Mr. Odenheimer officiated, and badly. He does not read well, and he spoiled that beautiful service.

Dick *s'ennuie* remarkably, but, being slow coach, he does not fidget much. He declines going to Washington, and I question a good deal if he would go into the next street without some prompting. A segar and a book is all he asks. Horace Walpole's letters, which I have, are too lively, however.

I shall bring home several books, and Horace among others.

I have seen Barton and the Willings. The latter are just opposite to me, at the Marvin House. I met Eliza Patterson in the street, and am to go and see her. Philadelphia is very *triste* on account of its money affairs. The State interest is not paid, though it is said it will be soon. Things are a little better within the last few days.

Barton laughs heartily at the lost chapter, and says it is unanswerable. The exception that proves the rule is exquisite. But Webb is figuring in the same paper as a bankrupt and as a manager of the Dickens Ball! Could this happen in any other country?

Mr. McIntosh went through here two or three days since. I asked after Lord Marpeth. He is at Washington amusing himself. Is he in love, or likely to be married? No—he is too sensible for *that*. Hum. He tells me he has one boy, and intends passing the summer here. I fancy Madame doesn't like it, on the other side. Perhaps he will agree with me now on the expediency of American girls marrying Englishmen. By the way, I am told Marpeth did pass a good deal of his time in Boston. Mrs. Willing tells me he greatly prefers Boston to New York.

Gardner has married one of his two daughters to a Louisiana senator. He resigns, and takes his bride south with him.

This is going to be the hardest summer we have had in years. Everybody is poor, feels poor, talks poor. Books sell very heavy, though near 2000 of *Naval History* have gone off. That book's sale remains to come. It ought to produce me $200 or $300 a year for eight and twenty years to come, and probably will. They print only 3000 of the *Admirals*. I like the book, though I doubt its very great success. The Effingham book produces no talk. It is said to be contemptible by some journals, which I fancy is the real fact.

Adieu, my dearest—kiss all the girls, and be very prudent in this treacherous weather. Two accidents have happened on the Pittsfield road, since we left home. One just before us, and one two or three days after us. In the last two men were killed. We shall not go back that way, the road being bad. God bless you all.

J. F. C.

FROM BISHOP DE LANCEY

New York, Feby. 9. 1842, I this evening had a conversation with Mrs. Davis, an old Lady 80 years old, born in New York, the wife of a tory Gentleman who left N. York on the evacuation in 1783. They returned in 1791. She and her daughter Mrs. Smith are boarding at the Rev. Dr. Hugh Smith's, where I am boarding with my family, two of my boys being under treatment for the spine complaint. Mrs. Davis is the sister of the first wife of the late Bp. Richard C. Moore. Mrs. Davis informed me that the author of the Song burlesquing the putting up of a Liberty Pole in the city of New York about the beginning of the Revolutionary war, was the Rev. Mr. Vardell. That the Individual called in the Song, Johnny S. was John M. Scott, Esq., a Presbyterian Lawyer, that William Smith, another Presbyterian Lawyer, was meant by the man "with hands so clean and heart so pure." That these two Gentlemen lived in Broadway on the opposite sides of Garden St., Mr. Scott on the south side, that the Liberty Pole stood in the middle of the street, about opposite to Ann St.—to use her expression, it was put up "in the fields." That the House of James De Lancey, called the Bowery House, was near the East River with a double row of trees from the bowery to the House, wh. trees were destroyed in the war, and Mr. De Lancey obtained for them one hundred guineas, from the English Government. She said that the above named William Smith, from being a whig, turned Tory, and was rewarded with some high office in Canada. Upon being asked what induced him to become a Tory, she said, "because it was more profitable."

Upon being told that he had been represented as having played a double part during the revolution and re-

vealed the secrets of the torys to the whigs, she said "it
was just like him."

W. H. De Lancey

Bp. Moore was son of Lambert Moore.

TO MRS. COOPER, COOPERSTOWN

Globe, March 22d, 1842

Cruger and his wife are separated again. Cutting's
affair has also produced a separation between Hosack *et
sa femme*. They say it is all passion in this last chapter,
and no criminality, the Doctor refusing to live with a
woman who has bestowed her heart on another man. Cutting went to Europe to dissipate his passion, which was
certainly better than dissipating it *à la nouvelle Angle-
terre*. Mrs. Willing said it was a novelty to hear of such
a thing as any passion in an American intrigue.

By the way, Mrs. Willing has let out the secret of
Irving's appointment. He wrote to Webster to remember him *if anything good offered*. So that instead of not
asking for the office, he asked for anything that was good.
There has been more humbug practiced concerning this
man than concerning any other now living.

TO MRS. COOPER, COOPERSTOWN

New York, May 13th, 1842

I wrote you a line from Fonda, to say that I had
beaten Weed, a verdict of $323. This was too little, but
it has proved a great source of mortification to *them*, as is
shown by their papers. Most of them do not speak of my
verdict at all, and all round we have proofs of their
mortification.

We go on to-day in the Stone case, though he is on

trial to-day in his indictment, and we may not get seriously at work until Monday. We shall be through time enough to get up to Saratoga by the 23d.

I have been so busy preparing for the arbitration that I have nothing to tell you. Dick and myself are well. A good deal of interest is felt about the Stone case, and I expect a large audience. I shall write on Sunday more fully and will then enter into details. Now, I am surrounded by lawyers.

TO MRS. COOPER, COOPERSTOWN

New York, May 14, evening, 1842

Dearest Sue,

In my last, I forgot to mention *The Two Admirals*. Spencer alluded to it in the trial at Fonda, observing that Mr. Weed had been praising it, and spoke highly of it. This was encouraging, you will say. Webb has extolled it, and so has Benjamin! All this is a part of a system of tactics, but the book is decidedly successful, so far as I have heard. Several individuals have spoken of it to me. In addition Lea & Blanchard stand firm.

Every thing shows that the late verdict has produced an effect. Not even a sneer has appeared against it in any journal here. Two or three have not spoken of it, but most have, simply announcing the fact. Weed is here, and I fancy pretty uneasy. He wishes to amend his plea in the next case at Saratoga, but we have refused to consent. Dick thinks they will not come to trial. Greeley wishes to refer. I cannot now say what we shall do.

I find the battery much more frequented than formerly. It is now covered with well dressed people every afternoon, and the young men resort there to smoke. It is very pretty, though not yet a villa rock.

I had a few minutes' talk with the Chief this morning. It was all about grasses and farming.

Sunday—1 o'clock.

Dick and I have just returned from a visit to the *Columbia* 44, Capt. Parker, lying in the Hudson. We arrived just as service was commencing, and heard it all. The Chaplain read a part of the morning prayer, and delivered a brief extemporary address on the subject of condition of the spirit after death. The men were attentive, and the discourse was a good one, and well adapted to the congregation.

The weather is rather raw, with the wind at South East, but I feel perfectly well. My labours will commence at ½ past 4 to-morrow, and when you get this letter we shall be fairly engaged in the subject. I think we shall get through by Wednesday and I feel great confidence in the power of truth.

You need scarcely expect to hear from us again before it is all over, though I may write, if anything particular occurs. I have not heard from home, though Dick has, and tells me you are all well.

Adieu, my love. Kiss the children, and rest assured of my tenderest affection.

J. F. C.

When Fenimore Cooper was preparing the account of the Battle of Lake Erie for his *Naval History* he reached the conclusion that an injustice had been done Jesse Duncan Elliott, who was second in command to Commodore Oliver Hazard Perry, and who was accused of failing to bring his ship, the *Niagara*, to the assistance of Perry, when the latter's flagship, the *Lawrence*, was disabled, as promptly as he should and could have done.

At this time Cooper did not know Elliott and had no motive

but the desire of accuracy in his account of the battle and of Elliott's conduct.

Perry and the Battle of Lake Erie were at the time looked upon as distinctly the property of Rhode Island, as was the *Constitution* of Boston, and any criticism of either was bitterly resented locally.

The accuracy of Cooper's account of the battle was attacked in the most venomous and abusive manner in pamphlets and by certain of the newspapers; among the most violent of the articles were the criticisms in the *Commercial Advertiser* written by William A. Duer. After nearly a year's delay Cooper sued William L. Stone, the owner and editor, for libel. Stone objected to the trial of the case by an ordinary jury, pointing out that only a trained lawyer would be competent to review the evidence. Cooper thereupon proposed that the decision should be rendered by three arbitrators or referees; and it was so agreed. Samuel Steevens, Daniel Lord, and Samuel A. Foot were selected, one by each of the parties and the third by mutual agreement. The cause was heard and the arbitrators decided every point in Cooper's favor— five of the eight questions submitted, unanimously, and the other three with the dissent of one arbitrator to a minor point in each case. They also directed Stone to publish the full text of the decision in Albany, New York, and Washington papers and to pay the costs of the arbitration.

The decision in effect found that Cooper's version was accurate in every particular and that the critic had not faithfully fulfilled the office of reviewer; that the review was untrue and was not written in a spirit of impartiality and justice.

It is an interesting fact, and perhaps as well stated here, that Cooper succeeded in every lawsuit which he brought, except one, in which the Court held that the statement made by one of the newspapers sued did not constitute a libel. The verdicts often seemed small, but the juries and the Court always eventually held that the plaintiff was justified in bringing the suit. Morally and legally Cooper was right and his opponents and critics wrong.

TO MRS. COOPER, COOPERSTOWN

Globe, New York, May 21, 1842

My dear Wife,

The arbitration commenced on Monday, at ½ past 4, P. M. I opened in a speech of about two hours. It is generally admitted that the opening was effective. Campbell followed—then came some witnesses on Tuesday, and a part of Campbell's summing up. He made a very fair speech, concluding it on Wednesday afternoon. Dick came next on the questions of law. After speaking very well for an hour, he was stopped by the arbitrators, who told him they preferred to hear the other side. This was tantamount to saying that his views so far were their own. As they never asked him to resume, we infer that they were with us on the law. Bidwell followed. He commenced about 8 on Wednesday evening, and finished about eight on Thursday, having spoken about five hours in all. I commenced summing up when Bidwell sat down, and spoke until past ten, when we adjourned. Yesterday, Friday, I resumed at four, and spoke until past ten again, making eight hours, in all. Here the matter rests for the decision.

At first the papers were studiously silent, and our audiences were respectable, though not large. The opening, however, took, and many attended in expectation of hearing my summing up. On Thursday numbers of Duer's friends appeared, and some twenty of my most active enemies crowded within the bar. Among others, Jordan came and took a seat directly opposite to me, and for three hours his eyes were riveted on Bidwell. When I rose, he was within six feet of me. For half an hour I could see that his eyes were fastened on my countenance; then his head dropped, and for an hour it was concealed. He could stand it no longer, got up, and went out. Stone's countenance changed, became gloomy, Duer went out, and I had not spoken the two hours before all that set vanished. The impression was decided on Thursday, when I closed, and the next day there was a throng. I now spoke six hours, and all that time the most profound silence prevailed. I do not believe a soul left the room. When I closed there was a burst of applause that the constables silenced, and a hundred persons crowded round me, two-thirds of whom were strangers. There is not the smallest doubt that we have carried all before us, so far as the impression of the audience was concerned.

I tell you this, my love, because I know it will give you pleasure. Dick has just come in, and says he has seen the Chief Justice, who tells him that all he has heard speak on the subject say we have altogether the best of it.

I am well, but excessively tired, and can only tell you my present movements. There will be no trial at Saratoga on account of Willard's indisposition. I shall remain here to make arrangements about *Le Feu-follet*, and be home about the 1st June. Dick will leave here to-morrow, and will provide you with money.

My last victory over Weed appears to have stopped his mouth. The tide is unquestionably turning in my favor, and the power of the press cannot look down truth as completely as was thought.

I have not yet seen May or anybody, and can tell you no news. Let me find a letter here, about the 27th or 28th. With love to all,

Tenderly yours,

J. F. C.

New York, June 17, 1842

My Dear Sir

I have this moment received the award in the suit against Stone. I have barely time to run my eyes over it, and to say that they decide eight points, every one of them in your favor.

1.—"That the plaintiff would be entitled to a verdict from a Jury—that the defendant within sixty days pay the plaintiff $250 for his outlays in the suit, and also $50 for his outlays, etc., under the arbitration—the arbitrators determine to receive no compensation."

2.—"That he (the plaintiff) has faithfully fulfilled his obligations as a Historian."

3.—"That the aforesaid narrative of the Battle of Lake Erie is true in its essential facts."

4.—"That it (the narrative) was written in a spirit of impartiality."

5.—"That the writer and publisher of said Review in writing and publishing the same, has not faithfully fulfilled his obligations as a Reviewer," and they assign the facts on which this opinion is founded.

6.—"That the said Review is untrue, in the following particulars"—(stating the particulars).

7.—"That it (the Review) was not written in a spirit of impartiality and justice."

8.—"That the defendant is bound to make reparation, and that this award shall be published at his expense in the manner, and within the time, provided in the above recited paragraph of submission."

The Award is signed by all three arbitrators. Mr. Foot gives an "opinion dissenting from parts of the award,"

which he desires to be published with the Award. I have
not time to read his opinion before the closing of the mail.
Very Respectfully and truly
your friend and obed Servt
Hamilton Fish

P. S. Mr. Campbell shewed me Mr. R. Cooper's letter
desiring him to hand me the award. The award and opinion together are written on seventeen pieces of paper; the
postage would exceed the sum mentioned in Mr. Cooper's
letter ($2). I therefore retain it subject to your directions.
J. Fenimore Cooper Esq., Cooperstown

TO MRS. COOPER, COOPERSTOWN

Globe, Tuesday, June 29th [28th?], 1842

Dearest—

I got here this morning: pretty tired, but much improved in stomach. The shaking has done this, at least.
I found Stephen Rensselaer in the boat, and he gave me
a berth in his state room, where I passed a cool comfortable night.

Stone *has* published the award. It is not long, and he
has made his arrangements to have it published in Washington and Albany. I saw Lord to-day, and he says
Foot—*entre nous*—is a *fool*. His published opinions are
anything but forceful, or elaborate. I can draw a coach
and six through them, but they seem to have made no
impression.

The arbitration has been a dear triumph. I do not send
the award, but Dick will find it in one of the Albany
papers this week.

Webb's duel makes a good deal of fun. They say the

wound looks serious from the condition of his body, but
I fancy it will not come to much.

Very tenderly yours,

J. F. C.

PART FOURTH

From July 1st, 1842, to the date of Cooper's death, September 14th, 1851. During this time he lived in Cooperstown, New York, and wrote The Wing-and-Wing; Wyandotte; Ned Myers; Afloat and Ashore; Satanstoe; Miles Wallingford; The Chainbearer; The Redskins; The Islets of the Gulf (*also published under the title* Jack Tier; or The Florida Reefs); The Crater; The Oak Openings; The Sea Lions; The Ways of the Hour; *and a number of biographies and short articles.*

1842-1851

FROM ELIZABETH F. ELLET

New York, July 6th [1842]

Dear Mr. Cooper

You so kindly encouraged me to apply to you for assistance or advice in the matter of the Revolutionary women, that I venture again to trespass on your time in their behalf. But it will not involve any trouble for you to answer my enquiries.

It is stated in Bolton's *History of Westchester County*, that you drew the character of "Frances," in *The Spy*, after Miss Mary Philipse, the daughter of Hon. Frederick Philipse. Is that true? The lady is one of my heroines, and I can obtain no particulars respecting her from her relatives, reverentially as they cherish her memory. Mr. Sabine has furnished me with almost all the details I have. The portrait in the possession of Mrs. Gouverneur is to be engraved.

Do you think it beyond doubt that Mrs. Gates taught school in Richmond, Virginia, previous to her marriage with the General? If you do, I will insert it, though Mr. Sparks is of the opinion that Gen. Gates married in England.

In the brief sketch of Alice De Lancey Izard, I have mentioned that Susan, the daughter of Col. Stephen De

Lancey, whose first husband was Lieutenant Colonel William Johnson, became the wife of Lt. Gen. Sir Hudson Lowe, and was the beautiful Lady Lowe praised by Buonaparte.

Charlotte married Sir David Dundas, and was the one whose mother hid in a kennel, and who was herself on one occasion concealed in a bin. I believe I have remembered this correctly.

I received a few days since a most interesting letter from Mrs. Martha Wilson of Lakelands, near Cooperstown. She favors me with some of her recollections of Mrs. Washington and others, and with a few particulars concerning herself. She refers me for further details of herself to her nephew, the Rev. Charles Stewart of the Navy. I have not heard from him, though I sent a note to his house, and doubt not he is out of the city. Should you see any of the family, will you have the kindness to mention that I have not been able to see Mr. Stewart? But do not take any trouble about it, as I may yet succeed.

My book is in press, and the printers proceed very rapidly; so that I am much hurried and full of anxiety for fear of mistakes. Scarcely any authorities agree with each other with regard to facts; and tradition I find cannot at all be depended on. I have received many interesting anecdotes which I am compelled to reject because they cannot be substantiated, and in some cases conflict with historical facts.

Should you visit New York again, I hope you will let Dr. Ellet and me have the pleasure of seeing you. My address is 624 Broadway. Mrs. Wayne of South Carolina (Miss Morris that was) expects shortly to visit Cooperstown, and wishes much to renew an early ac-

quaintance with you. I have promised her a letter to you.
I remain, with high regard
Dear Sir
very truly yours
E. F. Ellet

J. Fenimore Cooper, Esq.

Elizabeth F. Ellet was the wife of William F. Ellet, M.D.,
and the daughter of William A. Lummis, M.D. She was the
author of some fourteen books, among them *The Women of the
American Revolution.*

TO MRS. COOPER, COOPERSTOWN

Philadelphia, Thursday, [September] 29th, 1842
My dearest Sue—

You have seen Wilkes' sentence. It is just what I
expected; relieving him from opprobrium of all sort,
though the secretary's reprimand manifests feeling. Ballard, it is said, is suspended for a year without pay. It
is a hard sentence. It is now reported that Gallagher will
resign. There will good come of all this.

I have dined with young Charles, Barton, and Miller.
The latter was at my door early the evening I arrived
and has been very civil. If I were a young lady I should
expect a proposal.

Joe Ingersoll is well, and in tolerable spirits; though
he keeps quite out of the world. His brother Charles has
had a fall, but is better. Barton was really learned and
eloquent the day I dined with him. We were *tête-à-tête*.
It is a pity the *ménage* is not happier.

I have sold the *Autobiography* to Graham, 50 pages
for $500. I shall finish it as soon as *Le Feu-Follet* is off
my hands—but I must come home to write the three last

chapters. I have sold, on a check plan, to L. & B. I get some down, some notes—in all $500—with rights reserved. It is an experiment.

Verron's trial for perjury is just over—result unknown.

> Yours tenderly, with love to the girls—
>
> J. F. C.

Saunderson's, Oct. 2d, 1842

My dearest wife,

When I got here I found I had a great deal to do, or a very little. It has resulted in the first—and I have done a great deal. I have written a biography of Dale, and it is printed. So I am in *type*, already, for November and December. January, February and March we shall come out in the autobiography, and there will follow, Perry, already written, in April and May. This will leave me my own time, after about a fortnight's work on the autobiography, to concoct anything else.

Shubrick has gone on to New York, and I have not seen him—unless he got on to-morrow morning. Conner, who is here, however, says he must be in New York to-morrow. I shall find him there, on my way home. You will see me probably on Saturday next—possibly not until Sunday. This will make an absence of nineteen or twenty days, instead of a fortnight—but much will have been accomplished in the time.

I have all but one chapter of *Feu-Follet* written, and half the second volume is printed. I am to be through here by Wednesday at latest.

There will be scarcely any books, none having been published but medical works.

Books begin to move again, however, and times will soon be better.

Pennsylvania stocks look up a little, and the better opinion is that they will pay in the end. Biddle, however, thinks it still a matter of question, whether they pay *all*.

Webb is indicted for his duel, though I question if much will come of it. He is such a talking bully that men get wearied of him, and a portion of the community seem disposed to put a stop to his bullying at least. I fear this affair may throw some impediment in the way of his trial at Fonda. The least penalty, if convicted, is five years in the State Prison.

I send this to-night that you may know I am well, and my expectations. I have no letter, but hope to find one at the Globe. It is now five and I am going to dinner, breakfasting at eleven, and munching a few peaches about nine in the morning.

My tenderest love to all, and to none more than to yourself.

J. F. C.

TO MRS. COOPER, COOPERSTOWN

Ballston, Thursday, 3 P. M., Dec. 8th, 1842

Dearest,

Weed has come up, and his affair is settled. He has paid costs and counsel fees, agrees to pay the verdict last obtained, makes a full retraction of this libel, and a general retraction of all the others, and I let him off, until he misbehaves again. This is as complete a triumph as we could obtain—so every one here seems to think, and so we think.

Greeley has prepared a speech, and is anxious to deliver it. His friends advise him to retract, but he must have his speech—We shall try his case to-morrow and shall be home to a tea-dinner on Saturday: with a verdict of from $200 to $400.

There is an intelligent bar here, and we pass our time in gossip. Col. Young is here, and I find him an amusing companion.

Dick is well, and smokes. I never was better, and so the world jogs.

With best love to all, I am

Dearest Love

Yours as tenderly as ever

J. F. C.

Thurlow Weed, of the Albany *Evening Journal*, was born at Cairo, Green County, New York, November 15, 1797. He died at New York City, November 22, 1882. He was a noted American journalist and politician. He was educated as a printer, served in the war of 1812, was editor of various papers in New York state; but became famous as editor of the Albany *Evening Journal* (1830-1862). During the Civil War he supported Lincoln and was sent by him on a mission to Europe, 1861-1862. He worked in a printing house at Cooperstown when a young man.

RETRACTION OF THURLOW WEED

The Publication to be set out in full, embracing the letter from Fonda and the comments.

The above article having been published in the Albany *Evening Journal* of Nov. 22, 1841, on a review of the matter and a better knowledge of the facts, I feel it to be my duty to withdraw the injurious imputations it contains on the character of Mr. Cooper. It is my wish that this retraction should be considered as broad as the charges.

The Albany *Evening Journal* having also contained various other articles, reflections on Mr. Cooper's character, I feel it to be due to that gentleman to withdraw every charge that injuriously affects his standing in the community.

It having been submitted to me to determine the nature of the reparation due to Mr. Cooper from Mr. Weed, I have decided that Mr. Weed sign the foregoing retraction and publish it together with the article of the 22 of November, 1841, in the Albany *Evening Journal.*

Daniel Cady

I agree to publish the foregoing in the Albany *Evening Journal.*

Thurlow Weed.

TO MRS. COOPER, COOPERSTOWN

Albany, Jan. 4th, 1843

Dearest,

I had a good time down, though it was eight before we got in. Sarah was placed safely in her school, and I went to Lawdom. There I found Ben Nicols, who is one of the members from Suffolk, looking like a lad of five and thirty. He is a great humbug, in the way of looks, certainly. Cousin David is in the field, again.

Mackenzie's affairs look bad enough. The report he sent to Washington is considered to be the work of a man scarcely *compos mentis.* I never read a more miserable thing in my life—he has actually got in one of the prayers he read to his crew. To crown all he admits he told Spencer that he would not be hanged if he got in, on account of his father's influence, and he actually recommends his nephew to fill his vacancy. In a word, such a medley of folly, conceit, illegality, feebleness and fanaticism was never before assembled in a public document.

I am to dine with Stevenson to-day, and I shall go down *via* New Haven to-morrow. By this road I get a good night's sleep. The thermometer was 10 below zero last night, and only 2 above at ten o'clock. This is our cold weather. Tell Dick Col. Young got $900. damages. He had the good jurors, and some of ours. Weed has got back, but, as yet, has said nothing. The attempt on the legislature will be abandoned; first, because it won't succeed, and next because it might equalize the law in civil and criminal cases.

Tell Paul I saw Professor Webster yesterday, and he gave him a good character. He gave poor Phil as bad a one as possible. With tenderest love, ever yours,

J. F. C.

TO MRS. COOPER, COOPERSTOWN

Philadelphia, Jan. 10th, [1843]

Dearest,

Wing-and-Wing has only done so so. It is well received, but the sales but little exceed one-half of what they ought to be. About twelve thousand copies have been sent off. I consider the experiment a failure, though we may sell five thousand more. The season is against us. We should have done better in the summer. I shall touch about $500 here, this time. It is better than nothing, but not half what I expected to receive.

I dined yesterday with Harry Ingersoll, whose father was present. To-day, I am to dine with Ben Wilcocks. His nieces are with him. The two brothers live together, *en garçons*, at Washington. The Wilcocks family is not likely to be extinct.

Harry Ingersoll and I had a long *tête-à-tête*, after dinner, in which I got much navy gossip. He gave me the whole history of Charles Stewart's being sent home. It is a terrible story to tell of a chaplain, but cannot be written. He has no standing whatever, though of his *crime* it is possible he may be innocent.

Everybody is talking of Mackenzie's affair. As yet it looks worse and worse for him, though they say the secretary will sustain him. If he attempt it against the evidence, it will only break him down himself. Gen. Well, Govr. Kemble, and one or two more of us, at Gen. Cadwalader's, agreed last evening. Every man of mind thinks in the same way about it.

Griswold goes to Europe in the spring; how long to remain, I know not. Mr. Herbert, an Englishman, will take his place.

The taverns are thin, a few persons are moving. Ogden says New York was never duller in a business light, and he sees dullness in perspective. A little check to go aheadism will do no harm.

I am well, and in good spirits. The sight of a bridegroom fourteen years older than myself makes me feel young again, though he will swear more in a minute than I can swear in a year.

The weather is very mild—so much so that I feel no inconvenience in writing without a fire—I suppose you have a thaw.

I went alongside of the *Somers*, and saw the fatal yard at which Phil was swinging little more than a month since. I am told the old officers shake their heads.

With tenderest love to all,

Yours
J. F. C.

Globe Hotel, Jany. 18, 1843

My dear Sir,

I have hoped to have the pleasure of handing you the enclosed in person, but have not been so fortunate as to find you at your lodgings. Allow me to congratulate you upon your success thus far in combating the spirit of Evil, embodied in a work of that evil disposed person John Milton, the author of a defence of "the liberty of *unlicensed* printing."

Do me the kindness on your return home to present my compliments to the Ladies of your family, and believe me
with the greatest regard
most truly yours
Fitz-Greene Halleck

J. Fenimore Cooper, Esq., Globe Hotel

Sailors Snug Harbor, Staten Island,

January 23, 1843

Sir

Excuse the liberty I take in addressing you, but being anxious to know whether you are the Mr. Cooper who in 1806 or 1807 was on board the ship *Sterling*, Cap. Johnson, bound from New York to London, if so whether you recollect the boy *Ned* whose life you saved in London dock, on a Sunday, if so it would give me a great deal of pleasure to see you, I am at present at the Sailors Snug Harbor, or if you would send me your address in the city, I would like to call upon you.

I have lately been to the eastward and have seen Cap-

tain Johnson who is now well and in good circumstances.
should you be the person described Cap. Johnson would
be much pleased to hear from you.

Respectfully,

your obt servt.

Edward R. Myers.

Jas. Fenimore Cooper, Esq.

TO PAUL FENIMORE COOPER, GENEVA, NEW YORK

Home, Mother's Birthday, Jan. 28, 1843

My dear Boy,

You will have heard of my return, and that I went no
further than Philadelphia. The experiment of *Le Feu-
Follet* has done admirably, but would have done better
with a little more experience on my side. Next time, I
shall make a better bargain.

The *Somers* affair makes much conversation. The better opinion is everywhere against him, though there is a
desperate effort making to get Mackenzie out of the
scrape. Of the final decision of the country I entertain
no doubt, though there is an evident desire to shield him
among certain officials. All relating to the Court of Inquiry has been badly managed, and leaves a suspicion of
favoritism. Still all the captains with whom I have conversed think him wrong.

The leading points are these: Spencer tells Wales his
plans, to induce the latter to join him. He says he has
about *twenty*-seven concerned. These, then, were the *most*
he had engaged. Mackenzie reasons exactly the other
way; he thought twenty was the *least* number opposed to
him. *This fact, alone, proves the frame of mind under
which he acted.* Of course Spencer, in cajoling a recruit,

put his best foot foremost—he boasted of all he had, and, as his own muster-roll subsequently showed, he boasted of *more* than he had. This paper has four down as certain. One of these four was Phil, himself, and another was Wales. Wales was clearly uncertain. He enlisted at nine o'clock at night, after the lights were out, and he swears that this was the first he had heard of the mutiny. Of course his name was put down next morning, the day Spencer was arrested, and this list was then complete. Three men *certain*, did not make a formidable mutiny— but there were *nine* doubtful. The doubtful were sure to join the strongest side. But four of these doubtful were marked as likely to join before the rising. Well, this makes but seven in all, and surely a brig of 266 tons could hold seven, or seventeen, or seventy prisoners, if necessary. Suppose she had taken a pirate; what would she have done with the crew? Hang them, by way of precaution? Mackenzie had all the evidence in his possession of the feebleness of this plot, and yet he hangs one man, whose guilt, to say the least, was questionable!

I saw Elihu Phinney on my way to New York. He was on board the boat from New Haven, going to pass a few days with the Stewarts. He looked well, and seemed in good spirits. He says the work is hard at Yale, but thinks you could have led your class there, and fancies a deal of honor lost, in consequence of your tail being eight or nine instead of eighty or ninety. Rensselaer is toll loll, and he, Rens says, is loll toll. I fancy neither is in the first twenty.

Weed has given up, and paid his verdict. He appears disposed to be quiet. Stone's demurrer was argued on Friday; result not known. Greeley pays.

I had a merry time in Philadelphia, having got into the

middle of a wedding. The last steamer has just brought
me favorable news of *Feu-Follet* from England, where
the book has taken well. Dick has just been here, and let
me into the state of all the suits. At present we have but
two; one against Stone, and one against Greeley. Webb,
however, will probably come in for one or two, shortly. I
met Professor Webster in Albany, and was much gratified by his account of you. I wish, however, you would
pay more attention to declamation. Speak naturally—
endeavoring to speak slowly, take care not to halt, but to
divide the sounds on the different syllables. I think, too,
it may be of essential service to you to write well. Nature
and simplicity are the great secrets, as to style, as well as
to declamation. All fine writing must have its root in the
ideas. You never will want the last, and the embellish-
ments will follow, quite as a matter of course.

I have no gossip to tell you. Sam. Starkweather and
his wife, who have lived apart these ten years, have come
together again. The motive is probably her annuity.

I saw a person in Albany, whom I took to be an em-
ployé of John C. Spencer, that had been at Geneva obtaining testimony as to Phil's character. He told me it
was not so very bad. I told him, in answer, that I had
received the worst accounts of it. He then told me that
a letter desiring Phil to call on the writer, before the
Somers sailed, and signed "Eliza," had been found in
Phil's trunk. This letter was sent to Washington with an
endorsement on its back, to say that it was a *proof of
his dissolute habits, etc.* This letter was written by a
female relative, who had already given poor Phil, and
wished still to give him, good advice!

I have just heard that a flourish was made at Ballston,
about getting up a subscription towards paying Greeley's

verdict, and that $35 were subscribed; $15 by an inn-keeper who expected that the *Tribune* would puff his house; and then, the affair fell through!

We are all well. Dr. Bush is in your room. Last week there was a Mr. Griswold here, who announced that "a lady"—Mrs. Clark—"wishes to return thanks for her recovery, etc."

Our good bishop does ordain right and left. I hope *your* bishop has a little more discretion.

Give my love to all at Geneva—particularly to aunties. Aunt Cally has sent me a pair of mittens, of which, tell her, if the length of the fingers is to be taken for the measure of her love, had better never have been sent. They just reach to my knuckles. The next time let her take Judge Sutherland's hand for a measure.

Adieu, my dear boy.

Most affectionately

Your Father,

J. Fenimore Cooper

The facts of the "*Somers* affair" are briefly as follows:

In the winter of 1842 the U. S. Brig *Somers* was cruising off the coast of Africa under command of Captain Alexander Slidell Mackenzie. On board as a midshipman was Philip Spencer, a boy under nineteen years of age. He was the son of the Secretary of War. According to the statement of a purser's steward by the name of Wales, young Spencer confided to him a plan for mur-dering the officers of the *Somers*, seizing her, and turning pirate. This conversation took place November 25, while the *Somers* was on her way to St. Thomas.

Wales reported the conversation to the first lieutenant, and Spencer was arrested. On the 27th the main-royal mast was car-ried away, and Captain Mackenzie, thinking it part of a plan for the seizure of the ship, arrested a boatswain's mate, Cromwell, and a sailor, Small. Later on four more of the crew were arrested.

Mackenzie, seeing, or imagining, other signs of a mutiny, on December 1, after an informal discussion with some of his officers, hanged Spencer, Cromwell, and Small. There was no civil trial or court martial; no oaths were administered or witnesses sworn and examined.

When the above facts became known there was an outcry of protest throughout the country, and Mackenzie was ordered before a court martial, which, on March 28, 1843, acquitted him, finding that the charges against him were not proved. The charges were: Murder on the High Seas; Oppression; Illegal Punishment; Conduct Unbecoming an Officer; and Cruelty and Oppression.

The decision was unpopular and severely criticized by many, and was elaborately reviewed and condemned by Cooper.

FROM NED MYERS

Sailors Snug Harbor, Staten Island

February 22. 1843

Dear Sir.

I duly received your esteemed favor of January 28th. and I assure you it gave me much pleasure to hear from you, and to think that you would condescend to write to an old sailor laid up in ordinary.

In your letter you desired to know Cap. Johnson's direction, and through negligence on my part, or you would have had it sooner, his direction is "Cap. John Johnson, Wiscasset, Maine." I was on a visit to Wiscasset last fall, when we were conversing about our first voyage, and of course your name was mentioned, he enquired particularly if I knew any thing about you, and expressed a desire to hear from you, he is very old, and it would give him a great deal of pleasure to hear from you.

You mentioned that we had sailed on different tacks, which is a fact, yours being a smooth sea, and fair wind, while mine has been nothing but head gales, a head beat sea, sails spilt and spars carried away, and at last condemned as unseaworthy. I however have a pretty snug harbor to spend the last of my days in; altho' not as comfortable as it might, or was intended to be, by the noble donor, however better than no place to rest in.

I think however I have at last got on the right tack, making my bible my only chart to steer by, and trusting in a kind providence to bring me to a happy state hereafter. I was brought to this happy train of thoughts in consequence of a severe fall (which has crippled me for life) on a passage to Batavia, on board a dutch East Indiaman, the crew at the time being in a state of mutiny.

If not to much trouble I should like on your arrival at New York, for you to drop me a few lines, I feel very anxious to see you.

With Respect
Your obt servt
Edward R. Myers.

J. Fenimore Cooper, Esqr, Cooperstown

FROM W. B. SHUBRICK

Navy Yard, Gosport, Va., 10th March, 1843

My dear Cooper

This affair of the *Somers* is certainly the most extraordinary on record and one that has perplexed me beyond measure. When I first wrote to you on the subject I had not seen Mackenzie's narrative. The bad effect produced

on my mind by that singular production was in a measure
effaced by the full and decisive opinion, in his favor, of
the court of inquiry composed of men in whose judgment
and intelligence I have great confidence. I have always
held it to be a rule that a mutiny detected before an overt
act has been committed is a mutiny suppressed, and
Mack.'s crew must have been composed of very different
materials from any that I have ever seen, if with the ringleaders in irons, the officers, petty officers, and a part of
the crew with him, he could not have taken care of the
remainder. Large allowances must be made however in
these cases for an officer thrown entirely on his own re-
sources, with the responsibility of command for the first
time on him, surrounded by very young officers and
obliged to decide promptly for good or for evil; he must
certainly shew an imperious warranty for taking the law
into his hands, or rather thrusting it aside, and adminis-
tering "wild justice." We get the testimony given before
the courts in detached portions, and it is hardly safe to
make up a final opinion from it. I think however that the
court martial will follow in the steps of the court of
inquiry and acquit. What is to be done then? Can he be
tried by a civil court? Mr. Tarewell the great Virginia
lawyer says, yes, I think so—Mr T. says a court martial
is not a court of record, and therefore cannot protect him
from civil process; that if the court martial should con-
vict Mack. and the President should pardon him, he
could plead the pardon in bar of further trial—it would
be a *"nolle prosequi,"*—but that nothing else can save
him. This seems to me strange doctrine; I cannot understand it; yet Mr Tarewell is a great lawyer. Whatever
may be the result of this business Mack. is ruined for
the Navy and must fall back on his other vocation of

bookmaking. I do not think the Department is disposed to favor him *now;* the Spencer influence is too powerful— Mr. U. has not firmness enough to stand up against it. The appointment of the Judge Advocate was a bad one,—he is a young man and little known in his profession even in Baltimore.

Parker's squadron, *Brandywine* and *St. Louis*, is ready for sea—*Stewart* and *Trenton* ready for the Mediterranean, *Macedonian*, *Warren* and *Decatur* preparing for the coast of Africa—several small craft, such as [illegible], *Wave* and *Phœnix* for different places—store ship *Lexington* for Mediterranean, and a brig building besides—so you may suppose I am not eating the bread of idleness—I am heartily sick however of dock yard duty, and of navy matters generally; our affairs at headquarters are in the hands of "shallow men and irresponsible boys."

The bureaux except Warrington and Traver must break down. Goldsborough cannot stand twelve months. Barton is a scamp who ought to be kicked out of all decent society.

We are quite well and unite in most affectionate remembrances to Mrs. Cooper and the young ladies, and Paul.—We despair of ever seeing any of you in Virginia—after the summer we expect to have nothing to do but to travel about, but we shall feel bound to give Cooperstown a wide berth.

As ever your friend

W. Branford Shubrick

I must give you a coincidence for the biography of Hull—the *Constitution* was put out of commission the very day that we heard of the death of her gallant old commander.

Bedford, 15th July, 1843

My dear Cooper

I had last night the pleasure of receiving your kind letter. The Doctor, my Wife, and my Daughters have all conspired to send me a jaunting, and of course a jaunting I must go. It has been a question in what direction I should wander—North, East, or West? To move towards the fourth cardinal point, you know, is dangerous for such fanatics as contend that men are not chattles [*sic*]. But the question is settled—"I will go and see Cooper."

I propose setting out on Wednesday next, but as you are not to be at home immediately I intend giving my Wife, Sally, and Augusta a sight of Niagara, and calling at the Hall on my return.

That your answer to Mack. will be as plain as a pike-staff I do not doubt, and I am mistaken if he does not find it something of a "colt."

How piteously the Editors are squirming under the law of libel. It is certainly hard that they may not lie and slander with impunity. Why, it is by this craft that they get their living. Were they to print the truth only, their papers would be stale, flat and unprofitable. The public, I fear, would not read them, and they would be of but little use to the politicians.

As to the Church "bobbery" to which you refer, I have not made up my mind. The protest may have been very impertinent, and it may have been very proper. All I think depends upon the *facts* of the case, and with those I am not yet acquainted. I have seen a good deal of the clergy. St. Paul says they are *earthen* vessels. Many of them are cracked, and good for nothing. Others are indeed fit for the Master's use. The great fault of the great mass of them is that they are too anxious to increase their own power, and not anxious enough to save the souls of their fellow men. The exaltation of the clerical order is the foundation on which the mighty superstructure of Puseyism rests. But we will settle the affairs of Church and State when we meet at the Hall. I anticipate much pleasure from being the guest of my old friend. My regards to your wife. I knew and admired her before you did.

Yours truly,
William Jay

J. Fenimore Cooper, Esq., Cooperstown

FROM RICHARD COOPER

Cooperstown, July 23rd, 1843

Dear Uncle

I have just seen the *Commercial Advertiser* of Friday the 21st inst., in which Mr. Stone makes some explanations, as he calls them, in relation to your suit against him. You will see by getting the paper that he says the charge of "shaving" was mere badinage, etc., etc., and that he retracts it, in the "broadest possible manner." You will also perceive that he denies having ever told any one that you were a shaver. The article I presume will be used on the inquest in mitigation of damages, and I write this to suggest the expediency of your seeing, if possible, some one of the gentlemen to whom Stone stated in conversation that what he had published of you was true and asking him to come up. It will be important, I think, to shew this on the inquest, in case one should be taken. Stone has got in his article some statements about me, and the bill of costs on his demurrer in the first suit, that are all false. The truth, however, is not I presume of much moment to the world.

All well.

Yours very truly,
R. Cooper.

FROM EVAN EDWARDS

Charleston, So. Ca., July 25, 1843

Dear Sir,

In looking over some old papers I came across the enclosed letter from my uncle Lt. Edwards, who was on board the *Niagara*, at the battle of Lake Erie.

I do not suppose it contains any thing that would be new to you, but as you have in your naval history and elsewhere endeavoured to clear the character of Com. Elliot, from the charge of misconduct at Erie, I take the liberty of sending it to you, as the evidence of a gallant officer in his favor. I do this more readily as in a work called the naval book, lately seen by me, certificates of Com. Elliot's officers are published condemning his conduct on that occasion.

If the letter should prove in any way useful or interesting to you it would give me sincere pleasure, and if it does not, why it will give you no trouble.

Lt. Edwards died of Typhus fever soon after the date of his letter. As it is one of the few records we have of him, I would beg you to return it at your leisure.

I have the honor to be

Your obt. svt.
Evan Edwards.

J. Fenimore Cooper, Esq., New York

LETTER ENCLOSED WITH THE PRECEDING

Dear Charles

Your letter of the 9th. inst. I have just received, and was happy to hear from you, and that you were well. As regards the particulars of the action, I presume you have seen so many accounts of it, that a repetition would be tiresome, however to gratify you, I'll give you the occurrences. I joined the Fleet at this place about the 5th. of August at which time the British fleet was off we got out and chas'd them into Madden and then returned to this place in about three or four days after, where we were reinforced by 60 men and Officers we then went in pursuit of the Enemy but found them still in Madden we laid to of and on the place for several hours but they would not come out, which we attributed to their not having their new Ship the *Detroit* ready, we then kept sailing about the Lake for our amusement for about six weeks now and then putting into the different harboring places the last of which was put in Bay when about 5 A. M. on the 10th. Sept. the Enemy was discovered from our mast head standing under easy sail the signal from the Flag Ship was made to weigh which was immediately and cheerfully done, the wind was light and ahead which caused us some difficulty to beat out of the Bay at 10 the wind shifted which got us the weather gauge of them and entirely clear of the Bay; we then formed a line of battle in the following order the *Lawrence* Capt. Perry and Flag Ship ahead with the Schooners *Ariel* and *Scorpion* on his weather bow, the *Caledonia* Lieut. Turner, the *Niagara* Capt. Elliot with the Schooners *Somers* and *Porcupine* on his weather Quarter and the Schooner *Tygress* and Sloop *Trip*, Lt. Holdup [Thomas Holdup Stevens] astern of all. The Enemy in the follow-

ing order the *Detroit* Capt. Barclay and flag Ship ahead
with the Schooner *Chippeway* on his Lea Bow, the Brig
Hunter Capt. Bignal, the Sloop *Queen Charlotte* Capt.
Finis, the Brig *Lady Prevost* Capt. Buccan and Sloop
Little Belt at 20 minutes before 12 the *Detroit* commenced firing on our head most vessels computed at one
and one half miles which was superceeded by the rest of
them, at 12 the action became general on both sides which
was kept up with great vigor and destruction until half
past 2 (the Enemy from the superiority of their long
Guns and which at long shot cut us most damnably for
they drove their shot through and through us and made
the splinters fly like the devil) when the *Lawrence* from
her crippled state was compeled to strike, the *Niagara*
immediately made sail and shot ahead of the *Lawrence*
being all the time about 200 yards astern of her and laid
herself within half a Pistol shot of the *Detroit* pouring a
tremendous and galling fire into her with round and grape
which she gallantly returned for about 10 minutes and
then struck, about this time Capt. Perry came on board,
and Capt. Elliot who we consider in no respect second to
Perry in gaining the victory gallantly volunteer'd his services to bring the smaller vessels into close action, and in so
doing was very much exposed to the fire of the Enemy in a
small boat which he row'd through the fleet in, we then engaged the *Queen* and *Lady Prevost* raking them part of
the time and with the assistance of smaller vessels coming
up made them all strike in ten minutes more, the *Little
Belt* attempted to make her escape for Madden being only
18 miles of, when the engagement took place but was
caught by the *Scorpion*, the *Niagara* at the latter end of
the action fought both sides of her guns, I received four
Gun shot wounds besides being bruised by splinters, the

one in my head and groin were the severest, I was just touched in the small of the back and right side, but none of them disabled me materially I suffer'd mostly from the loss of blood being very much heated at the time, however I am as well now as ever I was, I did not give Bobbie much trouble for I thought him too much of a horse marine to touch me with an amputating knife, notwithstanding all the exertions of Capt. Elliot, you find Perry eulogised to the skies and scarcely any thing said of Elliot who brought his vessel into action with all the skill of a Sailor and fought her with all the coolness and courage of a hero, we brought the fleet to an anchor, and repaired the damages during that evening and night and the next day proceeded to put in Bay with a fleet of 15 sail, Harrison arrived then with his army and we took them across into Canada, and a damn job we had in transporting them, we found Madden evacuated, and all the public buildings burnt, Harrison then pursued Proctor and overtook him about the Moravian villages on the river Thames and after a small skirmish took all his forces, but himself, who ran like a Son of a bitch as soon as the action commenced.

I was about the mouth of the river with the *Niagara*, on Lake St. Clair, a short distance from the Army, and commanded her from Detroit to Buffalo near Lake Ontario with troops, and from there to this place where she with the rest of the fleet have haul'd up into Winter Quarters, and I have very little more at present than to dash about the Tavern keepers daughters and cut didos with them, I hope this will satisfy you

John L. Edwards

Charles Lee Edwards Esq.
    Philadelphia

P.S. Answer this, remember me to all the lads, I hope I shall be in Philadelphia in the course of 6 weeks, is Shippen as close as ever with his Ale, you will have to assist me in my answer to the President of the 76 association; you must excuse all errors, for I was interrupted all the time writing

FROM G. W. L. LOWDEN

Mansion House, Brooklyn, 29th July, 1843

Sir,

The succinct biography of my Grand Uncle Paul-Jones in the late numbers of Graham's Magazine, I have read with much gratification. Its generally just and impartial statement of facts is peculiarly acceptable; and this feeling is little affected by differences of reasoning on, and conclusion from, them, which on my part, arise mainly from thinking a greater justification of his defects might be found in the extent of the provocations and injustice Paul-Jones endured. Shall I candidly confess, too, that I had not been quite prepared for such a biography at your hands. Had a more extended notice of the subject suited your views, it would have afforded me pleasure to have contributed any information in my power, towards its efficiency.

All the biographies of Paul-Jones, hitherto published, of any authenticity, claim, for the most part, from the descendants of Jane or Janet Paul, with which those of her Sister, Mary Ann *Hamilton* (so called from a family of Hamiltons who assumed by marriage the name of Craik), have no connection. These biographies are more or less defective in several respects, and seem not always conceived, to my mind, in the best taste.

The publicity of private infirmities serve rarely a good

purpose, but even here, accuracy is not the less imperative. Delia and Madame T. were distinct persons; the
first, the Lady of a Scotch Baronet (a countess, it is believed, in her own right),—the second from her own report, a natural daughter of Louis XV. by the Countess
D'A [torn]. A system of great duplicity characterized the
conduct of Madame T. towards Paul-Jones, and was the
final cause of a disconnection which has been ascribed to
other motives. The name of Lavendahl is erroneously
given, in several publications, for Lowendahl. Catherine
de Bourbon, one of the natural (legitimatized) daughters
of ——— de Bourbon, married Count de Lowendahl,
afterwards Major General in the Danish Service, a Son
(if I do not err) of Marshal Baron de Lowendahl, so
distinguished in the reign of Louis XV. The Countess
bore an exemplary character.

Had the position of Paul-Jones seconded his wishes in
1790—'01, there is reason to believe, from Correspondence, on both sides, in my possession, that his marriage
with the daughter of Count Tomatis de Vallery was
affected solely by that Contingency.

No interments were made in Père la Chaise prior to
(I think) 1812. Paul-Jones was buried in the old protestant Cemetery situate near the Barrière du Combat. This
Cemetery (at that time, *hors la ville*) formed part of the
present ground of the Hospital St. Louis and the Rue
Grange des Balles. In 1815, many mourners returned to
Paris, intent on removing or discovering the remains of
friends or relatives, there inter'd; but the excesses of the
Revolution left few places sacred; and it would be impossible, at this day, to Consummate any such errand of
affection, on my part, so perfectly desired. Truly, "a
strange, eventful history"!

M. Marron, the protestant pastor who pronounced the Oration at the grave, perished afterwards on the guillotine. His Widow was recently, and is believed to be still, alive.

In your search after truth, the satisfaction you afford to others, having a prominent interest in the subject discussed, cannot fail, I feel persuaded, to be pleasing to you: this must be my apology, at least, for the present expression of acknowledgement from a personal stranger, and may, perhaps, justify me in subscribing

With esteem and Consideration

Sir, Very obediently, Yours

G. W. L. Lowden.

J. Fenimore Cooper, Esq., Cooperstown

FROM J. SUTHERLAND

Geneva, August 30, 1843

My Dear Cooper,

I have just read your Pamphlet on the Battle of Lake Erie. You certainly place your Adversaries in a very awkward predicament, and fully establish, as it appears to me, the accuracy of your historical account of that Battle. You have shown your usual moral courage in undertaking the Vindication of Elliott, in opposition to the universal Sentiment or feeling of the country. I have no doubt great injustice has been done him. There is no ground for imputing to him any want of personal courage in that affair. But still I have a *sort of feeling*, that a man of generous courage, a courage not merely above personal fear, but animated by generous impulses, would, notwithstanding the order of Battle, have gone to Perry's relief sooner than he did.

Your answer to this is that he did not know the crippled condition of the Flag Ship. If Perry required his more immediate support, he should have ordered it by signal. There is great force in this. It is undoubtedly a perfect *legal* defense. But still I can not but feel that he must have known, from observing the superior force which was concentrated upon Perry's Ship, that he required support, and that if his Heart had been exactly in the right place, he would have afforded it much sooner than he did, and I rather think this will be the final judgement of the Country on the matter.

I am very sincerely and Truly

Yours

J. Sutherland.

J. Fenimore Cooper, Esq., Cooperstown

TO MRS. COOPER, GENEVA, NEW YORK

Head's, Sunday, September 17th, 1843

My dearest Wife,

There is a *report*—I do not vouch for it—that Wm. Cox is to marry his cousin, Mrs. P——, with a fortune of $15,000 per an—for $15, however, read $10,000. She is about thirty, and still a very charming woman. Should it take place, she will have the soul-felt pleasure of making her husband's fortune.

I saw Pope a day or two since. He has two children, and has gone to live at New Orleans, where he passed the last winter. Charlotte was not with him, but goes this autumn. As Pope & Aspinwall, he was thoroughly emptied. Though, it is said, he behaves perfectly well. As he failed once before, it is to be hoped he will escape in future.

I have seen Elliott. He is content to rest on my case, and in this he is wise. Poor Mackenzie is losing ground daily. An old seaman, of the name of Sturgis, is writing against him, under his own name. Three letters have appeared; the two first are good, as far as they go, but do not go far enough, but the third is unanswerable. It is much the best thing—the only good thing, indeed—that has appeared on the subject. In a word, it is as good as it can be, on the point it treats, and makes Mackenzie thoroughly contemptible, as well as the government. I fancy the plan is to be silent on the subject of my pamphlet.

Head is quite full, and must make money. We have two scions of nobility here, besides lots of our own dignitaries. Among other curiosities, we have brides without number; no less than fourteen having graced the house since it opened.

The town is filling, though it is still quite warm. Mr. Miller is in the house, and is, at this moment, about to go and hear Mr. Odenheimer, who, he says, preaches, *tant soit peut*, too much about the apostolic succession.

Warrington's beautiful wife is dead, and it is said he intends to go to sea. Stewart comes ashore, and, quite likely, will take his bureau. I fear Bordentown is a sad climate. The commodore is said to have a large family, and I have just heard of three young Bonapartes, by two different mothers: one French, one American. The count married the last to his cook, but she tossed up a *vol-au-vent* of her own, and eloped with a third lover.

Mary Head has a cage directly under my window, which contains eighteen canaries. They keep up a great chattering, though Willy could make more noise than them all put together.

I have no more news from Penn. The stock keeps rising, and will go up as I have said. When the interest will come, it is hard to say, but most people here think before many months.

A gentleman from Paris tells me the de la Vallette *ménage* (*ci-devant* Welles, *femme*) is unhappy. She is jealous, and has had a shindy with *him*, on a race-course, before all the world. This must be fatal at Paris, as it is making herself ridiculous. I fancy she wishes Samival back, again.

I believe I told you that Mrs. Shinley was dead, in child-birth, she and her infant. Her cousins are her heirs. She died in Demarara. A Mrs. Willing (Miss Black-well) is at the point of death, I hear.

Adieu, my dear wife; my blessing to Caroline, and Paul, and regards all round. If you can get home without me, so much the better. Pinky will lend you money, and I shall be glad to find you at the Hall.

J. F. C.

COPY OF A LETTER EVIDENTLY WRITTEN TO STURGIS, THE "OLD SEAMAN" MENTIONED IN THE PRECEDING

Phila., Sept. 17, 1843

Sir,

I have read your letters in *The Courier* with great interest, and being somewhat of a seaman myself, can appreciate their justice. Your third letter, I hold to be one of the simplest and best arguments on the point it treats of, that can be written.

I regard the affair of the *Somers* as one of the darkest spots on the national escutcheon. Apart from the feeble-ness of the case that is made out in justification of her officers, it is a stain on the American character that a transaction of this nature should be treated as this has

been. Three lives were taken without legal process in any
form or manner. The very circumstance that the power
of the government was the agent in the act, renders the
case more grave. The enquiry, altogether ex-parte, was
so much worse than nothing that it was a mere mockery
of justice, instead of being conducted on its plainest principles. Thus Cromwell was hanged entirely on circumstantial proof. Com. Stewart has admitted to me there
was no proof against him, with the exception of the fact
that Spencer showed him the Greek paper. Unfortu-
nately, the witness to this point swore he said nothing
about this occurrence, until the brig got in. Now, the issue
was not the truth or falsehood of the mutiny, the reality
of the danger or not, but whether such a case was made
out to Capt. Mackenzie as *justified* him in believing, first
in the unquestionable guilt of the accused, or parties executed; second, in the imperative necessity of hanging the
men. This is clearly the issue, moral and legal; and it is
not easy to see how a fact that appears subsequently to
the deed can justify it! But circumstantial evidence always falls short of direct proof, and, in its nature, may,
in every case, be explained. Mack. raised the question of
life and death, as to Cromwell, more than twenty-four
hours before he caused him to be hanged. Now, did he,
or did he not, ask this unfortunate man to explain the
circumstances, during all this time?—did he hang a man
on *circumstantial evidence,* with that man at his elbow
for four and twenty hours, and not question him on the
subject of these circumstances? If he *did*, and I believe he
did, this single act stamps his conduct and his character.
What just man would correct a child, discharge a servant,
on circumstantial proof, without a hearing?

Then, for the proof itself. The turning point in the

whole affair was the loss of the mast. Capt. Mack. thinks
Cromwell instigated Small to swing out on the brace, in
order to bring down the spars, throw the boy overboard,
and seize the brig while the vessel was in confusion and
her true men were busy in saving the boy. I consider this
as the most infatuated reasoning that a human being ever
employed. It would be contemptible as an excuse for the
simplest dereliction of duty—it is frightful when urged as
an apology for taking life. How long a period could have
passed between the issuing the order to steady the royal
brace and its execution? Would not ten seconds be
ample? The coincidence could not be foreseen—I mean
that of the boy's being on the yaw, and the necessity for
steadying the brace—nor could the order be anticipated.
The last came from the mind of the officer of the deck,
and, of course, it could not have been anticipated. Small
was on the bitts within ten feet of the brace, probably
nearer, and ten seconds are quite sufficient for all he did.
In this brief space, the man in quick physical movement,
must this deep plot have been laid! This is only one side
of the case. If it were desired to do as Capt. Mackenzie
suspected, what was there to prevent Cromwell *from preparing his men*, which they could *not* have been in the case
of the mast, in the nature of things, to *throw* a boy overboard, to *toss a bit of iron* into the water, after dark, and
call out a "boy overboard," to order a boy into fifty situations out-board, when he might have been tipped into the
sea, under the pretence of helping him, and then effecting
his purposes? It is a libel on the common sense of Cromwell to suppose he could not have devised a hundred better expedients than that Capt. Mackenzie attributes to
him, under circumstances which render it morally impossible, I might almost say, to be true!

Every distinctive fact urged in the defense might be cut up just in this manner. I never looked into a weaker case, or one that is sustained so completely by fallacies. You should not be misled by the interested clamor of the towns. The country is strongly against Mackenzie, and, sooner or later, will vindicate its justice. Insurance officers are proverbially short-sighted, and, God be praised, they are not the nation. I do not know an officer in the navy, of any experience, whose principles and intellect I respect, and of whose opinions I am apprized, who approves of Mackenzie's conduct; I do know of at least a dozen captains, men of high character and intelligence, every one of whom condemns him. They are cautious in what they say, but to *me*, they say enough to let me understand them.

If Captain Mackenzie had any evidence before him, at all, he had ample proof that the mutiny had no extent. Even admitting Spencer's boast of twelve to twenty men to have been strictly true, whereas the true inference was that he had not half the number, what had he to fear from twenty men, with their names in his possession, the ring leaders in irons, and the arms and authority all in his own hands!

Something ought to be said of the atrocious principle that a man of war is to hang a citizen before she will ask a foreign state to receive her prisoners. If this principle be just, Capt. Mackenzie, had the *Somers* been lying in a friendly port, would have been compelled, under this view, to have gone to sea, in order to be able to hang his criminals! What could have more redounded to the credit of Capt. Mackenzie himself, or of his country, than to have gone into Guadalupe and told the Governor,—"I command a vessel of war, without marines. A mutiny exists, and I must either leave the ringleaders here, or hang them at sea, without legal process. I belong to a government of laws—the ship I command is commissioned to enforce, and not to violate, those laws—my country is tender of the life and liberties of the meanest citizen, and I prefer the self-mortification of asking your assistance, to robbing an American citizen of his rights in so grave a matter." The man who does not feel this moral truth is not worthy to hold an American commission.

But, I beg pardon. A total stranger, I have written you in haste, just after reading your third letter, and because I feel the deep reproach that must rest on the nation in connection with this sad affair. I wish it were in my power to send you a pamphlet of mine on the Battle of Lake Erie. That will show you the real character of Capt. Mackenzie. He has hanged Cromwell exactly as he has pressed facts into his own service, in making up his accusations against Com. Elliott. Public opinion in this country is more apt to go wrong than right, in the outset. The press is venal, corrupt, ignorant, and impervious to principle. It seizes the common mind, in the outset, but the intelligence and honesty of the community are brought to bear in the end, and then public opinion gets in the right quarter. Depend on it, sir, it is not in nature for a nation that boasts of having a government of laws, long to be blinded in this matter. But for the peculiar political position of Mr. John C. Spencer, the public mind would, long since, have been disabused on the facts and principles of this dreadful case. I hope we shall hear farther from you.

With much respect,
Your Ob. Ser.
J. Fenimore Cooper

Head's, [begun] Monday, Sept. 18th, 1843

Dearest,

I have seen the Ingersolls. Mr. and Mrs. Charles have
not been to Saratoga. The latter was at the Yellow
Springs in the state, where was Mrs. Pierce Butler, with
whom she seemed much delighted. It seems Mrs. B. is a
good fisherwoman, and she made a good deal of *cancan*
by wearing pantaloons, with boots and straps, a man's
hat, with blouse over all. It was the dress of a page on the
stage. She rode miles on horseback alone, in petticoats,
and fished in pantaloons, which Charles said was unreasonable, if not in bad taste. Still, Mrs. Charles says
she is charming.

I met Ben Wilcocks and his wife in the street yesterday. The last told me the baby was fat, which would seem
to be the consideration with you mothers. Joe Ingersoll
is to go to Congress again. I think it probable the Mc-
Calls will keep the house in the interval.

Head is not full, but increasing. I should think he
must be receiving sixty or eighty dollars a day, at a
moderate expense. I think he is making money as it is.
I think my money safe, and bearing a fair interest.

Wyandotte does not seem to sell well, although those
who have read it speak well of it. One or two judges give
it a high place in the series. *Ned Myers* has reached fifty
pages, and will be done soon—this is Tuesday evening.

Philadelphia is reviving, and you can tell your sister
that Penn. is looking up; the stock sold to-day at fifty-six,
and is firm at that price. I think the stock will go to
seventy ere long, whether the interest is ever paid or not.
They tell me, however, that they are paying off the
domestic creditors, contractors, and others of that clan,

and when this is got through with, it is believed by good judges, the state will resume. The great abundance of money, all over the world, just at this time, will aid exceedingly in bringing about this desirable end—desirable to Caroline and Pink, if to no one else. Tell Pink she must give an affair when she gets the back interest.

Philadelphia seems to be filling, and I never saw so many skippers in the streets, as I have seen to-day. The peaches and melons are abundant, and are getting to be good.

My pamphlet has sold well here, and has struck deep wherever it has been read. As yet, there is no answer. Griswold tells me he has conversed with several of Mackenzie's friends about it, and especially with Charles King. The latter admitted that Burges and Duer are used up, but said that Mackenzie would annihilate me when he came to reply. After some further conversation, he confessed he thought it doubtful if Mackenzie replied at all. After probing him, Griswold was of opinion he had merely skimmed the pages, and had studiously avoided the stony parts. *The Democratic Magazine* has a good article on the pamphlet. It commences well. The subject, it says, has been long in dispute, until Cooper, like Perry in the battle itself, bears down with his heavy metal, and settles the matter at once.

Adieu, my love.

Yours tenderly,
J. F.-C.

TO MISS SUSAN COOPER, COOPERSTOWN

Philadelphia, Sept. 22nd, 1843

My dear child,

I leave this place to-day, and shall be home in all next

week, but, what day, I cannot now tell, Fan and the convention interfering.

Tilly is not a catholic.

Ned Myers is printed, and will be published the 1st Nov. Those who have read it say it will take wonderfully.

I have got your manuscript, and shall sell all your tales together. This will be the best plan. I make no doubt of getting one or two hundred dollars for the whole. A name will sell the remainder, and a little habit will set you up.

The peaches are just getting to be delicious. I tear myself from them with regret. The melons are not so good, the rains affecting them.

You see what little Vic is about, and it shows she is up to a frolic. They tell me she is now on the best of terms with her mother.

The weather here is delightful, and promises so to continue.

With love to Charlotte,

Affectionately your Father

J. Fenimore Cooper.

Miss Fenimore Cooper

TO MRS. COOPER, GENEVA, NEW YORK

Philadelphia, Sept. 22nd, 1843

My Dearest Sue,

I have finished here, and shall go to New-York this evening. *Ned Myers* is printed, and I have sold ten thousand copies for $1000, cash in pocket. This, with the English sale, will make good business. I shall give Ned a handsome fee.

My pamphlet tells, wherever it is read. The circulation

is not large, but it goes into the right hands. Capt. Stockton is here. He tells me he was ordered on Mackenzie's court, but frankly told the secretary his mind is made up, and *that he should vote for hanging the accused*, if he sat. On this hint, he was excused. I am told several others got off, on the same ground. *He* feels confident Capt. Page was against him.

Shubrick quits the Norfolk yard on the 1st. Oct. A fine frigate is fitting for sea in each of the ports of Phila., New York and Boston.

I saw Mary Farmer in a store yesterday. She is looking very well. She has been to see Jane, and is so pleased that she is half a mind to turn nun herself. Her admirer the old Colonel (Payne), however, stands in the way a little. He is stationed at Baltimore. She does not return to Cooperstown this Winter.

Adieu, my dearest wife—expect me soon after you get this.

Love of course.   J. F. C.

FROM COMMODORE JESSE DUNCAN ELLIOTT

West Chester, Nov. 7, 1843

Com. Elliott's respects to J. Fenimore Cooper, esq., and would be very happy of his company at dinner with Col. R. M. Johnson, on next Saturday. He knows or expects, you cannot attend, but nevertheless feels bound to extend the invitation to such a "good and true" friend; and be assured there shall always be a knife and fork at the table for you, and if you are not present, some good fellow, worthy to represent you, shall take the seat, with "toast and speech."

All's well, and letter coming from headquarters.

J. Fenimore Cooper, Esq., Cooperstown

Hall, Cooperstown, Nov. 9th, 1843

My dear Paul,

You have doubtless heard, indirectly if not directly, of the safe arrival of your sisters. They got home in good season on Tuesday, after a tolerable passage from Fort Plain. We were all delighted to see them, especially as Caroline is looking so much better. Your mother, as usual, spent one or two evenings in useless villages, and that which Charlotte, with her German pedantry, calls smouse, came and went several times, until a particular chicken incurred great risks of martyrdom from my masticators.

We have an early winter here, and throughout the country, as I learn. The year 1796, the snow came in this month, and it remained until April. Many persons, now, have not gathered all their roots, particularly potatoes, and it is not improbable that they will be lost. It is said in this region that the potatoes this fall have the usual disposition to decay. I wish you would inquire if the same thing exists about Geneva. Remember, in getting your facts, they ought to be obtained precisely and with accuracy. A small collection of such facts is worth a dozen large collections loosely obtained.

Ned has left us, after a five months' visit. His book is not yet out, but will shortly appear. I think it will amuse you, and I really believe its incidents to be substantially true.

I have finished a lecture on the Battle of Lake Champlain, to be read before the Historical Society of New York, and am now at work on a review of the *Somers* mutiny case. This last would be soon finished had the record of the Court Martial arrived. I expect it soon, however. I find Mackenzie's case grow weaker and weaker, as I look into it.

We have made early dispositions for an early winter. The cider is in the cellar; the apples in the outer cellar; the pigs are on corn, and look excellently well, and the cows are already brought into the yard. The garden is manured, and laid up to winter, in better order than I ever knew it to be, and every thing is ready for the North-westers but the ice house, which is not yet thatched. The straw is in it, but the weather has been too cold for thatching. To-day it is much milder, and I am not without hope of finishing that job in a few days.

I shall probably go below and return before you come home for Christmas. We have given Mr. Tiffany leave of absence for the winter, *on condition he relinquishes the salary*, a condition that will render his departure doubt-ful. You may have seen the article signed A Lay Dele-gate from Otsego, in the *Churchman*. It is a little muti-lated and damaged in the close, where it speaks of the rights of the Bishop to absorb, in his own person, all the powers of decision, in question of order. I see Bishops Chase, McIlvaine, Eastburne and Meade are all out in opposition to our hard-headed diocesan, and the effect of a division in such high places will be, either to put an end at once to further discussions, or to bring about a perma-nent separation of the church. It really would seem, my son, that the *Catholic* church has an unhappy tendency to minute separations of its particles into their original elements. I suppose when every man in the country has a church of his own, we may suppose the tendency will take the opposite direction, though some among us would probably be sufficiently unreasonable to wish for two.

I hope you improve your leisure by useful reading. I

beg particularly that you would attend to your hand-writing. I am a living proof of the importance of such an accomplishment. It is just as easy to write well as to write ill, and all you have to do is to put yourself under a master *de novo*, as it were, and build up from the foundation. The best ideas have a mean aspect, if communicated through rude writing. Your hand, now, is boyish, and pride ought to induce you to wish to make it at least decided and manly. The only thing decided about it, now, is the circumstance that it is decidedly bad.

Attend also to your declamation. Read aloud, slow, articulating every syllable. The art of reading is easily acquired. Your natural utterance is quick, like my own. Quick utterance is never dignified, and you should correct this. The whole secret is to give equal time to the *syllables*, which prevents halting between words. A drawl is my aversion. I have none—you should have none. You have caught a few Yankeeisms at college, and they may expect no quarter at home. Without a drop of the blood of the glorious Puritans in your veins, you have no right to claim their excellencies, which are so exclusive according to their own account of the matter, and I hope you have too much self respect to put up with their blemishes.

The ground is covered with snow, here, and I begin to think Winter has actually commenced. I do not so much anticipate a severe winter as a long Winter. Snowy seasons are seldom very cold seasons. They are unusually healthful and fertilizing.

You have heard the gossip here. Your aunt Isaac has gone to her father's, and I question if she ever returns. It is probable she will spend the remainder of her days in the bosom of her own family. Occasional visits to her daughters may relieve the monotony, and still render the close of her life comfortable. The rent of her house, and the little property she has, may supply her personal wants.

You see O'Connell is arrested. This will terminate the repeal movement. England is not honest enough to put Ireland on an equality with herself, nor do I know that it would be wise. Theories in politics, that are founded on abstract notions of right and wrong, are never justly applied. So many other interests and rights are connected with the results, that even what seems justice may work gross injustice in practice.

John Nelson is in New York. He is troubled with some affection of the throat, and I believe dreads consumption, the disease that killed his mother. I think the apprehension is groundless.

This letter is finished Monday 13th, down to which date we are all well. Everybody sends love to you, and your two sisters say you were so attentive to them when last in Geneva, that they miss you even here. Adieu, my dear boy.

Ever affectionately
Your father
J. Fenimore Cooper

TO MRS. COOPER, COOPERSTOWN

Globe, Thursday, Jan. 18th, 1844

To my surprise *Wy and Dotti* has sold better than *Ned*, though the last has done well. I can trace 3000 copies sold here. I suppose 4000 may have sold in this city. They tell me *Wing and Wing* and *Two Admirals* continue to sell—I have not had a cent from either this long time. I am afraid all booksellers are rascals. In future, I act for myself.

Head's, April 9th, 1844

My dearest Sue,

Mrs. Charles Ingersoll has another daughter. Charles says it is hard, there being *two* sexes, that all his children should be of one.

Scandal is rifer and rifer. The old affair of Pierce has given place to a new one. The sister of the Virginian's *mare* is married to a Mr. Schott. It seems this gentleman and P - - - - - - were intimate. P - - - - - -, Sch - - -, Mrs. R - - - - - y, and Mrs. Sch - - - went to New York to attend the opera. They staid at Astor House, and while there Sch - - - affirms that he saw improper familiarities. There is a blow up, and a challenge was proposed. The lady's father interferes, takes the lady home, and she and her sister go before the mayor and complain of Sch - - -. He is charged with choking her, and menacing her with a pistol, previously to this affair at the Astor House. The character of the lady is good, and that of the husband is said to be none of the best. Public opinion is with the Willings. But this is notoriety enough for one connection, in one winter.

At the same time, Sch - - - has another affair on hand. He plays high, and a young O - - - - - - s of Boston, of the distinguished family of that name, and the son of *the* Mrs. O - - - - - - -, has lost largely. It is said *he* has challenged Sch - - -, on his side, and that there is a muss all round.

I give you this stuff as I hear it, the part that relates to the lady coming pretty straight. I have seen none of the family, myself.

I have been on board the *Princeton*, and have seen the gun. It is a tremendous wreck. Stockton will go on, how-

ever, and is confident of success. He had a bit of iron pass
through his leg, just missing the bone, and was much
burned. He is now about, again.

Adieu—yours most tenderly,

J. F. C.

Head's, Sunday, [April] 14th, 1844

I dined at Wilcock's Friday, and saw all the ladies,
including the youngest, which is really a beauty. The
Misses Wilcocks as usual. Miss Ann Ingersoll is engaged
to a Mr. Mings.

The S. H. affair begins to take a different aspect. It is
now said that he intercepted a letter from his wife to her
sister, in which he found these ominous words—"S. H.
seems quite determined, and certainly meditates either a
duel or suicide—*I hope the last.*" This drove him from
the house to a tavern, where he talked like a fool. It is
now said the parties have gone a good way south to fight.
They passed through Baltimore two or three days since,
as is reported by the police. Both have certainly disappeared from here. Enough of this.

There is an apprehension of trouble. The treaty of
annexation is certainly signed, and preparations are making to take possession of the gulf. Orders have been sent
to prepare one vessel, certainly, for that service. Many
persons think war with England will follow—I do not.

Head's, Friday, August 23rd, 1844

Dearest,

Your letter reached me Wednesday. I learn *here* that

Harrison Grey Otis and his daughter Mrs. Ritchie called at the Hall, although you do not speak of it. Neither do you say whether the ossifers are soldiers or sailors. I hope you ride out occasionally, and I now give notice that Pumpkin and the wagon will be put often in requisition, as soon as I get home.

We are on the last 100 pages of *Miles* [*Afloat and Ashore*], and I hope to be home towards the close of next week, making an absence of about nineteen days.

I have dined once with Barton, and once with Joe Ingersoll. Gilpin, the ex-attorney general, was of the party. Ingersoll has promised to accompany me on a pilgrimage to Cooper's Creek, before I quit Philadelphia.

I find Anne Penn's book will cost only $150, near a $100 less than I feared. I entertain no doubt of being able to sell it, and to make some $50 or $100 by the bargain.

Schott has come out with a pamphlet. He gives an extract from an intercepted letter of his wife's, which speaks volumes against her, if true. She tells her sister, she hopes he meditates suicide. I understand her sister admits that she received such a letter. They are divorced, on her application, he not resisting. He says his object was a divorce, and that he was passive in order that she might succeed, that he now conceives that he has a right to speak in his own vindication. He calls Butler very hard names, some of which are probably merited.

The cold shoulder is pretty well given to Mrs. W—. I am afraid there is a reason for it. I shall have something to tell you on that subject. They are now in Connecticut, and I have not seen them.

Charles Wilkes is in this house, superintending the publication of his work. It will be a very magnificent book, and I make no doubt will do him credit. He tells me Mrs. Henry has a second son in the Navy, though she felt the loss of Wilkes very deeply.

I have nothing more to say, than to send my tenderest love to all, of which the largest share will be yours, old as you are—Lucy makes me think of you.

J. F. C.

Wilkes was a captain in the U. S. Navy. He wrote *Narrative of the U. S. Exploring Expedition During the Years 1838-1842*, and a number of similar works.

FROM COMMODORE JESSE DUNCAN ELLIOTT

Philadelphia, Oct 8th, 1844

Dear Sir

In yeilding to a strong feeling of my heart, I cannot but offer my gratefull acknowledgements for your magnanimous and disinterested labours in a cause of Truth and Justice. Although I was personally unknown to you, when you first undertook the preperation of a fair and an impartial History of the Navy of the United States, and although attempts were made to mislead your mind upon many points in the War of 1812, after a long and tedious discussion before Impartial Arbitrators, a majority of whom were selected by your opponents and who were well versed in law you have made the "Truth triumph and prevail."

In your defense of Truth that cause and mine being so nearly allied in its maintenance you were unconsciously my deffender and I am therefore called upon by the impulse of my own feelings to make some expressions of the high estimation of the able and impartial manner in which

you have defended me, and pray you to accept the accom-
panying memento as a tribute from

Faithfully your friend
Jesse Duncan Elliott

James Fenimore Cooper, Esq., Cooperstown

TO MRS. COOPER, COOPERSTOWN

Head's, Sunday, November 17, [1844]

The Whigs are furious—so sore you cannot joke with
them. As sore now as they were insolent before. They do
not like to hear the election mentioned. In this place they
are worse even than in New York. Anything or anybody
has beaten them, but the people. Our people show great
moderation, though they feel particularly comfortable.

Our Bishop is in for it. Bishops Mead, Elliott, and
Otey sat two weeks examining his case, and then they
presented him to the Primus. Dr. Chase has convoked the
House of Bishops, to meet in New York on the 10th
December for the trial. Some of the more distant Bishops
have remained, in expectation of the result, and it is
thought that fifteen or sixteen will attend. I entertain no
doubt he will be degraded from the ministry altogether. I
have heard the substance of the presentment, and am told
the females concerned, the wives of clergymen, have made
their affidavits and will appear before the House. You
will see a second letter of ——'s in the *Churchman*, in
which the character of his defence is made to appear. He
speaks of cases that occurred several years back. Now, an
innocent man would spurn such a justification. All the
cases occurred since he has been a Bishop, and it is folly
to speak of the statute of limitations in a case of this

nature, unless it can be shown that testimony is lost in consequence of time. In this case, or in these cases, I understand all those who know anything of the matter are still living and willing to testify. Then, I am told cases within six months can be shown. I do not entertain the least doubt of his guilt, though I do not say so openly.

Doane is in difficulty, too, they say, through his efforts to screen his two colleagues. It is said that H. U. would have been degraded altogether, had he not kept back some of the testimony. It would not surprise, were something to grow out of his tricks. A clergyman told me this anecdote yesterday. Richmond (of New York) was very zealous in obtaining a grant for Dr. Chase from the Missionary fund. When the vote was taken he sat on the stage and near Doane. The latter, contrary to expectation, adopted the side of Dr. Chase, voting and speaking in favour of the grant. As soon as the vote was taken, New Jersey spoke to Richmond, and said, "Now, Richmond, you see I have gone with you in this; be liberal and drop this prosecution of Bishop Ben." "I am concerned in no prosecution of any Bishop, nor have I anything to do with the matter." "But your brother has—he can be influenced by you—persuade him to withdraw for the good of the Church." "It is too late. He has brought his charges, and must prove them, or be degraded himself." "Let him withdraw his charges, and I pledge myself no proceedings shall be had against him."

The story was told me by the clergyman to whom Richmond related it!

Little has been done in books since I went up. Everybody has been too much occupied to think of books. About 2500, however, of second part has gone off. I may be detained a day or two longer than I supposed, but do not yet know. I am well, and send love to all; to yourself the largest share as ever.

Adieu,

J. F.-C.

New York, December 30, 1844

Esteemed Sir

It is the particular desire of the Tammany Society to have the honor of *your company*, answering the enclosed Invitation.

Beside the Vice President Elect we expect to receive upon that occasion many distinguished men of our Country none more cordially than the Veteran Sailor, whose Fame Connected so intimately with that of our Common Country you have in the Integrity of your mind given a proper position before the World, Commodore Jesse D. Elliott.

Permit us to hope that we shall not be disappointed and myself to remain your

Obt Ser'vt Paul K. Hubbs

Chairman of Special Com.

for this purpose.

Cap. J. Fenimore Cooper, Cooperstown

The above accompanies an invitation from the Society of Tammany, or Columbian Order, to their annual ball, to be given at Tammany Hall, New York, January 8, 1845.

FROM COMMODORE JESSE DUNCAN ELLIOTT ‡

City Hotel, New York, Jany. 9, 1845

My Dear Sr

I had hoped the pleasure of a sight of your pretty face

at the Tammany Hall last night, a more dense and crowded hall I have never seen.

My hand has been so much embraced and my arm almost drawn from the socket that you will not have a very ledgible letter. The Medal has taken well is in possession of the President of the U. S. the heads of departments, Expresidents of the U. S. or widow if no widow eldest child John Q. Adams claimed two and asked me to allow him to hand one to a nephew and suggested father that I send one to each of the Philosophical societies of the U. States numbering 12, I wrote him a note enclosing the medal for his nephew remarking that you would estimate the compliment more could you know that the presentation came from the frank of the fathers of the House of Representatives and of the Senators of our country, they are now on the way one to each of our Embassadors abroad and to the Ministers representing foreign courts at Washington, to the Gov^n of our states of birth and adoption to Co^l Polk, Mr. Dallas, Shubrick, Warrington, Strangham, McNeal and a host of others, when all is done Geo. M. Dallas, cheif justice Gibson and some other distinguished person will witness the breaking of the die and their certificate of the fact will be *sent you*. Thus my dear Cooper I shall have discharged a debt of gratitude and set an example of a proper reward for the labor and trials of the Historian. You were very much wished for here and I regret you did not come down, I am at Philadelphia as you will have seen and will be glad to take you by the hand there.

Very truly yours

J D Elliott

I have not seen that scoundrel Mackenzies book, where is it and in what form did it come?

The medal referred to bears on the obverse a profile of Cooper and around it the legend "The Personification of Honor, Truth, and Justice"; and on the reverse an oak wreath and the inscription, "To J. Fenimore Cooper, The Offering of a Grateful Heart for His Disinterested Vindication of His Brother Sailor, Jesse D. Elliott."

FROM COMMODORE JESSE DUNCAN ELLIOTT

Navy Yard, Phila., Jany. 13, 1845

Dear Sir

Every days experience satisfies me of the propriety of having the medal struck of you. Cooper, *answer* me *right* to the *point*, I am urged to take a position at Washington, how would you like to *fill* the *Navy* office?

I have a letter of Congratulation from Genl. Jackson saying no Man on earth rejoices more than he that I am in full possession of all my honors and long may I live to carry the stars and stripes successfully through every clime and sea, that Mr. Polk is my warmest friend, and the old man sends me a lock of his hair to be divided in my family and as I want you to allow me to adopt yours I send a portion for them and for your good Sister Mrs. Pomeroy. What you lost by not coming to New York! The Interview of Dallas and I with Mr. Gallatin was rich in the extreme. Judge Gibson says if you had have been there enough would have [been] suggested for a Book. Imagine the Statesman impeling the young Warrior on to battle, subsequently at Genets, the youthful Dallas at his side, he with one foot in the grave, he seeing now the one at the head of his profession, still in vigor, the other with apparent premature old age still in the possession of all his rigging, Vice Prest. elect of the

U. S. Gibson says there is both poetry and music and you
are the man to bring out the sound, thanks to Graham.

I am very Truly
Yrs
J D Elliott

I have had search made for Mackenzies article, where
is it, let me know, I hope in your next you will annihilate
him.

J. Fenimore Cooper, Esq., Cooperstown

FROM JAMES H. MILLER

Baltimore, Feb. 14, 1845

Sir, Knowing and indignantly feeling the unjust cen-
sure passed upon you for your noble, generous and efficient defense of my early and most inhumanly persecuted
friend Com. J. D. Elliott, I am in a manner urged over
any delicacy in obtruding upon the attention of one of
the most distinguished writers in our language, in presenting my feeble testimony in behalf of our common
friend. . . .

During the Campaign of 1814 I was for a short time
thrown in company with Com. Perry. In a conversation
I enquired particularly concerning Cap. Elliott, when
he frankly declared that the victory of Erie was mainly
due to him, "not entirely," he remarked, "to his bravery
and skill but also to his confident manner, which restored
my drooping spirits and rearroused us all to a resumption
of energetic action. For when I left my ship to go to his,
I feared that all was lost, but his undaunted manner and
confident expectation of a successful result cheered me on
to victory. I know that our success has raised us enemies,
but they shall never make us enemies of each other." The
next incident connected with E. that I recollect, was this:

On a visit to Washington during this period of unsettled affairs with France, I visited the President in company with a distinguished Senator. We found the venerable chief alone and smoking his pipe; he invited us to join in the smoke, and then this senator left us to make some other calls in the neighborhood. In the midst of a lively and interesting converse, a messenger entered and presented the Pres. a packet, which he promptly opened, read and handed to me. It was from our Minister in France, declaring the refusal of that Gov^t to pay the indemnity claimed. After I had read it, he familiarly asked what I would do. "Just what you will," said I; "that is, compel them to be honest." "Yes," he rejoined, "I'll sink some of their ships." "Permit me," said I, "to suggest that duty for my friend Elliott." "It shall be so," said he, and drew paper to him and wrote a note to the Sec. of the Navy to that effect.

On Elliott's return he presented me individually and as President of the Washington University of Balt. a number of antiquities, amongst which was a mummy from the Catacombs of Memphis, which, as Professor of Anatomy, I unwrapped and demonstrated to a large concourse consisting of my class and other literary and scientific gentlemen of all professions. Portions of this I have presented to many distinguished friends and still retain an appropriate portion for your acceptance. (Please inform me how and when I can transmit it safely to your hands, provided you honor me so far as to receive it.) . . .

For a long time I have cherished a hope that now when wars have ceased and the world is beginning to cultivate a desire to prolong rather than shorten life, that some of our ships of War shall be converted into floating hospitals for the benefit of such invalids as require change of climate. From a very early period our profession has known the value and importance of change of residence for Consumptives and all labouring under chronic affections of not only the lungs but also of all other vital organs. The experiments that have been and are still making are very unsatisfactory, it is true, but the reason is obvious: the patients are hurried off from all the endearments of home, without friends, nurses or physicians or indeed without any of the absolute requirements. For then they must go wherever the ship is bound without reference to weather, peculiarity of localities, etc.

What I wish is that some large vessels with ample accommodations should be placed under the charge of competent physicians to accompany the patients wherever they may deem most salutary and be thus enabled to choose the climate, season, etc., etc., best adapted to their exigencies. I believe that it might be made a matter of profit, or at least would be of no expense to the gov't having ships lying idle or rotting in ports.

From my experience in the treatment of Bronchitis, Laryngitis and other affections of the Lungs, the chest and collateral parts I am confident that all we now require to save the lives of thousands is the means of placing patients in places adapted by latitude, temperature, etc., which this scheme would afford.

You and you only can achieve this desideratum. If you think it worthy your attention I will sketch out the scheme in detail.

Excuse the liberty I have taken in inflicting so tedious a letter upon you.

                              Your sincere admirer
                              James H. Miller.
James Fenimore Cooper, Esqr, Coopers-town

Stevenson's, Sunday morning [probably March
          2, 1845], while James has gone to Church.
Dearest,

I never had a better time, thus far, than I had yesterday. We went to the corner on wheels, thence eight miles
on runners, where we found another open carriage waiting for us, changed the horses, and got down an hour and
a half before the necessary time. I saw the oldest Miss
Berthoud on the road, and learned that the family was
well.

Sutherland, his wife, James Wadsworth and family
were in the cars. We are all bound to Joe Head's. I dine
here at one, and go down in the *South America*, at five
this evening. The rest will follow in a day or two. Sutherland looks ill, but not as ill as I expected to see him.

I met Mrs. Clark at the station. Her face is full of
wrinkles, her flesh is gone, and she looks seventy—or
rather, she looks ill. There is an end of coquetry in her,
faute de moyennes. She told me that Mrs. Jenkins has a
daughter. I understand Ben Wilcocks has another.

I send, by mail, John Jay's pamphlet, and a copy of
Weed's paper. The last is to be read by Paul, and *then
kept for me,* as I wish to use it in the new book. The anti-
Rent speech is the matter I am in quest of.

The opinion here is all against the Bishop. Wadsworth
told me of a case that occurred in the house of Fitzhugh,
the party insulted being a Miss C——, a young lady of
perfect purity of manners and character, whom he had
hardly seen before. The place, the stairs; part assailed,
the *legs;* and the young lady kept her room until he
quitted the place. You will see that John Jay alludes in
the plainest manner to two more cases in Westchester. It

is supposed a hundred cases might be adduced. Dr. Potter is against, as is Stevenson. Chief Justice Spencer is against; John N. Murray is against, etc., etc.

Most tenderly yours,
J. F.-C.

TO MRS. COOPER, COOPERSTOWN

New York, March 5th, 1845
St. Polk's eve—Festival of Democracy

Dearest,

I got here early on Monday morning, and have been hard at work since. I have discovered that the old books are worth something, and have actually sold the right to print 250 copies of each for $200. These books are likely to produce me two or three hundred a year, in future. I have been offered to-day $1200 *in cash* for the right to print these books, *Afloat and Ashore* included, for the next ten years. I have offered to accept at *five* years, and thus we stand at present. I have sold the edition *entire* of the new book [*Satanstoe*], 2500 copies, for $1050. This is $100. better than what L. & B. gave me for 10,000 copies. The bargain now on the *tapis* may keep me here a day or two longer, but, if made, I shall not remain in Philadelphia more than a week, this time.

The Bishop's affair grows worse and worse. Cases start up like mushrooms. I have heard of a dozen new ones in town. Two in Westchester, one a sister of Mrs. Clancy's. Ludlow Ogden's daughter relates another. Rev. Mr. Johnson of Long Island says openly, since Mrs. Bean's veracity is impugned, he will give his own wife as a case just as bad. Mrs. Joseph Delafield mentioned a case up the river, last evening. In short, there are so many one does not know how to count them.

There is to be a new pamphlet charging the Bishop home. He will be compelled to resign. I am sorry to say the dissenting Bishops will and do suffer, though your brother will probably escape better than the others.

A case in New Rochelle this moment mentioned, and one, another, as recently as thirteen months. The feeling of the community is thoroughly aroused, and the man is lost.

Mrs. Laight is well. Susy Watkins dying. Mrs. Beale, gone South to join her mother. Gay has had scarlet fever, and Mrs. Gay looks like a girl—fat as a pig. Mrs. L. very anti Bishop. The clergy are giving way in all directions, Gil Ver Planck shaking and David B. Ogden also.

This is a glorious May day—bland, bright and exhilarating.

Love as usual, and most where most belongs.

J. F. C.

FROM MRS. WILLIAM L. STONE

Saratoga Springs, March 17, 1845

Dear Sir,

I am wholly ignorant of the technicalities or practice of the Law, but am induced to present myself before you at this time, in consequence of a letter from my nephew, who is my agent in N. York, in which he mentions that you are again pressing the collection in case of the libel suit, which my friends assured me, after the death of my lamented husband, would not have been revived. I do not write however by his advice or suggestion, but to let you know how I am situated in regard to it.

My husband lost all that he realized from the sale of his books, by friends whose liabilities were thrown upon him, and he forced to stand in the gap. During the rage for speculation he was, by reason of his unsuspecting nature, drawn by designing men into the vortex, and determining to keep his office free from embarrassment, he laboured with an assiduity at his books, which, in addition to other labours, anxiety of mind, etc., prostrated his nervous system completely. He died intestate, having made a will, but it was not signed; he dropped away suddenly at last. All his Estate consists of the amount paid for his share of the office, and a house, 14 Clinton Place, on which he had made some payments. By advice I administered, and the office had to be appraised and sold. Pending the negociation, there was much demurring between the parties; at last Mr. Hall agreed to pay the sum of $15:000 for Mr. Stone's share of the office, provided the estate assumed the Cooper case. My Lawyer consented to this arrangement without consulting me. If I had been consulted, I should have objected, for it is of all things the one I should the most have dreaded to assume, not only from taste, but from the state of my mind.

In regard to the verdict rendered in Mr. Stone's favour, in the Stone case, and which Mr. Stone directed to be divided with Mr. Hall, not a cent has been realized, as yet, nor is it likely from present appearances there will be, so that the costs fall upon me, and are a dead loss.

Some delay took place of course in the investing of the $15:000, the proceeds of the office, which at the end of six months will draw an interest of 6 per cent. There are many debts to pay, which we are endeavouring to pay off as fast as we can, and if you press the payment of the verdict in your favour, it will put me to great inconvenience. I have practised the strictest economy, and intend still to do so, in order to have every honest claim settled.

For I would practice any self denial rather than be in debt. When I heard you were pressing your claim I supposed it must be from a misunderstanding of the true state of the case, as you certainly would not wish to distress the widow and the orphan.

It is with inconceivable pain I have brought myself to make this communication. For it forces upon me the instability of Earthly Friendships, at a time when I have little spirits to contemplate anything so sad. I have a letter from Mr. Stone, written after making you a little visit in the country, while I was absent from the city, in which he describes the interesting interview—your reading parts of the MS. of one of your novels, or making maple sugar; in which he breaks out into the most enthusiastick expressions of delight, at the bright prospects of literary fame opening before his friend, who was a Cooper'stown boy. I have others from you, and addressed to Mr. S. after your arrival in Europe, written in all the confidence of friendship, and speaking of your success with a frankness evincing a consciousness that you were writing to one whose heart throb'd in unison with yours, and rejoiced heartily in your success and advancement.

Mr. Stone always prayed for his enemies. During his last illness, I said, why do you pray so earnestly for your enemies; what enemies have you? Why, said he, I do n't know that I have any with the exception of Mr. Cooper, and one other he named, and he added, I am sure if Mr. Cooper knew all the truth, as I have endeavoured to have him made acquainted with it, I cannot conceive how his enmity should continue. For, said he, you know how proud I used to be of him, how I used to boast of his talents, before our little "Den," and in my paper, and in conversation and every way. And this having been uniformly the case, I was greatly wounded when he came out with his first attack upon editors, when he knew how much I had praised him in my paper, and brought his books into notice from pure love to them and their author. All the attacks he complains of, *he knows* I did not write, and I was absent from my post when the most of them appeared. He certainly is aware the most offensive were written by a young gentleman who was with him in Paris. As a dying man, I do think I have done everything a christian man could do to settle the dispute. I have always felt in honour bound to retract any error I may have been led into through haste or misapprehension. If you could have known the gentleness of his spirit and his hatred of strife, and how sorely his feelings were wounded by the course you pursued towards him, I am sure you could not feel it in your heart to pursue the enmity even beyond the grave. For it is but a point of Time, ere we shall each enter upon those untried scenes, and render an impartial account of our stewardship.

If you are so obliging as to answer this promptly, it will be a great convenience to me. In such case please direct to Mrs. Wm. L. Stone, care of the Rev. Francis Wayland, Saratoga Springs, as myself and little boy are here, at my Father's.

Very Respectfully,
L. P. Stone.

To J. Fenimore Cooper, Author of *The Pioneers*, etc.

RICHARD COOPER TO WILLIAM H. SEWARD

Cooperstown, March 21st, 1845

Dr Sir,

I have received yours of the 15th inst. It is my present

intention to argue the case of Cooper vs. Greeley and
McElrath at the May Term. I do not see a probability
of any thing occurring, to make me avail myself of the
condition annexed to the arrangement between us, in
January last.

As you expressed, in your letter, a wish that the suit
should be settled, I have asked Mr. Cooper on what
terms he would be willing to arrange the matter. His
answer was the same, substantially, as in like cases it has
always been. I give you his words: "The suit will be
dropped, on Greeley and McElrath publishing a full retraction of the libel, and paying the costs and expenses.
No other condition will be accepted by me."

As I have never known Mr. Cooper, when offers of
compromise have been made to him during the course of
his suits, to depart from these terms in the least degree, I
suppose any arrangement, short of them, would be un-
practicable.

Respectfully
your obdt Servt
R. Cooper

TO MRS. COOPER, COOPERSTOWN

Globe, Friday, 16th May, 1845

My dearest Sue,

We left Philadelphia, yesterday at 12, and got here
at seven. The girls will tell you their own story. Peter
and Abraham Schermerhorn, with several of their children, were in the cars with us. Our passage was easy
enough.

My money has been duly received, and I am $2200
better than I was. It came very apropos, as did the Philadelphia money. This makes $2330 received since I left

home, your carpet was paid for to-day, and I have ordered a new stock of wines.

The box has been opened, and contains some little matters which I have sent to the girls. Judging by the superscription, I should think they were all for Fan, though I've a notion a purse is intended for me.

Poor Sutherland! He was three days dying, Chester tells me, had his senses to the last, and had all his family around him. One of his lungs was nearly gone.

Dick's argument, I hear, was strong, and sound, on the whole, declamatory. Wessels and Comstock are both in town, and both at Astor House.

Dick tells me that he remembers to have heard a story, similar to theirs, to George's prejudice, many years since. The matter was rectified by himself at the time, but not until the story reached his ears. Forgery was then imputed.

I learned to-day that Gil Verplanck says the Bishop *must* resign. Tyng, it is said, will be elected to Pennsylvania, though he is unquestionably called to St. George's, as poor Milner's successor.

I magnetized Miss Sally Peters at Shubrick's with a good deal of success.

I think I shall write to Nancy before I come home. It will take off the edge of the meeting.

As the weather is bad, the girls wish to stay till Tuesday evening, which will keep me from seeing you until Wednesday, the 21st. They do not wish to stay longer, and it is best I should see them home. Otherwise, I should have left town this afternoon. Bentley must have accepted the draft.

Adieu. Yours as ever,

J. F. C.

TO PAUL FENIMORE COOPER, COOPERSTOWN

Head's, Tuesday, 27th May, 1845

My dear Paul,

As I have written to your mother twice, this letter shall be sent to you. No doubt you have got all the military news, which is highly favorable. Gen. Taylor seems to be perfectly master of his movements, and knows what he is about. He is clear-headed and cool, and made his call for volunteers at precisely the right moment. Notwithstanding the alarm that existed here, he appears to have been under no apprehensions. As early as the 6th April, he informed the government of his intention to build a fort that 500 men could defend, when it would leave the rest of his command free to act. Everything has turned out as he foresaw. The 500 men have, so far, defended the fort, with a loss of 13 in killed and wounded, and the remainder of his force has proved sufficient for all his exigencies. The volunteers are wanted for a forward movement. Near 2000 of them had arrived on the 14th, and Conner could reinforce with as many more. Our people must now be in Matamoras, unless the Mexicans have reinforced very largely.

The important feature is the course of England. If she secretly sustains Mexico, we shall certainly have an English war; if she be wise, she will endeavour to persuade Mexico to make peace. I think the issue doubtful. The war is well sustained, though the Whigs dislike the popularity it may give the administration.

I am getting on very well, and shall leave here early next week. Yesterday I dined with Gen. Tom Cadwalader. Major Ringold was his kinsman, his mother having been a Cadwalader, a sister of Gen. Cadwalader of the revolution. The poor fellow was shot through both thighs, the shot going through his horse and killing him dead. Mary Farmer's old beau, Col. Payne, is among the wounded. She must volunteer to nurse him.

Tell the girls Peter McCall is engaged to a Miss Mercer of Maryland; a daughter of Major John Mercer, an old acquaintance of mine. She is a belle and twenty-two. As Peter is thirty-eight, he will not wait a great while.

The Capt. McCall in the army is of the Philadelphia family and Peter's brother. Mrs. H. McCall's little girl was christened in St. Peter's church, yesterday afternoon. Wednesday Morning, 28th.

The southern mails merely confirm the good news from Point Isabel. A great many letters are in town, from officers of the army and navy, to their wives and friends. Among others, Lt. Mead, of the Topographical Engineers, who is married to the Miss Sargent who looks like Sue, has written to his wife, and Harry Ingersoll to his. Ingersoll is the first lieutenant of Conner's ship, and was sent up to the camp with communications for the general. I heard his letter read last night. He boasts largely of his own exploits *on horseback*, flattering himself that none of the army people could have done much better than riding sixty miles in two days, though he hints that his seat of honour is none the better for the exercise. But the material part of his communication is this—Taylor and Conner are certainly arranging a joint expedition against Matamoras. The letter was dated the 13th, and unless the Mexicans have been largely reinforced, or the general should choose to wait for the volunteers, the attack was probably made by the 18th. If so, we must get the result in a day or two.

I think the Mexicans have left the left bank of the

river entirely. So Gen. Taylor reports, and so the result will show, I make no question, unless large reinforcements are sent to Arista. The opinion is general that the war will be short, it being thought that a revolution will supervene. I am not so certain of this. Outward pressure usually has the effect to suspend internal revolutions. Then our government will wish to compensate itself for the expenses of the war by some signal advantage. California must fall into our hands in the next sixty days, and I think our people will wait for that result. I expect to hear it is sold to England.

I forgot to mention that poor Ringold sent for Ingersoll, and died with his own hand in that of the last. He was quite free from pain, and had his senses to the last. His troop was commanded by a Lt. Ridgely in the last battle, and appears to have behaved in the noblest manner. All our artillery behaved in the best possible manner. As Major Erving's name does not appear, I fear he is on the sick list, he having been left behind at Corpus Christi, on account of his health. Still, he may have joined. The Mexicans have probably lost a thousand men in the two affairs.

There is a report here that Capt. Thornton showed no judgment in his affair, while Harder behaved very well. Capt. May has highly distinguished himself. The Mexican Lancers charged Ridgely's guns, but he drove them back with canister. They also charged the 5th Infantry, which received them in square, and set them to the right about with a rattling fire of musketry.

Taylor will doubtless be made one of the new Major Generals; Scott, it is said, will be kept back, though it is difficult to see how. The Whigs complain, for they wish to use him as a candidate and float into office on his glory.

But all this is nonsense, popular feeling being so very capricious. One mishap would lose him all the popularity purchased in the war of '12. Adieu—love to all.

J. Fenimore Cooper

FROM RICHARD COOPER

New York, June 3rd, 1845

Dear Uncle,

Your case with Stone stands at No. 11. I have seen Spencer, and find, as I suspected, that he is of the opinion that the case cannot be argued until Stone's representatives are made parties. I don't know whether Mrs. Stone is sole executrix or not. I think, however, that she stated in her letter to you that she was. If so, then, according to their view of the case, she must be called in to prosecute the writ of error. I cannot learn that the practice in the Court of Errors, on this point, has been settled. I have followed what I believed, and still believe, to be the Supreme Court practice. I think I am right, but it is not improbable that the court may decline to hear the arguments until the Executrix is made a party, or all the personal representatives if there are more than one. When the question comes up, it will be of importance, I think, to them, that Mrs. Stone has received notice from you of your intention to go on with the case, which I take it for granted she did in your answer to her letter. I want you, therefore, to draw up and make oath to a short affidavit, substantially like the form of one I give you below, and send it to me by mail, at No. 51 Walker Street, where I am staying. I should like to have it as soon as possible.

Very truly yours,

R. Cooper.

In the Court for the Correction of Errors

J. Fenimore Cooper, Defendant in Error
versus
William L. Stone, Plaintiff in Error

Otsego County, etc. J. Fenimore Cooper, the defendant in error, in the above entitled cause, being duly sworn, says that sometime in the month of   last he received a letter from (given Christian name) Stone, the widow of William L. Stone, deceased, the plaintiff in error, in this cause, on the subject of the judgement rendered by the Supreme Court in this deponent's favor against the said William L. Stone, and to reverse which the writ of error, in said cause, was brought; that this deponent answered said letter soon after he received it, and informed the said   Stone, in substance, that it was this deponent's intention to proceed with the case in the Court of Errors, and that it would be brought to argument at the then en-suing term of the Court. And he further says that his said answer was sent to the said   Stone by mail, directed to Ballston Spa, which the said   Stone stated to be her place of residence, in her said letter to this deponent. And further this deponent says not.

I have written the above to give you an idea of what I want. Of course the affidavit must be adapted to the facts. The main point I wish to shew is that Mrs. Stone was fully apprised of the pendency of the Writ of Error, and of your intention to go on with the case. If you know of any fact which would make the affidavit stronger, you will of course put it in.

R. C.

Hall, Cooperstown, July 4th, 1845

Runaway,

You may have missed me at Syracuse, but you can not imagine how much you have been missed here. For a day or two, I was about to call out "Matie" every half hour, and your daughters were mistaken for you at every turn.

It rained here, dearest, Monday, Tuesday, Wednesday, Thursday. At first we moaned about your decision, but when we found how long the storm continued, we were glad you went. To-day has been charming, a little cool, but no rain and a bright sun.

Wednesday the two fratelli Beads appeared. The younger accepts, but asks leave to take off the wire edge of his wit upon his friends at Louisville. He appears in the paint next week, when we hope that the new broom will begin its work.

No news from F. Adley. He is doubtless from home, busy, as he has been written to and does not answer. By this time, I should think it done. Dow has answered, *is very grateful* and accepts. The affair, however, is by no means terminated. I think the P - - - - - s much easier on the subject. Mrs. P - - - - - seemed quite relieved this morning and P - - - - - really in good spirits.

I am sorry to say my unruly ox has done much damage to my very best corn. Some of it may recover, but many bushels must be lost.

Your cook has made a cream cheese which looks well, and as most of what she does *tastes* well, I live in hopes of success. A day or two will decide.

This day has been as quiet as last year's 4th was the reverse—a great many boats on the lake, but that is all, with the exception of crackers and some most infernal bell ringing last night—even Napoleon could not have stood it.

No news of the *Toe* [*Satanstoe*]. I wait to hear from the publishers.

As yet no news from Detroit, and I may be compelled to go to New York. Opposition is so active that we can leave home at 6 A. M., and reach Albany by 1 P. M. There are two lines on the Canajoharie road, and, what is odd, the old line thrives under it. The price, however, is very low, and will fall to 75 cents, I think, all round.

We had chickens to-day, but I shall pull up on them, for our company. Peas promise, as do cucumbers, and potatoes. We had potatoes in the soup yesterday. To-day, Paul and I emptied a pint of champagne to "the day and all who honour it."

Tiptongue was weighed this morning, and bore down 820 llbs. This is gaining 92 llbs. in 84 days, not as well as he has done, but pretty well.

Eight of the youngest turkeys have vanished at a swoop. These were on the hill, and with a mama turkey, who wandered too far. Forty is all I hope for.

I have written to Mr. Fort, and expect he will be here to-morrow morning. I have nothing to add but love to your sisters, Fan, Mrs. De L., Lucy and all hands.

As for yourself, you need no assurances. The girls have just said they intend to have their bee to-morrow. Adieu.

J. F. C.

FROM GEORGE BANCROFT

Confidential.

Washington, July 21, 1845

My dear Sir,

Your daughter having had the good nature to say she

desired to see my handwriting, I answered your letter through her. But as yet you have asked for nothing about Old Ironsides. It will give me pleasure and I shall hold myself as doing good service to the Navy, if you will freely direct me as to the papers, of which copies would be useful to you.

Your young friend, the Commander, shall have his claims considered with that respect which your recommendation warrants. He is an applicant for either of two positions, and I hope to gratify him in the one or the other.

The case of Ned Myers is more difficult. But I am turning that over in my mind and hope to have it in my power to meet your wishes. Yet I am not clear about it.

A recent event has given me much concern. A Naval Court-Martial has found one of its officers, a captain, guilty of scandalous conduct, and the specification is falsehood, and they have *not* dismissed him. Were you near me, I should take your advice as to the mode of relieving the navy from the disgrace of a sentence which virtually declares immoral and dishonorable conduct to be no obstacle to a place of equality in rank, command, and emolument with the captains of the Navy.

Very Faithfully yours,
George Bancroft.

J. Fenimore Cooper, Esqr

TO MRS. COOPER, COOPERSTOWN

Head's, Friday, [August] 8th, 1845

Dearest,

Here I am at last, coming on last night. I was detained by an arrangement made with Burgess & Stringer, by which I sold them a right to reprint certain *old* books, for one thousand dollars in cash. They have paid me, and I might now return home, to-morrow, but, having come so far, I shall remain until next week, in order to save time next trip. I shall quit here about Thursday, and be home three or four days afterwards. So far, every thing has been done very favorably. A full edition of the new book is sold, and a good thing made out of the old one. Something remains to be done with *Afloat and Ashore*, which B. & S. are anxious to get.

I have also met Gurney Smith. He says the impression is very strong against both bishops, more particularly ours. Your brother's friends here regret his mistake. Every hour about brings out some new facts. *Three* cases in West-Chester, a new one at New Rochelle. Quite twenty are openly reckoned in New York and on Long Island. More all over the State.

John Gay says it is now believed he kept a mistress, and thought the visit to the brothel was a fetch. Actual guilt is also spoken of, in a case in his own house. The determination is to drive him out of his chair, if a new trial be had. His friends desert him, and his foes increase. *Even Maria* gives him up—Dr. Coit do., other clergymen the same. Dr. Cushman also—these I have seen, Dr. C. excepted, and of him I have heard directly. . . .

TO MRS. COOPER, COOPERSTOWN

Head's, Oct. 3d, 1845

Dearest,

Here all are well. Mrs. McCall says her child looks just like a monkey, to begin with. Miss Wilcocks is well. Mr. Ben Wilcocks was thrown from his wagon about three weeks since, and much hurt, and he has since had influenza. The effect of both has been to render him nervous and low spirited, and apprehensions have been felt that he might fall back into the state from which he emerged only six or eight years ago. I saw him this evening, when he was said to be better than he had been. He has let his large house for $1500, and removed into a smaller one, though sufficiently large, for which he had no tenant.

In convention, I saw an old friend Rev. Barton, who is strongly anti-bishop. I also saw Mr. Bonven, who is ditto. The clergy did not behave well. Most of them think ———— guilty, and yet they voted, looked and talked, as if they thought him innocent. It will take ten years of exemplary behaviour in the clergy of the diocese to recover lost ground. Men insist on something more than the observance of forms—they require a little of the substance of religion. The whole will terminate in new charges, and a deposition. When that occurs, there will be a party to dispute the sentence, and to maintain that deposition from orders does not infer deposition from the diocese.

The close of the convention, nevertheless, was harmonious and respectable. The peaches *here* are good yet, and I do wish you could eat some of them. I shall try to get a basket for preserves—October peaches, which are hard and keep a good while.

Chainbearer is a good book I think, and *Satanstoe* has been a good deal read. The edition of 3600 is nearly sold, and Burgess is negotiating for more. . . .

TO MRS. COOPER, COOPERSTOWN

Head's, Saturday, Oct. 11th, 1845

Dearest,

I believe I will send another tinpinny before I quit

this place, to let you know how I get on. My book
[*Satanstoe*] will be finished this afternoon, and I shall
go to New York to-morrow night. One week in town, and
then for home.

Tell Sue I have her $100, in *gold galore*, for her. The
book will appear in November, as will my own. I shall
bring her the new preface, and shall send the sheets to
Bentley with my own.

The fair does pretty well. It had received $4500 at
the end of the second day, and it closes to-night—though
there will be a raffle on Monday. The raffles are numerous
and illegal. I have put in $2.50, one chance in thirty, in
hopes to get some law books, though without any expectation of succeeding. Miss Peters had taken $400 the
third evening, divided into $200—$130—$70—, resem-
bling a lady's waist.

Mr. Bancroft is here with his family. I believe one of
his children is unwell. I have been asked by Ingersoll to
meet him at dinner, but could not on account of clearing
off my work. He is to pass an hour with me to-morrow
morning.

Bishop Potter is at work, but opinion is suspended. To
own the truth, the clergy have lost so much ground in this
affair of ours that no one seems disposed to bestow unnecessary faith. It will take years of good behavior for
them to recover their lost ground. Ingersoll has not yet
been to see his own bishop.

I have had an interview with a Mr. Granville Vernon
M. P., a son of the Archbishop of York, and the cousin
of various great persons. A niece of his, a Miss Harcourt,
is married to Lord Norreys. He gave me all the gossip of
London, knew everybody I knew, and knew all about
them. He says Lord Abingdon *had* about £15,000 a year,

but, without any vices and by pure negligence, has suffered himself to get so much involved that his estate is at reverse, and he lives on £2000 a year. Norreys he says is a veritable monkey, being the greatest mimic he knows and a perfect chatterbox, though good natured, and not bad principled. He will be cut down to the entailed estates, at about £7000 a year, which is quite as much as I supposed the father to have.

Old Rogers is well, and very little altered. Lady William has gone to join her husband at Berlin, though he keeps the beautiful Jewess openly, to the great scandal of the pious King and Queen.

Lord Kerry's widow was the admiration of all London, for a few years, but has given away at last, and become the wife of a certain Charles Gove, as *roué* a second son as England contains!

None of the Greys had a child till they wed a parson, who, with a parson's luck, has a house full. My pretty Mrs. Grey—the young Duke—has got nothing from her banker-father, and doubtless works as we all do to help feed the household. The present Earl is married, but childless.

Mr. Vernon says that Stanley was in love with his present wife when he came here, but was thought too young to marry; that Labouchère was in love with the late Westley, has since married; Westley in love with the present Lady Grey, and Denison in love with someone else.

God bless you all. With tenderest love,

J. F. C.

"Stanley" was Lord Derby, who as a young man visited America in the early 1820's and, in company with Fenimore Cooper and Mr. Wortley Montague, made a trip up the Hudson

River to Glens Falls and thence to Niagara. It was in consequence
of a suggestion of his that *The Last of the Mohicans* was written
and a part of the plot laid at Glens Falls.

FROM RICHARD HENRY DANA

Boston, Oct. 25, 1845

My dear Sir—

I left home early in August, returned for one day, and
was off again till just now, so that I did not get your
letter at all and was only able to call upon your son a day
or two since.

One of my sons called during my absence, but your son
failed of seeing him or getting his card. I am now going
from post to pillar and from pillar to post; for our house
is still getting into order, that is, into most admired disorder, preparatory to our winter's sojourn—White-wash-
ing, paint-washing, floor-washing, carpet-mending, carpet-
making, carpet-laying and all the numberless doings that
go to the making up of domestic quiet and comfort. I am
truly sorry that my absence and, next, the condition of
our establishment, should have so long prevented my paying that attention which it would give me much pleasure
to do, to a son of yours. A few days into the coming
month, and bureaus, chairs, and tables will have ended
their whirl and dance, and have taken their several places.
From the account your son gave me of himself I have my
fears, however, that he will have found it necessary to
leave us before that time. I hope that his disease may not
be such as his physicians consider it,—it would not be
the first time that physicians have pronounced indigestion
of stomach to be congestion, or some other disease, of
lungs. Should he leave us, I trust that you will keep him
in exercise in the open air, so that he may come back to us

a strong, healthy man. Let him be here when he may, we shall all be glad to see him. For the few minutes that I was in his room, he quite pleased me. He looks and speaks like a man of brains and he is natural—no thinking about *self* all the while. As I was away your son took from the office your letter to me, and destroyed, I presume, as he said it simply related to a matter which had been adjusted. A letter to me directed to Cambridge might be there for a twelvemonth. Do me the favor to direct one soon to me at Boston, and excuse my interlined words—I am forever leaving out.

Most sincerely, my dear Sir, Y'rs,

Richd H. Dana.

J. F. Cooper, Esq.

Boston, November 10, 1845

My dear Sir—

I have three sufficient reasons for not having sooner replied to yours of Oct. 30th, which are as many as so reasonable a man as yourself would ask for. 1st, Your letter was about a week on the road; 2nd, I was so busy for two or three days after as not to have a moment to myself; and 3rd, have since that time been so miserably sick as not to be able to bear the sight of paper or pen. I will speak as "frankly" as you ask me to do. I can only give you my general impressions, being too little in the world to have any distinct knowledge of particulars as respects feelings, opinions, or rather notions, afloat here or elsewhere. You must consider that Perry being a New Englander and from a State bordering close upon us, and one with which we were in intimate relation, it almost necessarily followed that our people should take a peculiar pride in his success—something beyond that merely of his being a fellow-countryman;—they felt and claimed the honor of near relationship. After the peace he visited Boston, and through all the attentions paid to him bore himself modestly. He was a young man also, and, as I remember him, with a mild expression of countenance, which you know is particularly pleasing in military men to those in civil life.

In consequence of this and of the stories then current, a contrary feeling towards Elliott may of course have been stronger here than elsewhere. When some few years back E. came here he came among a people more or less prejudiced against him; and the first act done under him (and, as understood, *by* him) at *our* navy-yard, was to put the figure head of Jackson (a man then generally most heartily hated here) upon Old Ironsides, *our* Old Ironsides, *born* among us and one of us: it was felt as if it were a personal insult to us. Looking at both instances, you see how naturally the state of feeling prevailing here was produced, seeming to grow up unconsciously out of the run of circumstances.

I have very little belief that people have been saying— we won't read Mr. Cooper—our "minds are made up." And I much doubt whether they have read more of Mackenzie and your other opponents than they have of what you have written. I suppose their reading to have been principally confined to the newspapers, and what may have appeared in our Monthly Rev^s etc., among other articles. I have gotten this impression—for it is nothing more—I scarcely know how; and I have another still stronger, that as concerns you personally, if there is any ill feeling, it is very slight and confined to the most ignorant, and entirely unworthy your notice.

Now, as to your lecturing on the subject. I do not see how one situated as you are could come here and lecture upon the matter without *appearing* to take advantage of your place as lecturer to turn what should be a mere public affair at such a time into something personal to yourself. It seems to me that on all such occasions the true course is for a man to avoid all that may even *appear* to bear upon himself. Allow me to ask, would it not be calling out towards you a deeper feeling of respect to make no allusion to the subject, than you could possibly excite even by a defence of your ground that should be *conclusive to the minds of your audience?*

Besides, were you to take a contrary course, some would say, let us hear the other side; and your antagonists might claim a right to be heard, and the lecture-room would be turned into a battle-ground. In your long and manful struggle to put down the slanderous character of our press I am led to believe that the better part of our people feel that you have done a good service; and I trust that should you come here and lecture on any subject upon which you and they can meet upon common ground, you will be received with every attention, and be most gladly listened to. You must understand me as having laid entirely aside the *merits* of the case, considering that they do not belong to the question of lecturing or not lecturing upon it. May I, as a private individual, express the hope that you will be so able to manage your subject, if you are on a battle, as not to excite the vain-glorying of our countrymen?—a hard matter, I know, on such a subject. I fear for our country, when I look forward; for the *permanent* health of a nation must lie in its *moral* constitution; as that is so, first or last, must be its physical;—and I thank a righteous God that it is so.

I called a second time to see your son, and learned that he had been gone a couple of days. I am truly glad to hear from you that he is less ill than he feared. However, he has "run up" too fast, and needs exercise and open air to strengthen and spread in. After that to books again! Our Law-school is an excellent institution for the study of his profession. Send him back in good time, and tell him to let me know when he returns. My son, with his younger brother, is doing well in the Law. He has a good constitution, though not the Boreas face and timber-hard arm that he brought home from sea. He is much confined to business, and exercises too little. I warn him, but it does no good. He has two nice little girls—quite enough to make an old fool of a grandfather.

Don't wait for matters of business to write again, I pray you.

Most sincerely, my dear Sir,
Yrs, Richd H. Dana.

James Fenimore Cooper, Esq., Cooperstown

Did I not send you a small pamphlet upon Marsh's Address last year, before the New England Pilgrim Society, New York? If not, I will do so. It was by my second son, E. T. D.

TO MRS. COOPER, COOPERSTOWN

Globe, Tuesday afternoon, Nov. 18th, 1845

Chainbearer will be published early next week, and not before.

It is May weather, here; positively pleasant without fires. Last night was one of the pleasantest I ever passed on the river. My berth was wide, and I slept it out until eight o'clock, the first time I ever did so. Craft, the *Hen-drik Hudson*, a boat as much superior to any thing you ever saw, as the best boat you ever saw was superior to the second boat on the river. Every way a noble vessel, and as swift as a balloon.

With tenderest love,

Yours

J. F. C.

Alas! How I miss the Laights.

Mrs. Laight, so often mentioned in this correspondence, was Elizabeth Watts, a daughter of John Watts and Jane de Lancey.

She was born about 1793; was the wife of Henry Laight, and a cousin and very intimate friend of Mrs. Cooper's.

TO MRS. COOPER, COOPERSTOWN

Head's, Sunday, November 30th, 1845

My dearest Sue,

I supped with old McAdams and Kit Hughes, at Joe Ingersoll's last Friday. The old man was in good spirits, and well disposed to talk, but also disposed to listen. On the whole, I was pleased with him, though I think he is very strong headed. I did not name Mrs. De Wint to him.

Elliott is here, and in an advanced dropsy, not only of the body and limbs, but of the heart and chest. He cannot survive, I should think, though he seems to think he may. I have seen his wife, and thanked her for the "few little matters." Elliott, himself, believes he is getting better.

Read is going to the coast of Africa, and the Mediter-ranean, with a broad pennant. This is the service for

which Bothe was designed, and I fear a reason has induced the secretary to change his mind.

Griswold, to my surprise, is still here, though his name
he tells me, is on a door plate in Savannah or Galveston,
I forget which. His wife is with the door plate. How
long he will remain here is more than I can say, though
some time, I fancy. It is altogether a queer operation.

I have seen no lady but Mary Wilcocks, and my kins-
woman, Mrs. Vincent, who is a nice little body; handsome and the picture of health, though the mother of a
house full of children, and very fine children too. I shall
make a sally with Paul, however, to-morrow, or as soon
as the weather will permit.

I can hear nothing of *Chainbearer*. The papers are
mum, as usual, but I know it sells pretty well. They cannot put me down entirely, though they do me infinite
harm. A precious set of dishonest knaves are they!

Everybody is on the *qui vive* for the message. Oregon
or no Oregon—peace or war. The reports are a little more
peaceable than they have been—as for Mexico, that point
is essentially settled. There will be no war with her, and
I expect the difficulties with France are at the bottom
of her moderations.

Douw, *the* Van Rensselaer's husband, is staying in the
house. He spoke to me of Otsego, and of Cooperstown
in particular, without my knowing who he was. Is there
not a suit for divorce pending?

Bishop Potter is making a little talk, by consenting to
lecture before the Mercantile Library Association. The
Philadelphians are used to such scholastic escapades in a
prelate, but the Episcopal character stands low just now.

Elinor will be published in a few days. I have given
the quietus to the Pocket Handkerchief story by saying

firmly that I wrote the tale myself, and would not have allowed my name to be affixed to anything that I had not written. I have spoken to Graham about the autograph, and he has asked for the manuscript to look it over. I shall ask at least $25 for it and I think he may take it.

Do not fail to write me immediately, for I was quite uneasy at not having heard from you for twelve days. Paul I think decidedly improving, and, as for myself, I am as ever,

And yours in the bargain,
J. F. C.

TO MRS. COOPER, COOPERSTOWN

Head's, Saturday, [March] 28th, 1846

Dearest,

I got here on Wednesday, in a most inclement night. Frederick Prime and Lewis Rogers were my companions. The last told me that Madame la Marquise de Lavalette had abandoned every thing else for politics. She had been at work all summer to get the Marquis into the Chamber, and had succeeded by one vote. He left Paris in June and returns next month.

I suppose you have seen the death of poor Dr. Foote. All I know about it is a sentence in a letter from Matamoras, which announces that Drs. Foote and Wharton were both dead at Levacca. Poor Mary! She has a hard time before her.

Wessels had arrived at Matamoras, a month since, and will no doubt be sent to Tampico with his regiment. Young Chapman was at Camargo, at the same time, on his way to join the 2d Dragoons, at Monterey. Phil Kearny was at Matamoras with his troop, and would probably be employed to keep open the communications.

My affairs look pretty well. The manuscript [probably *The Islets of the Gulf; or Rose Budd*] is gone, and an arrangement is on the *tapis* that I find to my liking. It will give me a $1000 at no great trouble. I shall not complete it until next week, when I turn my face north. I hope to be home at the end of the week.

Adieu, with best love to all,

J. Fenimore Cooper.

TO MRS. COOPER, COOPERSTOWN

Globe, April 1st, 1846

Dearest,

An hour after I wrote you this morning, I effected a sale of literary property, to the amount of $1,500, which will enable me to return home at the close of the week. I have the cherubs, picture, and $500 in England in reserve, amounting in all to $600 more. This will pay off Ogden and other demands, leaving all my affairs in a small compass, and perfectly manageable. I am happy enough to be through with that western affair, leaving what remains of it to come in, and not to go out.

As I wish to press a bargain with Graham of Philadelphia, I shall stay here until Friday morning and be at home on Saturday—possibly a day earlier.

I met young Phil Kearny this morning. He resigns in a day or two, in the intention to push for a Majority, should there be a war; a project that will probably succeed.

With kindest love to all, I remain

Yours tenderly,

J. F. C.

Every body speaks well of *Elinor*, but its price kills it.

Hall, Cooperstown, June 9th, 1846

My dear Sir,

Understanding you intend to come and see us, *en route* for town, I write to make the following statement—

Mr. Beach, our clergyman, is a deacon, and very desirous to be ordained priest in his parish. We hear the money has given out, and *point d'argent, point de suisse,* meaning no money no bishop, as well as other things, your visit will offer the only chance of having things as we wish. I hope, provided that he get the regular documents from our standing committee, you can ordain him, and write that you may not have the excuse of having left your pontificals at home. If you say *yes*, be good enough to send a missive ahead, a day or two before your own arrival, that preparations may be made.

I saw Ned on my way up, looking as if he might occasionally study.

With kindest regards to all,

I remain very truly yours,

J. Fenimore Cooper.

Head's, Friday [Thursday], 27th [August], 1846

We got here last night, Mrs. Shubrick a good deal fatigued. Our passage from Providence was not "rough and ready," but "rough and rainy." Mr. and Mrs. Mutter were on board, as were several other persons of our acquaintance. Newport is breaking up for the season. Thousands have been there. It very fairly rivals Saratoga.

Boston is a very fine town, and has charming environs. I can easily believe, nevertheless, that the climate is infernal.

Mrs. Shubrick sends quantities of love, as I do myself. She had a bitter moment at parting, and in thrusting her head out of the cars to look after him, came near having it knocked off by a post. For an hour she was silent, after which she revived, became conversible, and has been in very good spirits since.

Redskins is making quite a sensation, in the high deb. to my surprise.

TO MRS. COOPER, COOPERSTOWN

Head's, Sunday, August 30th, 1846

My dearest Sue,

Here I am again, well and sound. We left here Thursday afternoon, and reached Baltimore at eleven that night. I bethought me of the telegraph just as we left the house, and sent the enclosed note to Mr. Lewin Wethered, who got it, just as you see, from the office, a few minutes later. In consequence, young Wethered was on the wharf ready to take charge of his aunt. Asa Fitch and Moncure Robinson were among the passengers, and rendered the trip pleasant.

I was too lazy to come back on Friday (having no motive, since Graham will not be here until Tuesday at soonest) and passed the whole day at Baltimore. I did not see McNally, who I rather think is out of town. One of his daughters is married to a Mr. Chatard, who is second lieutenant of the *Independence*. He was a widower when he married her.

I left Baltimore yesterday morning, at nine, and got here at three. I found Comm. Stewart and Gov. Hamilton of South Carolina at table, and the old set. In New York I saw Col. Payne, who is waiting to have the ball extracted from his back. It went in just over the hip bone, and lodged near the back bone. He continued on horseback to the end of the fight, and this nearly cost him his life. He is now much better, however, can walk with a cane, and once rid of the lead will do well enough.

Joe Ingersoll is re-nominated for Congress, but Charlie's success is doubtful. *He* is strongly opposed by democrats. Joe was nominated unanimously. Joe will get in, as a matter of course. Miss Virginia looks interesting when he is mentioned, but there is no engagement talked of. Poor, laughing Annie Payne has been at death's door, but is convalescent.

Gurney Smith told me your sisters were at Mrs. Welch's, a little out of town. I will manage to see them to-morrow, if possible.

A good long snooze, last night, has quite refreshed me, though I went to bed much fatigued, with the eternal shaking of a bad rail-road. They tire me much more than the old carriages.

Did I tell you that *Redskins* is in great favour with the better classes? The praise I have heard of it has been warm, and is, I doubt not, sincere. Its time is just coming. The common sense of the book tells. With best love to the girls and Paul,

Yours most tenderly,
J. F. C.

FROM J. E. DE KAY

New York, September 16, 1846

My dear Cooper

This will serve to make you acquainted with my young friend the Reverend Mr. Harwood, who is on his way to Cooperstown by command of his ecclesiastical Commander, Bishop De Lancey. I fancy you will like Mr.

Harwood on his own account, and I feel sure that you will receive him with more cordiality when you learn that he is shortly to be my son in law.

Do you not feel some presentiment of an impending evil? Your worst apprehensions are realized. Webb of the *Courier* has undertaken to *praise you!* How *can* you stand it?

The best *mot* of the season we owe to the actual Pope. When applied to, to have a rail road through the Papal States he threw himself on the maxim *"Stare super vias antiquas"*—but this may possibly be a naughty low church bit of waggery. Adieu, dear sir, and with kind remembrances to Mrs. Cooper and the young ladies

I am
Yours truly
J. E. De Kay

TO CHARLES GAYARRE, LOUISIANA

Hall, Cooperstown, Dec. 14, 1846

Sir:

Quite recently, while I was in town, Messrs. Burgess and Stringer gave me the copy of the book that you did me the favor to send to their care, together with your obliging letter. This delay in the receipt of the communication and the history will explain to you the delay in my acknowledging the compliment. It happened that Mrs. Cooper was much engaged in reading a work on Louisiana that had been given to me in Paris, by Mr. de Marbois, and the moment she saw your history she seized it, and has been reading it since. Consequently, I have had no opportunity to look over your work, but shall do so on some early occasion.

There is little probability, Sir, of my ever venturing

so far from home in literature as to attempt the sort of work you mention. It properly falls to the share of Southern writers. My time, moreover, is nearly done. At 57 the world is not apt to believe a man can write fiction, and I have long seen that the country is already tired of me. Novelties are puissant in this country, and new names take the place of old ones so rapidly that one scarcely learns to distinguish who are in favor before a successor is pointed out. My clients, such as they are, are in Europe, and long have been, and there is no great use in going out of my way to endeavor to awaken a feeling in this country that has long gone out. I am, notwithstanding, very sensible of the honor you have done me. Should you ever come North you will find me at no great distance from some of the most celebrated of our waters, and ever ready to offer you the hospitalities of my roof in the modest manner that my means will permit. I am, Sir, your most obliged,

J. Fenimore Cooper.

Charles Gayarre, Esq., Louisiana.

Charles E. A. Gayarre was a very distinguished resident of New Orleans. He wrote a number of histories of Louisiana, most of them in French. The book mentioned here is probably his *History of Louisiana* in French, published in 1846. He wrote one novel.

FROM AN UNKNOWN PERSON

Franklin House, 25th March, 1847

James Fenimore Cooper, Esq.

I have just finished reading your new work *The Pathfinder** and am delighted with it, you have here surpassed

* *The Pathfinder* was published in 1840.

yourself, and credit me, Sir, it gives me no little pleasure
to find the advice I gave you, somewhat gratuitous you
will say, has been followed, the press are, and always have
been your sincere well wishers. improve the present opportunity and you can make them your warmest friends, your
very able supporters. In fine leave *libel suits and satirical
poems* to men who have no reputation to lose, you, Sir,
should not have ought to do with the one or the other.
You have regained your former foothold in the public
favour—beware lest your eminence turn your brain again
and tempt you to the edge of the precipice. *I say Sir
beware, for should you forget the arm that helped to rein-
state you,* for in this the prophecy is but the forerunner
of its fulfilment you may bid an eternal farewell to
fame—*for you shall be striped as bare as the forest in mid
winter,* and envy the poorest scribbler that ever held a
pennyless happy insignificance.

A Friend.

James Fenimore Cooper, Esq., Cooperstown

FROM AN UNKNOWN PERSON

England.   April.

Sir

Having Read your most interesting novels, viz., *The
Borderers, The Pathfinder, The last of the Mohicans,
The Pioneers,* and *The Prairie;* I beg leave to inform you
that they are universally esteemed, and that Hawk eye or
the Scout, together with the Mohicans, are very favorite
characters, and have created great interest. It would be
useless for me to attempt to point out, any *particular*
interesting part in them, as they are equally good all
through, especially all relating to Indians and the Scout.
I therefore request, if agreeable to yourself, that you will

oblige *England* by writing some more novels of the same kind, about Indians, and the Scout, such as about various exploits alluded to by the Scout, and along his Prairie Career, and about the Mohicans, in the times, when their Tribe was in its best days. There are many People who are anxiously awaiting some more of your interesting Tales to appear, and it will be a great pleasure to myself and them to hear of your Tales being Published. I therefore wish you success, and that you will continue to outstrip all your competitors in novel writing, who are nothing as authors compared with yourself.

I therefore subscribe myself

Your obliged

P.S. Any thing about Indians will be read with Pleasure.
J. Fenimore Cooper, Esqre.,
    Author of the *Pathfinder*, *Prairie*, etc.

TO MRS. COOPER, COOPERSTOWN

New York, June 16th, 1847

Miss Cruger told me yesterday (old Ditto's daughter) that Mrs. James is a showy woman, but that her sister was the better woman of the two. Mrs. James loved show, etc., and would like to figure. Her great recommendation was walking particularly well. Harry Munro is completely used up, and Mrs. Bailey with him. Jim seems to be very well understood. He is looking unusually well.

Cortlandt Parker is about to be married—to whom, I did not learn.

Ogden's company is completely ruined—lost everything, and is about to close. They blame Ogden, whose

day is gone in his own set. He keeps up his spirits, however, and will take care of himself. His decline will not
be happy, I am afraid. Now a wife and children would
be a relief to him.

TO MRS. COOPER, COOPERSTOWN

American Hotel, Buffalo, June 20th, 1847

I went to the City Bank to beat up Tom Rochester.
He was at Canandaigua, but his father took me in charge,
covered me with civility, and pressed me to stay some
time. I went with him in a carriage even to the landing,
saw the outside of everything, and found Rochester a
far pleasanter, as well as larger, place than I expected to
see. The country is very fine, and this town the base of a
really noble place. Some say it has 30,000 and some pre-
tend as many as 40,000 inhabitants.

I have just come from church. A Mr. Schuyler
preached; and very well. He reads far better than common. Grosvenor Clark knew me, and gave me a seat.
The church was greatly crowded, having but one parson
for three congregations.

TO MRS. COOPER, COOPERSTOWN

[Philadelphia] United States Hotel,

Wednesday, 11th [August], 1847

Dearest,

Stephen Rensselaer was on board. He told me he was
getting on well enough with his tenants, selling to raise
money to pay his debts. His brother has mortgaged and
left Beverwyk—the popular notion being that he is
ruined. Of course, this cannot be so. I was sorry to find
that Stephen spoke coldly of him, as if he had few com-

munications with him. Abraham Ogden told me that
Phil Schuyler's friends thought Stephen had been hard
with *him*, but when I told him that Stephen's furniture
had been sold to pay Phil's debts he got a new idea.

I have nothing more to say, unless it be to tell you
how much I love you. Eat chicken and all other nice
things in my absence, but leave enough for Mr. Hand.

Adieu, dearest—

TO MRS. COOPER, COOPERSTOWN

United States Hotel, Thursday, Aug. 12th, 1847

Dearest,

I wrote you yesterday, and resume to-day, journalwise.
I forgot to say in my last that I met Maitland in the
street. He told me that he was not going to Europe and
would bring his wife up himself. How serious he was,
I cannot say. He asked how we liked the niece. I told
him very much. He seemed to demur and then complained that she was captious. On asking an explanation,
he seemed to think that she was extravagant. But allowances must be made for a bride, and I daresay the trus-
tee was a little in the affair. Sometimes such persons like
to hold on to the cash. They cannot have spent much this
Summer.

Here, everyone appears to be in the country. Yesterday it was furiously hot, though it is not so much so to-day.
I miss Head's intensely and shall not pay long visits here
in the future. There is not now a gentleman-like tavern
in the place. I have not seen Head, and fear he cannot get
a new establishment. I have seen about five and twenty
pages [of *The Crater*], and have the promise of some
twenty more to-night. Six chapters remain to be read,

and five to be printed. Home I shall be, *deo volente*, next week. Fagan arrived from Cape May last evening and was here this morning. He says that in six days I shall have my discharge.

Sunday afternoon—August 15th.

Last night I saw 114th page of volume IInd, leaving about four more days' work to be done. As it is safest to finish while about it, I will do so. I expect to leave here Thursday afternoon and to be home Saturday, the 21st. Should Mr. Hand appear, with or without his brother, ask him to stay with you. I expect, however, to meet him at Fort Plain, on Saturday. Perhaps I may get home on Friday.

Joe Ingersoll has gone to Athens in Georgia, to deliver an oration! Hot times for that. Miss Leslie is staying in the house. She gives me a terrible account of Griswold's propensity to misstate the truth. I have not seen him, and do not much desire to, after what I have heard. Charles Ingersoll and wife are here, and I have seen them. Also the Henrys. Biddle is expected home in October. I think he must be here sooner.

I do not think I shall write again, for the letter would scarcely reach you. I shall expect to find one from you at the Globe. Henry Carey has lost his wife. She was a sister of Miss Leslie's, you know. The latter told me her cookery book had made her between four and five thousand dollars. I told her we had not succeeded with cream cheeses, and she said she got her receipt from a woman in the market who was celebrated for them. But she added that she had found that persons who lived by making anything often suppressed some ingredient, or particular, in giving her their receipts. This she had found out. She has published a new volume, which I shall bring up. The cookery-book has reached its 28th edition. She has been aided much, I should think, by having had Carey for a brother-in-law.

I like my new book [*The Crater*] exceedingly, and the part which I was afraid was ill done, is the best done. I mean the close. Altogether, it is a remarkable book, and ought to make a noise. If anyone else had written it, it would be the next six months' talk. As it is, it will probably not be much read in this country. Well, there is not much love lost between us. It is a contemptible public opinion, at the best.

No news from General Scott, though important tidings are hourly expected. Of his success when he does move, there can be but little doubt. Conner is in Maryland, and I have not seen him. Parker was here a day or two since, and he tells me that some imputations are endeavored to be brought against Aulich's courage. He is accused of refusing to give a seat behind a good cover to a wounded officer. The facts are, that, while waiting for ammunition, everybody was ordered to keep covered. Aulich and two or three more got a good place, and sat there for some time. At last Aulich got up and went to some other part of the battery. While gone Mr. Baldwin was wounded—no blood showing—and was put into Aulich's berth. When the latter came back and said laughingly "Why, you have got my place," whereupon Baldwin offered to relinquish it, but Aulich refused to take it. But Aulich is thought to be a tartar, and everything he says or does is judged harshly.

One of the best things going is an apologue on Perry and Hunter. A party went out to kill a wolf. They drove the animal into a hole, and set one of their number to watch him while they went for hoes and dogs. The wolf stuck his head out, and got it caught in the hole, when the sentinel killed it with a club. Presently the rest came back with loud demonstrations of what they meant to do. Great was their rage at finding the wolf killed. "Why did you do this?" they demanded. "You had no hoe at all, not so much as one dog, and here we have a dozen hoes and a whole pack, and yet you presumed to kill the wolf. Go home—we are going to kill a possum this evening, but you shan't go along—you spoil everything."

Parker told me that Perry was much out of favour at the department. His movement against Alvarado is said to have cost the country an enormous sum of money by cutting off Quitman from his supplies, already agreed for, and retarding Scott's march many days. Conner is said to have given up the squadron in a pet, on receiving unexpected orders to let Perry have command. He ought not to have done it, and I believe now thinks so himself. Parker laughs heartily at Perry's reporting Mackenzie wounded at Toussan, because he got hurt accidentally the day after the fight. All the navy men have seen his folly and laughed at it.

It has been terrifically hot here. To-day it is much cooler. I have now slept five nights within six feet of an open window, and most of the time without even a sheet on me. I keep quiet, and thus keep cool. I eat light meals and little fruit, drink three glasses of wine at dinner, and am as well as I ever was in my life.

Yesterday I met Joe Miller fanning away. He was going to Bordentown for lodgings, the town being too hot for him. Mrs. Miller was at her daughter's. Joe greeted me with a hearty laugh, but fanned away.

Adieu. By the time you get this I shall be about packing up. My stay in New York will not exceed one night, if it be even that.

Yours tenderly,

J. F. C.

The Miss Leslie mentioned in this letter was born in 1787; she died in 1858. Her *Domestic Cookery Book*, which by 1851 had run through forty-one editions and 100,000 copies, was sold about 1857.

TO MRS. COOPER, COOPERSTOWN

Globe, Sunday, Nov. 14th, 1847

I hoped to have arranged with the publishers by this time, but they wish to get the next book for the price of the last, which would be a loss to me of $150. Some arrangement will probably be made, as they are very desirous of getting the next book, this having done so well. In the meantime I am endeavoring to sell the cherubs.

With Cruger I dined yesterday, several ladies being of the party. He says Mrs. Cruger writes most amicably to her sister, but proposes nothing definite, and until she does he can and will do nothing. I suspect the poor woman finds herself alone and homeless, and begins to see some of her folly. They are all at Graffenburg, and in the baths, even to the nurses. It is a general wash.

TO MRS. COOPER, COOPERSTOWN

Globe, Nov. 17th, 1847

I am glad to see that Wessels is honorably mentioned, as having distinguished himself at Contreras. I have not seen the report of Col. Riley, but from the manner in which his name is introduced by Scott, I think he must have been conspicuously engaged in the great charge of Riley's brigade, when they stormed the Mexican camp.

I have not seen Mrs. Laight, but shall call to-morrow or next day. Jim and his wife, with young Van Cortlandt, I found in lodgings, in Houston Street; two rooms with folding doors, gas lighted, and a game dinner at six. Everything was handsome and at, I should think, at least $50 per week. Perhaps his income will stand it. She looks well.

By the way, butter is about 18 cents in Otsego. This makes farming more profitable.

Phil Kearny has lost his left arm above the elbow. He suffered intolerably until the arm was taken away, which was about three hours after he was hit. I saw his father to-day. *I think* Wm. Davidson is courting Miss Maitland.

TO A LITTLE GIRL

Otsego Hall, Cooperstown, Dec. 25th, 1847
Chère Petite,

In the first place, I wish you, and your parents, a very Merry Christmas. I have just come from church myself, and have met a great many happy faces, this morning, particularly among my great nephews and nieces—my own nephews and nieces being now so old that Santa Claus (good old St. Nicholas de Flue) will no longer call on them in his annual journeys. Watches, Dragoons, Tusks, Dolls, Tops, etc., etc., are very numerous in the family, just now, to say nothing of cornucopias filled with sweets.

I am very grateful at being honoured with one of your first efforts with the pen,—I do not know but it may have been the very first,—and hope you will recollect what I told you of my being a bad correspondent, in explanation of the delay in answering it.

It is very true that I was at Rochester, under the circumstances you mention. For the first time in my life I passed through your place this summer, and what is a little remarkable, I have been four times in Rochester already. On the first occasion, I passed half a day there, and was the whole time with Mr. Rochester, who had the civility to take me to all the points worth seeing. I thought of you, and inquired of Mr. Rochester concerning you and your family. He did not know your father, but was aware of his being in the town, but I could not quit him with propriety to make the visit I intended. On the second occasion young Mr. Rochester took me to see the falls, and my time was fully occupied. On the two other occasions I merely made the stops of the cars, and did not go any distance from them.

Next June, I shall again be in Rochester, *Deo volente* (ask your father what that means), when I hope to make your acquaintance. Remember, you are not to expect a smart, handsome young fellow, with a poetical look, but a heavy, elderly gentleman, with gray hairs, and who has begun to go downward in the vale of years. I was fifty eight on the 15th of last September—a very safe age, I trust Mama will think, for our correspondence.

And, now you have begun to write for yourself, let me take an old man's privilege, and give you a piece of advice. Write what comes uppermost, naturally and without any more effort than you would use in conversing with one you respected. In this way, you will soon come to make a very nice little correspondent. With my respects to your parents, I remain

Chère petite, votre affectionné
J. Fenimore Cooper.

Mademoiselle Doolittle

Washington, 30 Dec., 1847

My dear Sir:

I thank you for your letter, which I read with much interest. Your views are vigorous and forcible, and I shall certainly give them a very careful consideration.

I have always denied the power of Congress to impose on a State, on its admission into the Union, any restrictions not to be found in the Constitution. In respect to territories, the whole power of legislation resides in Congress, and I doubt exceedingly the expediency of surrendering it until the people become sufficiently numerous to be represented in Congress according to the ratio adopted for the States. Any declaration which should involve such a consequence I should consider inadmissible. We know not what may be the condition of territory hereafter to be acquired by us in respect to the capacity of the inhabitants for exercising the powers of self-government. If a pupilage more were necessary, it would seem to be so for the mixed races, which hold, or rather occupy, northern Mexico.

But I am too much pressed now to answer your letter or to discuss this important question *in extenso*. I may be compelled to do so on the floor of the Senate, though I am always happy to escape any such compulsory service.

With sincere respect, Yours

John A. Dix.

J. Fenimore Cooper, Esq.

John Adams Dix was born in Boscawen, New Hampshire, July, 1798, and died in New York City, April, 1879. He served during the war of 1812, under his father, Major Timothy Dix. In 1819 he was appointed aide-de-camp to Gen. Jacob Brown, and stationed at Brownsville, where he studied law. Later he was admitted to the bar in Washington. He resigned from the army in 1828, owing to ill health, and settled in Cooperstown, New York, where he began the practice of law. In 1830 he removed to Albany, having been appointed Adjutant General of the state. He was a prominent member of the "Albany Regency." He was United States senator from 1843 to 1849. Nominated for Governor of New York by the Free-soil Democrats in 1848, he was defeated by Hamilton Fish. He was Secretary of the Treasury in 1861, and took a prominent part in the Civil War. In 1872 he was elected Governor of New York.

He sent the celebrated despatch at the outbreak of the Civil War, "If any man attempts to haul down the American flag, shoot him on the spot."

TO MRS. C. J. WOOLSON, CLEVELAND

Hall, Cooperstown, Jan. 3rd, 1848

My dear Hannah,

Your daughter left us yesterday afternoon, along with Alice Cooper, both attended by the latter's father. They went to Hyde to pass the night, and were to go, and doubtless did go, to Albany to-day. Owing to a little legerdemain, the holidays covered two complete weeks, and a little more, as Georgianna was with *us* just fifteen days; long enough to make us all love her. You have reason to be satisfied with your daughter, my dear. She is a great favorite here, I can assure you, and will be most welcome when she repeats her visit, as she has promised to do, *if she can*—a very proper salvo, for a young lady of her time of life. To me she appears to be ingenuous, very warm-hearted, sincere, and quite clever. She strikes your aunt in the same way, and Paul says she is one of the cleverest girls of his acquaintance. Paul being a miracle himself, you are to be highly flattered by his opinion. We are all obliged to you for letting your daughter come, and trust you will hear her story and let her come again.

Was there ever such a winter! In these mountains, there was something like one week of *cold* weather in December, the remainder of the month was almost warm—many of the days like April, as we have April. There is no ice in the lake; not even a bay for the boys to skate in.

You know that your aunt Mary and three of her children are here. Mrs. Foote has the rectory, and Mrs. Wessels and her two children live with her; Dr. Foote left some ten or twelve thousand dollars, and we hope to get her half-pay, which will add $360 per annum to her means. If she gets the pension, she will be quite comfortable.

Wessels turns up a trump, after all. He was at Vera Cruz, Cerro Gordo, where he charged up the hill under Niles, and at Contreras. At Contreras, he was detached the first day, and covered a flank against cavalry, behaving well. In the charge he distinguished himself, and actually was present with a small party that compelled 200 horse to surrender. In this last affair he was wounded in the ankle. But mounting the horse of one of his prisoners, he continued on with his regiment, and was even warmly engaged at Churubusco. Nor did he go into the hospital until after the 2nd. His regiment entered Mexico, where it had quite a sharp street fight. Then he laid up, and was about to return to duty when his wife last heard from him. He is mentioned with marked credit in the dispatches, and will doubtless get a brevet, if he gets nothing else. Two years since he was halfway down the list of 1st. Lieutenants in his regiment—now he is the ninth captain. His wife evidently expects to go to the Hall of the Montezumas, nor do I think her expectations at all unreasonable. If the Whigs make their alliance with Mexico a little more active, the war may yet last five years. If *they* will be neuter, six months will bring it to a close.

All here unite with me in affectionate remembrances— we wish also to be remembered to your husband and to Mrs. Campbell. Georgianna said the other day that Mrs. Campbell was making some enquiries about Wm. M. of that ilk. I got a letter from a friend in Florence, a day or two since, which was written to acknowledge the receipt of a letter of Introduction I had given to W. Campbell. The latter had sent the letter from Geneva, not going to Florence, in consequence of having been suddenly recalled to London. I am afraid that the house on which he had his credits may have stopped him on his road to Italy. This is purely conjecture, however, though it is conjecture entertained by a report that he is expected home in a few days, and by a knowledge of the state of the London money market.

Adieu, my dear—

Your affectionate uncle

J. Fenimore Cooper.

Mrs. C. J. Woolson, Cleveland, O.

TO E. F. DE LANCEY

Hall, Cooperstown, March 10th, 1848

Dear Ned,

As soon as you send me a line to say that the boats will run in a day or two, I shall come down, as I wait only for the ice to move. It is possible that I shall stay twenty-four hours in Albany.

Mr Sabine is to answer me this week, when I shall answer him. The whole story will be told in my next letter, as to your success.

1.   Peter De Lancey of West-Chester was a country gentleman, owning a considerable estate, with mills, etc., at and around West Farms. I cannot tell you *when* he died. He represented the borough, and played a considerable part in local politics. In character, he was a gentleman, only rowdy, racing horses, fighting cocks, etc., but always maintaining his social position, and being remarkable for impressing the blackguards of the cock-pit and race course with his manners.

2.   John, Mrs Yates' father, was a chip of the old block. His second marriage threw him out of the circle of his natural friends.

3.   Mrs Yates' mother was a Miss Wickham.

4.   I know nothing of the Rowleys except from Aunt Polly, but have understood *her* that Lady Rowley was a grand-daughter of Lady Draper. I can tell you nothing of the issue of Mrs. Payne-Galway, for the latter was the name by which she was known.

5.   Your grandfather's eldest brother, James, served as a young man, and was an aid of Ambercrombie's at the defeat of Ty. His father died intestate (of apoplexy) and he succeeded to the whole real estate. He was educated at Cambridge, England, and married Margaret, daughter of Chief Justice Allen, Penn. He was the head of the court, or church, party, and represented New York. In the revolution, he went quite early to England, leaving his family behind. Your grandfather accompanied the last, when it went to join him. In England he lived at Bath, in considerable affluence, having saved a good deal of his personalty, and receiving at one time £25,000

indemnity. This sum, I think, was subsequently increased to £60,000. Even this last amount was less than what the Bowery Estate sold for under the hammer, which was $202,000 specie, or specie value. His losses were probably double the indemnity. He was an indolent man and lived at his ease, the reason for quitting America, as he did; in this country, he lived in the highest style known to the colonies, and was deemed a principal personage in New York.

6.   Oliver, Peter's son, was in the navy. It was said he refused to serve against this country, and resigned. It is certain he left the navy, and lived and died at West Farms. He married beneath him as to family, and above him as to morals. He was a very elegant man in appearance when dressed, and also as to manners when he chose.

7.   The commander of the Cow Boys was Lt. Col. *James* De Lancey, Peter's son—the Lt. Col. James De Lancey mentioned by Sabine, and whom he confused with your uncle James. He had been sheriff of West-Chester, and his corps was held in that county, to keep open communication and to cover the arrival of supplies. Hence, the sobriquet of Cow-Boys, as probably when the beeves would not come of themselves, they made them come. This James did not marry the mother of his children, who were numerous, until all, or nearly all, were born. He said it made a woman proud to marry her; this was doubtless Mr. Sabine's "Martha"; who she was, I never heard, but of common extraction, no doubt.

8.   Warren entered the 17th Light Dragoons as a cornet, late in the war, and remained in it, a few years in Europe. He first married a Miss Taylor, a woman of great respectability, and a sister of the late Mr. Francis Bayard Winthrop of New York. She divorced him. He

then married a Miss Lawrence, a relation of the Morrises, and a granddaughter of old Lewis of Morrisania. Not content with this, he intrigued with her niece, and when his wife died, he married the niece, who is now his widow. One or two of his children were born out of wedlock. There are now about as many De Lanceys of the illegitimate as of the legitimate stock. The Guernsey De L.'s, all of Gaines' (West-chester) descendants, and a good many of Warren's, belong to the illegitimates.

9.   I do not know who the James De L. is that Mr. Sabine says was a collector at N. P. It is probable, however, a son of either James or Stephen, of the West-Chester Branch.

10.   I know little of Stephen, of West-chester, beyond this. He filled some office at Albany, before the war, as clerk of some court, and was a considerable man there. He had a large family, and they all removed to Nova Scotia.

No. 11 is too long an answer to be given now.

12.   *Ancienne noblesse* means nobles of so many ages—four centuries I believe was the period. They had the privilege of riding in the King's coach, etc., etc.

The *Major* Leake, afterwards General, I believe, who married Miss Watts was a brother of the Mr Leake who left the funds of the Leake-Watts charity.

Lt. Col. Stephen (Bloomingdale Branch) married Cornelia Barclay.
Adieu—

J. Fenimore Cooper

Aunty says she thinks Warren's first wife was a Miss Lawrence, Miss Taylor the second, and Miss Lawrence the niece the third.

Don't forget to give me an early hint about the river.

Washington House, Phil., March 27th, 1848

The season is very backward here, as yet. I have not seen a single spring bird. The spring is commencing, however, and the grass begins to show itself in favourable spots. I passed last evening with Dr. and Mrs. Hare, and Mr. and Mrs. Charles Ingersoll. The former are quite alone, all their children having left them. The Primes are in Italy, and intend remaining there some little time. His eldest daughter is seventeen. The son, who had an *appartement* in the rear of the Dr.'s dwelling, is in Maryland on a farm. The Dr. grows old, and Hare-Powell, I am told, is very much broken, a decrepit old man, though five years his brother's junior. Mr. and Mrs. Clark Hare were there, and *discussatory*, as usual. Joshua Fisher was also there.

The Ingersolls, as is their wont, had much to tell me. Mrs. Willing is reviving a little. Her sister unwell—water-curish. Uncle Joe well and gay. The McCalls in deep mourning on various accounts. A child, a cousin, Peter's brother, down at the south, and two aunts, Mrs. Cadwalader, and the oldest Miss McCall, all of whom have gone off this winter. Mrs. Erving with her husband, at Cincinnati. Miss Mary Wilcocks, still Miss Mary; staying with her sister.

I saw Stockton in the streets, but could not get near enough to nail him. Biddle looks uncommonly well, I hear, and is rejuvenated. Have not seen him. David Colder dined next to me to-day, on his way to Washington. Says Mrs. Wilkes is well, active and with all her faculties, at eighty-six. The race was tough, about a hundred years since. Lady Cochrane is living and well. Her

son, Sir Thomas, has been commanding in the China
Seas.

Globe, April 1st, 1848

Dearest,

I could not see Mrs. Laight. She has been ill, and does
not quit her room, though better. Mrs. Banyer is better,
and John tells me will get well. She begins to sit up. The
Maitlands are all well, and the children actually exceedingly pretty. Martha is a curious little thing and is rather
the prettiest. They are painting, and the house is very
uncomfortable.

Last evening I went to see Christie's minstrels with
Cruger, Miss Caroline Cruger, Miss Matilda Oakley.
It was amusing, but I got enough. That I am pretty well
you will see in the fact that I walked from Mechanics'
Hall to Twenty-third Street at ten P. M., and then
down to the Globe, a distance altogether of near five
miles—a large four certainly. Cruger was with me. We
stopped at a fashionable confectioner's ½ past ten, and
took some Roman punch by way of keeping up our courage. Several parties came in from the opera in full dress,
à la Naples—but it was *gros de* Naples, rum folk, rum
fashionables and rum punch. New York always reminds
me of the silk purse and the sow's ear.

I saw Mrs. Ellet yesterday. She is so-so. Ardent and
hard working, but with a husband and no children, which
lessens one's interest in her labours. She told me that she
was coming to see old Mrs. Wilson, in whose father's
house *her* grandfather, a Gen. Maxwell, had died.

By the way I hear that *Jack Tier* takes unusually well.
Griswold told me yesterday that it is thought one of the

very best of my books. I do not so regard it, certainly, but condensed I dare say it reads off smoothly enough. *The Crater* is worth two of it. It is selling well. I have bought *Now and Then*, but Griswold says that people are disappointed in it. Something *Eyre* is much talked of, but he puts *The Bachelor of The Albany* among the very best books of the season, or, as he very politely expressed it, "After *Jack Tier*, *The Bachelor* comes next." I should think there is nothing in common between them.

To-day, J. J. Astor goes to the tomb. It is said that he sent checks of $100,000. each to several grandchildren a few days before he died, in order to place them at their ease from the start. Irving is an executor, and report says with a legacy of $50,000. What an instinct that man has for gold! He is to be Astor's biographer! Columbus and John Jacob Astor! I dare say Irving will make the last the greatest man.

I met Bovel in the street the day his grand-papa breathed his last. He has letters from Paris. de Remusat was in the palace on the morning of the 24th—when the *maitre d'hôtel* announced breakfast. de Remusat's feelings then broke out, just as the king said to him—*"Allons—déjeunez avec nous, Mons. de Remusat—la reine sera charmée de vous voir." "Sire, abdiquez—abdiquez en faveur du Comte de Paris—peutêtre il-y-a encore du temps—abdiquez, Sire, je vous en prie."* The king laughed, told him he was *"un peu"* disordered in mind. In less than half an hour after that conversation, the king and queen were wading through the mob in the place de la Concorde, to get into a *citadine*, and were driven off at a gallop! You have doubtless seen all the details of his escape. I shall bring up some foreign papers—possibly some French.

The changes produced by this last revolution will be very great. I shall not be surprised if Austria is compelled to concede, though I am persuaded France will be torn to pieces by factions.

Thorn has just lost a suit with Mr. Gauncey. I believe he thought of setting up the defence that the children were not his sons, but was persuaded not to do it. Mrs. Thorn, however, talked very strongly against her daughter-in-law, who has now got $3500. per annum for herself and children. The other son-in-law, de Ferussac, has also prevailed against his papa, and the whole family is broken up. Thorn himself is eyed jealously, and has more suits depending with Gauncey's heirs.

Young Neirs is to marry Miss Barclay in May. Several other engagements are spoken of, but I do not know the parties. The affair of Eliza Gay seems to be forgotten.

Yours very tenderly,
J. Fenimore Cooper.

TO MRS. COOPER, COOPERSTOWN

Detroit, Sunday Afternoon, June 18th, 1848

Dearest,

At the falls I hear the river is passed constantly in an iron basket, and by means of an iron wire. Last week a young lady of 17 *would* go over. She got into the basket, but as soon as she found herself suspended over the cliff, she shut both eyes and made two trips, there and back again, without opening either eye for a moment. On landing she began to cry, and cried like an infant for half an hour.

Garrett Smith, wife, son, Dan Fitzhugh, and a niece, a Miss Backus, were among our passengers. Mrs. Smith is so fat I did not recognize her. Altogether, we had a pleasant time of it. The night's work was fatiguing, but I was not as dull Friday as I expected to be. Paocand was in the stage, and he kept up a fire of words the whole distance. Among other things he said, *"Madame Colt est une galante femme."* Has the word two meanings? Wm. Wadsworth gets no better. His wife has a child, and Miss Elizabeth remains unmarried.

Tell Paul Mr. Hand says that S. Carolina and Georgia will both go for Cass, and in all Northern Ohio the Whigs are out against Taylor. I have no little doubt of Cass' election. He got home only on Thursday, in the night. All the north-west will be strong for him.

Tell him, also, they are getting up a wire over the Horse Shoe, and intend to take people in a basket and suspend them within a few feet of the cataract, in the Mists.

There, I can tell you no more. I am well. The water is good, and the country much in advance of us. Beets, peas, etc., are on the tables. Peas, in abundance, were on the table in Utica. Strawberries in any quantity.

Adieu, with tenderest love to all,

J. F. C.

TO GAYLORD CLARKE

Hall, Cooperstown, July 8th, 1848

Dear Sir,

I have desired one of my daughters to translate the letter of Prince Dolgoroucki, and I enclose the original of Mr. Brown's, both as you have requested.

I am very sensible of the civility you have manifested in taking so much trouble on my account, and desire to thank you.

I have had several letters from Constantinople, in my

time, but never one so completely [torn] as this from Teheran, which I shall place among my family archives, too, on account of its singularity, as well as on account of its amiable language. I have ever found the better class of the Russians among the most accomplished people of Europe, and it has been my good fortune to know a great many of them. In saying what I did to Prince Dolgoroucki I was perfectly sincere, and I would go out of my way sooner to oblige a Russian, than any man I know, on the mere ground of nationality. To myself, personally, English, French, Italians, and Russians were equally civil,—all nations indeed but the Germans—but the Russian manifests consideration for the American name, which no other European people do,—unless indeed it may be the Swiss.

Very Respectfully yours
J. Fenimore Cooper

Mr. Gaylord Clarke

LETTER ENCLOSED WITH THE PRECEDING

Teheran, 16/28 March, 1846

Sir,

The new and distant destination I have just received has deprived me of the honour of sending an earlier answer to the letter you were so obliging as to write me.

Notwithstanding all the pleasure it has afforded me, I must confess it has entirely missed its end, since instead of increasing the number of my autographs it shall remain forever among my family archives, as a precious testimonial of your goodness. If my personal admiration can add anything to the just tribute of homage rendered by two hemispheres to your great and noble talent, I shall at least reserve for myself the privilege of assuring you that the sentiments of esteem with which the two nations whose future is most brilliant have inspired each other, belong exclusively to the relations between Russia and America.

I shall be very happy, sir, if I could associate my name, with those of my countrymen, whose memory you have been pleased to recall, and could flatter myself with the hope that in future you will count me among the number of your most sincere friends.

Believe the assurance, Sir, of my most distinguished consideration.

Prince de Dolgoroucki

Mr. Fenimore Cooper

FROM FREDERICK HOWES, JR.

Salem, Mass., Aug. 4th, [1848]

Dear Sir

I take the liberty of addressing you, to express my sympathy for the cause of honesty, decency, and gentlemanliness, in your contest with the blackguard Editors of the State of N. York.

I congratulate you on your victory over their abusive vituperation, and vulgar calumny. Every honest American ought to thank you for your exertions in the cause of honour, and truth.

In this country of mob despotism, where every man bows his head to the pitiless storm of opinion, you alone, Sir, have had the courage to stand up against it, and dared to tell the truth to the American people. You have met the reward of daring to tell the truth, the abuse of a low press, and the hatred of our democrat radicals.

The Editors of this country will never forgive you your "Steadfast Dodge" in whom you have so admirably

depicted with the pen of a Defoe, the impertinent, ignorant, conceited editor-demagogue, to whom the guidance
of public opinion is intrusted, or rather abandoned in this
"land of liberty."

Every one, every true American feels his heart glow
within him at the perusal of your noble ocean tales, which
have illustrated the deeds of our countrymen, every lover
of true beauty reads over and over your unrivalled pictures of woodland scenery, and a woodsman's life, with a
renewed delight. But, your admirable *dissections* of
American society and manners in your later productions,
are I fear appreciated by but few. The nice tact, the delicate irony, the discrimination, displayed in them, can
only be enjoyed by those who are conscious of our
deficiencies, and honest enough to say so.

To those who have once entered the lists with the
"press-gang" of America, the line of Dante, *"Lasciate
ogni speranza voi che entrate,"* is applicable. From that
moment every act of calumny, of detraction is exhausted
on them. Lies are forged, stupendous and palpable, every
species of abuse is showered on their heads; no fraud, no
invention is spared.

"Non ragionam di lo, ma guarda e passa."

I feel it presumption in an insignificant individual like
myself, to address a man of your eminence, but I cannot
help expressing my sympathy with the cause of justice
and of honour.

Your volumes on English society were received as
might have been expected, with the blackguardism, the
falsehoods, and the mean insinuations of the *Quarterly*.
In a word, they were too true to be relished.

From my boyhood I have lived in the Elysium of your
forest and ocean romances; your Leatherstocking Tales,

like the successive pictures of the Henry V plays, in turn delighted my youth, and never have I felt a more pleasing surprise than when in *The Deerslayer*—"Long absent Harold reappeared at last." His last scene with Judith has often brought tears into my eyes. Your charming book on Italy "like the sweet south that steals upon a bank of violets" breathing of a southern clime, of Italian ease and elegance, I have read again and again, and it has been my companion in many a journey. And now, sir, pardon the liberty I have taken and believe me

Your obt. humble servant,
Frederick Howes, Jr.

P.S. If, sir, you intend to gratify me with an answer to this, please address Frederick Howes, Jr., care of F. Howes, Esq., Salem, Mass.

J. Fenimore Cooper, Esq., Cooperstown

TO SAMUEL L. HARRIS, WASHINGTON

Otsego Hall, Cooperstown, Sept. 5th, 1848

Sir:

Much more is said about the veto than is understood. Properly speaking, there is no veto in this country. A veto is absolute and final, and places the will of the sovereign in opposition to legislation. In this country the authority of the Executive extends no farther than to send a bill back for reconsideration, along with his reasons, leaving to Congress, in its collective character, power to enact the law without the consent of the Executive.

But, it is said by these late dissentients, a majority of two-thirds cannot be had, and this is effectually giving the President an absolute veto.

It follows from this very objection, that the President does not oppose Congress, in its collective character, but only the small majority that happens to be in favor of the law. In the face of this obvious truth, a cry is raised that the Executive is counteracting the measures of Congress, regarding Congress in its collective character, when the veto is used, but disregarding that collective character when the powers of the respective functionaries come to be considered in general principles. In other words, the Executive opposes all Congress in using the veto, but all Congress does not vote in trying to get the two-thirds' vote, but only the difference between, that number and a simple majority!

The King of England does not use the veto, and why should a President do that which a King does not attempt to do?

The argument is singular were the fact as stated. What has the President in common with a king? The powers given to the first, in the Constitution, are given to be used, or the instrument is a puerility. Why not carry the parallel throughout and say that, as the King transmits his authority to his eldest son, the President should do the same!

But the reason why the veto is not used in England is so very obvious that one is surprised any sane man should attempt the comparison. The king has, inch by inch, been robbed of his prerogative by the aristocracy, until under the form of a ministerial responsibility, he can do nothing of himself but name his ministers. On the other hand their ministers are so much in subjection to Parliament, that they resign when they cannot control that body. Let what is termed a ministerial question go against the ministry and the latter retire. There is no one left to apply the veto, which requires a responsible agent for its constitutional exercise. Then when ministers lead parliament a veto becomes unnecessary, for parliament does what the minister desires; and when parliament is opposed the minister gives way. It is no wonder that the King does not use the veto in such a system. If it be liberty thus to limit the prerogative, it is a liberty purchased at the expense of the boasted balance of the English estates.

Gen. Taylor quite evidently does not understand the constitution. He is not disposed to set up his personal judgment (through an exercise of the veto) against the wisdom of Congress, except in cases in which the constitution has been violated, or there has been careless legislation. Now, in what is his personal judgment better in judging of what is, or what is not, constitutional, than in judging what is, and what is not, expedient? A plain man, who is at the head of affairs, may form a better opinion of what is expedient than a very clever man who is not behind the curtain; but any man who is a constitutional lawyer can say what is and what is not constitutional, as well as the President. Then there is much less necessity for vetoing an unconstitutional law than for vetoing one that is simply inexpedient. An inexpedient law has all the force of one that is expedient, and must be equally executed; but an unconstitutional law has no power *ab initio*, and there is a tribunal expressly selected to pronounce it of no avail. The veto is not necessary to kill it.

Washington and Jefferson, it is said, rarely resorted to the veto. That is true, and for an obvious reason. The Congresses of that day were in harmony with the Executives and followed their lead. When such is the case the

1848]   JAMES FENIMORE-COOPER   597

veto becomes unnecessary, for laws can be passed only by
inadvertency, to which the President is opposed.

But the true argument in favor of the American veto,
if veto it can be called, is this: All legislative power is in
Congress, and the veto of the President is merely a check
on its exercise. It is consequently a provision made in the
interest of liberty; precisely as the power of the Senate,
in the case of appointments and treaties, is a check on the
appointing and treaty-making powers of the President.
It would be just as rational, nay, more rational, to declaim against the negative of the Senate, in these last
cases, on the ground that it is opposed to liberty, than to
declaim against the veto, for the same reasons; more
rational, because the veto of the Senate is absolute, while
that of the President is merely a check.

In the point of practical consequences, the use of the
veto is probably more needed in this country than the use
of any other power belonging to the system. Congress has
a natural disposition to be factious regarding success more
than principles, and being totally without responsibility
it needs checking far more than any other branch of the
Government, for these two reasons.

As respects Gen. Taylor's notion of letting Congress
lead the Government, it appears to me that it is throwing
away the principal advantage for which the office of
President was created. We had such a system under the
old Congress, and it was found to be inefficient. Enough
is conceded to liberty when the power in the last is given
to the Legislature, and something is due to efficiency.
I have a great respect for Gen. Taylor, but should he
carry out his project in this particular, I apprehend that
it would be found that he would make the administration contemptible. All the provisions of the Constitution

show that the intention was to give the President just this influence which he seems inclined to throw away, while it secures the country from danger by bestowing all power, in the last event, on Congress. This is the division of authority that is most conducive to good government; an efficient Executive whose hands are tied against usurpation.

I have been amused with Mr. Clayton's logic. He dislikes an exercise of power, in which one man controls the decisions of many. Now, if there be any force in such an objection, it is true as a principle, and varies only in degree when the Senate applies its absolute veto to the acts of the other house. But who is Mr. Clayton? He and his colleague represent some 100,000 souls. Messrs. Dix and Dickenson represent some 3,000,000. What claim have the two first to a power equal to the two last? The Senators of Rhode Island, Delaware, Iowa, Wisconsin, Florida, Arkansas, Vermont, Connecticut, New Jersey, New Hampshire and Missouri have, all together, fewer constituents than New York alone; yet they give 22 votes to our two. Whence comes this aristocratical preference? From the Constitution, as does the veto of the President. Shall one of these powers be put down by the slang of democracy and equality and not the other? All this cant is unworthy of enlightened and fair-minded men.

I have little doubt that General Cass will be elected; should he not be, I leave with you this written opinion— *viz.:*—That General Taylor's administration will be a complete failure, and give as much dissatisfaction to those who put him in as to any other portion of the country.

Your obedient servant,

J. Fenimore Cooper.

Occupation has delayed this reply.

Hall, Cooperstown, Dec. 7th, 1848

My Beloved Daughter,

Your letter reached me last night, along with its companion, and I cannot express the astonishment it produced. To me the whole thing was unexpected and new. I had not the smallest conception of any thing of the sort.

And now, my child, I shall be as frank with you as prudence will allow in a letter. In the first place your happiness will be the first consideration with the whole family. Under no circumstances must there be coldness, alienation, or indifference. You are my dearly beloved child, of many noble and admirable qualities that I have always seen and appreciated, and you shall be treated as such a child merits. My heart, door and means shall never be closed against you, let your final decision be what it may. I say this not only for myself, but for your devoted and tender mother, who has done so much for you, and is ready to do so much more.

But that which you ask is of so serious a nature, that it cannot be granted without reflection—without closest and free communications with yourself. Your visit has been a pretty long one, and you had better prepare your aunts for your return home. Paul shall come for you before the holidays—say week after next. Come as fearlessly as your own frank and generous nature will dictate, and rely on being received with open arms by every member of your family.

In the interval be prudent, write no notes or letters, and give no pledges. You must hear what I have to say, unfettered; as the counsel and information of one who is still your best male friend, depend on it, and after you have heard I shall leave you to decide for yourself.

All send their love, and mother unites with me in giving this advice. I write to Mr. Phinney to-day, begging to defer an answer to his demand until after your return. I enclose ten dollars—your little New Year's gift, thinking it possible you may find it convenient. Paul will bring the means for the road.

Your most tenderly affectionate father,

J. Fenimore Cooper

Miss Caroline Fenimore Cooper

TO ANSON GLEASON

Hall, Cooperstown, Dec. 16th, 1848

Dear Sir,

I have delayed this reply from a sheer inability to answer your question. I do not remember what I said in the address at Geneva, and the manuscript was destroyed, but I very well remember that the highest authority I have ever been able to get for the phrase *"vox populi vox dei,"* was one of the English Archbishops, at a coronation sermon. Who was the king crowned, I do not now remember, but I think it was John. At all events, it was a Plantagenet, and one of those who had but a doubtful claim to the throne. It might have been Henry. I have had a good hunt for my authority, but can not find it, though I perfectly well remember to have had it formerly, and to have been familiar with it.

After all, I will not say that the axiom does not come from the ancients, though I can discover no authority for it there. The Latins commonly used *deus* in the plural, but they sometimes used it in the singular, when meaning a divine providence. I do not suppose that they believed in a plurality of Gods, but that their mythology was intended to be a poetical representation of the attributes of a single deity.

This country furnishes a living illustration of the truth of the axiom. It is perhaps fortunate it is so, there being great danger that the people will shortly respect nothing but themselves. King Majority may reign as well as any other monarch, and by dint of constant struggle it is possible that we may keep his majesty within bearable bounds.

It is when one remembers who they are who give utterance to the royal thoughts that one is induced to doubt the future. Divine Providence reigns over even Majorities, and the *"vox dei"* may interpose, after all, to save us from its miserable counterfeit, the *"vox populi."*

Respectfully yours,

J. Fenimore Cooper

TO H. F. PHINNEY

Hall, Jan. 9th, 1849

Dear Sir,

I have conversed with my daughter, and the result is an acceptance of your proposal.

I believe it is the wish of Caroline that nothing should be said on the subject, beyond communicating the state of things to your own family, which always includes your uncle Harry, until she and you have conferred together.

Of course you will let us see you shortly, and I trust your visits, in future, will be free and as frequent as may comport with your own convenience and wishes.

Yours truly,

J. Fenimore Cooper

Globe, Sunday, Jan. 14th, 1849

Dearest Sue,

We got down in good season, and Paul was soon off. I had to wait near two hours. I reached Albany at dark, and remained there until Friday morning, when I came on here *via* New Haven, where I slept.

I saw both Stevenson and Gansevoort. The latter is just *re*-married, the third Mrs. G. having been a Miss Lansing.

Stevenson told me all about the Rensselaer affair. First, as to the lady. They had lived very uncomfortably together for some time, he manifesting both undue economy and jealousy. One day he came home and found a gentleman and lady from New York at dinner, and he broke out in such a way on the subject of the extravagance of the dinner that she ran upstairs. It seems she sent for her father, who came and had an interview with Mr. D. A violent quarrel ensued, and D. ran up stairs for his pistols. An old servant intreated the general to quit the house, and he got into his carriage, where Mr. Johnson, the guest, soon after handed Mrs. D., who went with her father to the manor house. A scene followed, in order to obtain the younger child, which was at the breast. Her sister went for the child, and he flourished his pistol about, declaring he would shoot the person who offered to touch the infant. She is said to have manifested great coolness, and to have told him to lay aside his pistol, for she was not afraid of *it* or *him*. This had such an effect on him that he obeyed. After a long negotiation the child was had, and still remains with its mother; the eldest, a boy, is with him.

There are no legal proceedings, nor are any likely to

take place. He has had a private examination of servants, but it is supposed their gossip is all he has to sustain him. Now, who do you suppose is the gentleman implicated by these precious domestics? Her own uncle, Westerlo! He is about of the age of his niece, has always been fond of her, was brought up with her, played with her, and, it is said, used to kiss her, occasionally, after she became Mrs. D. Those who know the parties, seem to think nothing of it. As for Dr. C., there appears to be no proof at all. The whole affair wears very much the air of a design to extort money from the father, suggested by some levity of manner in the daughter.

The son's story is this. He was sent to Marseilles to remain in the ship, and return here, as a sort of genteel cooling off. He left the vessel, went to Paris, contracted debts, and ran away. A *Wm*. Bayard, the uncle, has gone to France; it is supposed he intends to settle the debts. The boy came to Albany, but did not go home. His father followed him to New York, and was down on that business when I saw him. He took him home, and for a short time he remained there. But he was soon detected in buying goods on credit, to sell for a trifle to obtain cash, which is a State's Prison affair. This would never do, and his father *apprenticed* him to the navy, where he now is! Thus the heir apparent of this old family is now an apprentice on board a man of war. The boy is said to be very weak. Still he might be honest. Low companions must have been his destruction.

I have met three or four acquaintances in this house, Ogden included, but learn nothing. There is no snow here. We lost it between Hartford and New Haven, going from Springfield to Hartford on runners.

I have escaped everything like a cold, taking care of

myself. I can say I have not been cold since I left home, though often uncomfortably warm. The thermometer has been a good deal below zero, but I have hardly felt it in the open air. I left Albany with it at 7° below zero at six o'clock in the morning, and yet I did not know it was so intensely cold.

The Bishop-war waxes warm. Potts is almost abusive—he is worried, and manifests a desire to make a false issue that does not tell well for his logic.

I expect to go to Philadelphia Tuesday evening. I am afraid *Ned* has not done much after all. No one I meet appears to know anything of it, and, you know, these people wait to be told what to do, say, or think, by the newspapers. The last have maintained a dead silence.

Nothing but murders appear to move the public mind now, and even murders begin to be stale.

Adieu my love. Keep yourself as warm as you have contrived to keep me, and you can stand zero admirably. Love to the girls.

Ever yours,
J. F. C.

Globe, Wednesday morning, Feb. 21st, 1849

Dearest Sue,

I did not suffer with the cold at all, especially in the feet. Wearing the leggings and the big boots, I had not a cold foot all the way down. I carried Mrs. Fish her letter; found them at table with Stevenson, Mrs. Brainard, Miss Granger, De Witt, Walter Church, one of the Gaineses, and a Mr. John Johnson, he a senator from New York and of the Stratford family. Bob Norris of

course. I sat down and staid a couple of hours. The Fishes
all kindness, and wished me to stay with them. Christine
had been up, and passed a day in Albany, and sailed yesterday for Europe. By the way, Mrs. Johnson said that
Mrs. Cruger has come up home, came up last week,
passed a day at Herkimer and returned. This was all she
could tell me. I fear, from the circular I got, that the
scabbard is thrown away.

I met Mrs. Smith's brother, Fitzhugh, at Albany, and
we came on together yesterday. The Senator Nicholas
was of his party, and we passed the day in company. The
last is a sensible man, but not a first-rater. There are very
few of the last, unhappily. At this house, I found De
Kay, or rather he found me, for he got in last from Washington, where he had been to see about the Commodore's
affairs, who, it seems, had bought a house in W. and
intended to live there. He died of dropsy on the chest,
among strangers, and none of his family with him. He
left home only the week before, and the Dr. says he told
him he would die on the road. Die he did, and has left his
affairs in terrible confusion. His widow and seven children, all young, are at the Dr's.

I have not seen any one, as yet. The picture is opened,
and Mr. Wight's nails have fortunately gone through the
frame only. *That* is a good deal injured, but the woman
and the tree are both standing.

Fish has a controversy with your old admirer, J. B.
Scott, who is now recorder. It is likely to prove fierce.
His friends told me that Weed was getting too much
influence over him. If so, I may have done good, for I
gave an instance of Mr. Weed's propensity to lie, and a
pretty strong one. I am afraid that Hamilton is surrounded by too many very bad men for his own good.

In coming down I passed through Sawpits, so altered I did not know the place. I got a distant glimpse of Rye, passing a hundred rods in the rear of Penfields, and somewhat near Pretty Land. I saw the Rye House, for an instant, more than half a mile distant. It appeared to me that we crossed Sheldrake just under the hills that lie behind Mamaroneck, crossing Sheldrake at a point a little below the Scarsdale road. There are so many changes, however, and the country was so covered with snow, and we went so fast, I could hardly recognize anything. I did not see Union Hill, nor any other object I knew, until we got to Harlem. At 27th Street we took horses, and stopped in Canal Street, near Broadway, at ½ past seven. We were nearly two hours behind our time, though we came 195 miles in about twelve hours. We experienced two considerable detentions in waiting for other trains. I paid but $4. The whole distance cost about $10, including taverns. This brings us very near New York for the winter, but we shall be much nearer.

Hand dines with me to-day, and we both dine with Cruger to-morrow. I have not been out this morning, but may take the air after dinner. Mrs. Cruger, *he* thinks, went to Albany to see the judge who was to decide her case; as she saw the Vice Chancellor, before. But the court he was on adjourned before she arrived. He came down, and gave his decision without seeing her. Since then he has consented to modify his opinion in Cruger's favour, so far as to exonerate him from the interest on his brother's bonds.

Finding nothing to do in Albany, Mrs. C. went on to Henderson. There she *took* lodgings in the porter's lodge, making a great stir about the hardship of her case. At night she prayed for him in a voice so loud as to be heard by all in the lodge. The community is much exercised with all this, some siding with, and some against, her. Such is the statement of one side.

TO MRS. COOPER, COOPERSTOWN

Globe, Tuesday, March 6th, 1849, 6 P. M.

Dearest,

You will be glad to learn that I have at length got all my sheets in the mail for the English steamer to-morrow. I have also made an arrangement with Stringer and Co. [Stringer & Townsend] that gives me the control of my books, the cheap editions they publish excepted, and have agreed with Mr. Putnam, a very respectable, though not a very rich, publisher, for a fine edition of *The Spy*. He thinks he can sell some 3000 copies. As there has never been a decent edition in the country, I am willing to try. I chose to own the plates, which will cost me near $400, but which will be good at the end of two years. I am to have 25 a copy, or $750 on 3000 copies. This would give me the plates, and near $400 of benefit. I do not think there is much risk, and am willing to try. Lea owns not quite as many books as I own, and, on the whole, not as good a set. I find he asks Stringer $3000 for his copy rights and plates, and they have been half disposed to purchase. All with whom I converse appear to think a fine edition, well advertised, will sell, and that extensively. The sale of Irving's books had altogether stopped, but several thousands will go off, and have indeed gone off, under this new plan. Each tale will sell for a dollar, bound in one volume, and printed on very fine paper.

I saw Russell in the street yesterday. He says Mrs. Watts is well, and that the Mrs. Stuyvesant party has gone to Pau, in the Pyrenees, for a mild climate for Mrs. Rutherford, whose health is very delicate.

As for Mr. Walsh, if he can get through the spring into warm weather, he may recover. I have all along regarded him, however, a very bad case, and have greatly pitied his sisters.

Caroline's dress has come. So far as I can see, it is quite rich and pretty; quite as much so as the dress of a woman whose husband is burnt out once a month ought to be. Tell Fred I condole with him. They have nothing to do, now, but to fill the vacant lots with thoroughly fireproof buildings, with outer doors so fastened at night that the incendiary will get burnt himself should he conceal himself in the day, in order to set fire to the buildings at night. It will turn out that one little suspected has done the mischief. We must all watch, if we don't pray.

Mrs. Butler is making a furore up town, but I seldom get there. I work hard in the mornings and shall have to get *The Spy* ready for the proofs before I leave town. I am waiting for an English revised copy, which I expect from Philadelphia to-day.

Were you not surprised at the sale of the naked lady? I must confess I never expected to see that 1000 francs back again; yet here are near 700 of them in my trunk.

I am sorry for poor Almira, but it is the will of God. John will get another wife, and she will soon be forgotten. You say nothing of Mary, from which I hope she remains.

Adieu; my work calls me off; with best love to all, and to your self the most—

J. F. C.

TO MRS. COOPER, COOPERSTOWN

Globe, New York, Sunday, March 11th, 1849

My dearest Sue,

Yesterday I packed my trunk, signed a contract with Putnam's, and executed all my orders, intending to leave town to-morrow, and be home on Tuesday. But an interview with Mr. Monroe has induced me to remain a day, and possibly two, in order to see Mrs. Cruger, in the hope of inducing her to come to terms. The suggestion is her own, and it may be well to attend to it, though I have very little hopes of success. At any rate I shall be home, nothing unlooked for preventing, by Thursday, and perhaps by Wednesday.

I have put the "Tribute Money" into a great sale of pictures, for the 22d instant, limiting the price to $600. I hardly think it will sell, but shall try it. I could wish to be in town at the sale, but cannot spare the time. It may do as well as the treeless lady.

I passed an hour with Mrs. Laight. She was very curious, asked a hundred questions and was gratified with my answers.

I have been to see Mrs. Butler, and to hear her. It was *The Tempest*. I went prepared to yawn and be bored; but, from the first instant she spoke, to the close, I was wide awake. I have not been so much amused at a play since I was a boy. It is true there was room for criticism, and the attention was, in a degree, kept alive by tracing the speakers, but, on the whole, it was a most extraordinary effort, and I would much rather hear her read any one of Shakespeare's plays than to see it performed as they are usually played. The audience really resembled an old-fashioned New York assembly. I saw more acquaintances than I have met for years, in any collection of persons. Next day I received a great many calls. "I saw you at Mrs. Butler's reading, last night," was the general story. The Sedgwicks were there, in force. Bob Watts, the Brevoorts, Mrs. and Misses Scott, Mr. and Mrs. Arthur Middleton, Mr. and Mrs. Lowndes Brown, and a lot of others, all close around us. Heads were bobbing the whole evening. I believe I was a sort of lion, myself, being so seldom seen.

I have got the rice, rose-water, and Caroline's frock. This is all that was commanded.

I have not seen the Californians. I am glad Wight has proved a true man, and thank him for the picture, which can go up in Paul's sanctum, but not in the family gallery. It is like, but is no miracle of art.

I met Dan Boden in the street, and had a talk with him. He expects to go, by June at least, and seems resigned.

Amariah says the Nelsons are to be here to-day. I shall look them up. Rens has gone through to New Haven. The Judge is delighted with old Zoo, they say, and likes the cabinet. The weather is now magnificent. In a few days I should think the ice must move. Amariah has just come in, and I must conclude by sending my best love.

As ever yours,
J. Fenimore Cooper.

FROM P. A. BROWNE

Philadª, April 25th, 1849

Dear Sir:

I am making a collection of the hair of the head of distinguished individuals. I have locks of all the Presidents of the U. S. except two, of many of the signers of the Declaration of Independence, beside many eminent divines, jurists, Statesmen, and Literary characters, and I am desirous of possessing yours to place alongside of Wash^g Irving's and James'.

you will enclose it by mail directed to

your ob^t Ser^t

P. A. Browne

Philad^a

J. F. Cooper, Esq., Cooperstown

TO MRS. COOPER, COOPERSTOWN

On board the *Oregon*, Wharf at Albany, 3 P. M.,

[April 27, 1849]

My dearest Love,

Our western goers so stimulated our driver that we got in before the first run down arrived, and reached this place at ½ past 1. I saw Mr. McHarg at the station, and as he promised to report me, I suppose you know the first part of my journey in advance.

I felt a good deal of pain in my right foot—now the worst—while sitting still in the stage. This troubled me a little, as a bad symptom, but I soon discovered that the foot was over a large hole in the bottom of the stage, and that the sensation *came from cold*. This encouraged me, as the *per contra* was warmer weather. On removing the foot, the sensation went off. My feet, after walking quite half a mile on a pavement, are now about as well as they have been any forenoon this week, very slight tenderness existing in the heels. From all these signs I am much in hope that the warm weather will remove most of the difficulty.

I got my fish, 48 llbs., to the tune of $5. This is quite enough, but I shall not send for any more, unless these take much better than I anticipate. Pier says there are some eight or ten of goodish size, and the rest are all small. I can't help it.

I have not met an acquaintance. I have secured a state-room, $2.50, and have my time to myself. The town is building up well, and is quite as much improved by *this* great fire, as it was by that of half a century since.

Adieu, my best love—with kindest regards,

Your tenderly attached husband,

J. F. C.

TO MRS. COOPER, COOPERSTOWN

Globe, Saturday, April 28th, 1849

My dearest wife,

I write to-day, though with little to say, in order to make sure of the letters getting through on Monday. I got here at the usual hour, and am very comfortably in-stalled on the first floor with parlour and bed room. The house has more company than was in it last month, but is very comfortable.

Stringer has so closely sold the first edition of *Sea Lions* (5000 copies) that he did not like to give me four copies, begging me to wait for next edition (1000), next week. I am told the book sells very well, and this without the aid of a puff.

Mrs. Butler reads Henry VIIIth, to-night, and I shall go and hear her. The furore has greatly abated, and the readings have not been at all crowded during this last engagement. Nothing does, or can, last long in this inconstant town.

Ned came down to the boat, and sat two hours with me. Hamilton came down with his two eldest daughters, a *bonne*, and Richard Morris. Dr. Hale made his appear-ance next, and Jerry Rensselaer. Stephen Rensselaer

came next, but did not come down. William Pierrepont
and family followed. I passed the evening talking doctor's stuff with Jerry and Morris, went to bed at ten and
slept like a top. After all my exercise yesterday and to-
day, the feet are about as well as when at home. It is true
walking on the pavements here is walking in the mud, and
soft mud, too.

I have been to see Leeds, but he is out, and I shall not
get the news of the picture until Monday. Putnam will
publish *The Spy* next Wednesday.

Monday next—possibly to-day, if it clear up, for it is
a drizzling rain here—I shall buy three or four or half a
dozen shad, and a dozen pines, and confide them to the
express. They are all cheap, and I shall put the shad in
ice. If I can get any birds, not an easy thing at this season,
I shall put a few in for your especial eating. Pigeons are
plenty here, but very dear. But I shall write and say what
the basket will contain. As oranges are cheap and very
good I may put up eight or ten dozen of them. The difficulty will be to make a stowage that will stand our stage,
but I'll try.

Do not hesitate about ordering the carriage and taking
plenty of air.

Do you see that that rantipole Brisbane has got himself ordered out of France, and says he will not go without force. He must be in a delightful agitation in the
affair.

I have just walked across the room, on resting ten minutes, after a walk of quite a mile on the pavements, the
severest trials I find, and my feet have less sensibility
than when I left home. Warm weather is what they want.
If you and I could pass a month near the sea, it would set
us both up.

The town is supremely dirty. City Hotel is to be converted (in part, I presume) into stores, as Blanchard is
losing money there. By the way, I believe I got that
piece of news from the corn-cutter, as I have scarce seen
a soul here but Cruger and the booksellers. The day is so
bad no one is in the street that can keep out of it.

I picked up a book on the City of New York, and have
been looking it over. It contains lists of all the city dignitaries, in regular succession from the settlement down to
the present time. It gives as the Mayor in *1688* "Peter
De Lancey." Is this a mistake? or, if true, who could he
be? The recorder was a Graham, and all the Aldermen
had Dutch names, and by no means the best. In 1687,
"Peter De Lancey" appears an alderman of South
Ward. Same in 1686, as assistant Alderman. In 1691
"Stephen De Lancey" appears as an alderman of South
Ward. This was your ancestor, but who could the Peter
have been? Peter appears in 1686, and disappears, as
mayor too, in 1688. I must enquire into this, or set Ned
at it. 1691 was full early for old Stephen to appear as
an assistant Alderman. It was only five years after his
arrival, and when he was quite a young man.

Rensselaer told me that the decision of the Court of
Appeals was of great importance to him, while it was of
none whatever to the tenants. The law was settled when
the demand should be made, as Dick knows, and the decision also settles the point as to interest's being recoverable
on rent. Previously to this case, the decisions conflicted;
now it is settled law that rent bears interest. Steve said
that formerly all the use he could make of this question
of interest was to use it as a bug-bear to compel the
tenants to pay their rents; whereas now, he can collect it
just as well as he can collect the rent. The Court stood

6 to 2. It is a most important decision in these unsettled times.

Adieu, my excellent Sue. With tenderest love to all beneath the roof and the one that has quitted it, I remain as ever

Yours most affectionately,

J. F. C.

TO MRS. COOPER, COOPERSTOWN

Globe, Sunday 29th [April], 1849

Dearest Sue,

Yesterday I dined with Cruger, on Otsego Bass and a beef steak. There was a small party, consisting of Mrs. Oakley, her daughter, and Mrs. Middleton. The latter lives with her uncle. The bass were extolled. In the evening we went to hear the Butler. By the way, Mrs. John Butler *is* married, and to the Mr. James mentioned. He is a lawyer in Philadelphia, who saw a great deal of her during her husband's absence, and who was necessarily in her confidence. The marriage took place some months since; all the women desperately scandalized.

Mrs. Butler was much admired, though I liked her less than in *The Tempest*. There was too much of the tragedy queen in her manner to be agreeable or natural. Mrs. Cruger was there, but quiet; she came in late, and could not penetrate the mass. The house was full, but not a squeeze. I sat on a stool in an aisle, and it was the hardest seat I ever filled. Perhaps my personal discomforts coloured my judgment! I know how to pity you, now, without a back to the wagon. I should think there might have been $500 clear in the house.

I got no news at my dinner. Miss Cruger, who obtains almost as much information as Mrs. Laight, though how she gets it I hardly know, was indisposed, and we lost her budget. I saw her shawl, however, and had a talk with the ladies about mantillas, shawls, etc. It seems Miss Cruger's shawl was purchased at Paisley, and is considered altogether above the ordinary run. I was mistaken as to its figure, though not as to its colour. One sees so many of these things that it is no wonder I should get a little wrong. This shawl is extra warm, extra fine, and every way extra. Its colour is a dark gray, without cross bars of any sort, but with a broad border in subdued colours. All agreed that such a shawl could not be bought here, but others very like it might be at from 8 to 10 dollars; that is, shawls of the colour and fashion as to ornaments. There will be time to write me on the subject. As for mantillas, the high caste fashionables wear them small, equally without ruffles or fringes, though the last might be tolerated, and very pretty ones could be had from 10 to 15; with judgment, for 10, perhaps. Fanny can send me her last word on the subject. It has cleared off pleasant, and May day promises to be fair. My feet after pretty fair exercise on the battery feel pretty well. Cruger walked with me, and said that his Uncle Peter had had neuralgia so severely as to prevent his walking. He was trying galvanism, and one leg was well under the treatment. Cruger came back to my rooms with me, and sat a couple of hours.

And now, before I go out to purchase my shad, and pines, and oranges, all of which you will receive per express, I must correct a false report sent you in my last. Mrs. John Butler [Fanny Kemble], it seems, is not married after all. Little Mrs. Nettie Middleton, Cruger's niece and who is staying with him, has always manifested a strong reluctance to believe the story. Last evening, as soon as I appeared, she broke forth with the joyful announcement of the untruth of the story. The little woman really seemed delighted to have it in her power to contradict what she considered a scandal. It seems Mrs. Rutherford solemnly denies it, and the following strange incident is told. Mrs. Butler got into an omnibus, and there overheard some common woman talking of "the widow Butler's having been privately married some months and her husband not dead a year." This was the first intimation she had that such a report was in circulation. And now, having repaired this wrong, I go to look for my fruit and shad.

Monday, noon. I have just given to the express a box and a champagne basket, freight paid to Fort Plain $1.50. The box contains six fine Connecticut river shad, in'ards drawn and cleaned, six cocoanuts and two yellow legged snipe for yourself. I tried for quail or woodcock, but could find none. The basket has a dozen pines, and 4 dozen oranges. I also bought a box of fine Naples figs, but could not get them in. As I shall send another box or basket next week, I will squeeze them in then.

Tom Cadwalader arrived this morning, and Robert McCall is expected at two. I dine with them. I have sent a message to Ned, and shall see him next Sunday, I suppose.

I have been on my feet all the morning, and am surprised to find how little they are affected by it. On the whole, they are certainly materially better, though they change about like boys at play. The right foot was the most sensitive until yesterday, and since then it is almost well, while the left is the weak one now, though nothing like what it has been for months past. I am in the hopes that the warm weather will restore me.

Cadwalader says Mrs. Butler is not married. James is a son of a professor in the University. The *old* W. Morse of Philadelphia, about 35, a lawyer, and quite intimate with Butler. He managed his property, and something *may* happen, but has not happened *yet*.

I am compelled to close, and indeed have no more to say. No attempt has yet been made to sell the picture. *Sea Lions* doing very well.

Adieu—God bless you all.

With tenderest affection—

J. F. C.

Globe, Tuesday, May Day, 1849

Dearest Love,

I begin a letter this morning, with the intention of making it run through two days, as I glean material. Yesterday I dined and made an evening with Cadwalader and his party, who are still here. Henry is one. He tells me that Biddle left over $70,000, divided equally between his sisters. Mrs. N. Biddle has now $7000 per annum, and is regaining her health. Major Biddle, whom I met at Detroit, told his brother he was a sick man, with a very improving estate, and wanted no nurse, and desired him to make the disposition he did.

Worth told me yesterday that a powerful effort would be made for Ogden, but the President is for Gov. Young. In the mean time, Cornelius W. Lawrence continues in office. I am now going out, and may pick up something. A very fine day. I got 13 per cent on your bank stock yesterday, and shall get eight more on Friday, making 21 per cent altogether.

I called on Mrs. Laight, yesterday, and was received.

John De Peyster's three children were there, and fine
children they are. Mrs. John came in while I was there.
She said that her husband had told her Mr. Powell died
of cholera. Dr. Jackson said cholera we must have, but
it would be of a mild type, and easily controlled by those
who are prudent. As yet, there is no report, nor any
alarm. Alvan Stewart is dead, but of his old infirmities,
I fancy.

I also went to see Mrs. Cruger and was admitted. She
soon started off on her case and talked more than an hour
about it. She is high strung, and there will be "no peace in
Israel" very soon. Indeed she told me that she should
stand out until driven to the wall. She seemed to take a
delight in compelling her husband to work. I incidentally
mentioned Mrs. Middleton. "Yes," she cried, "she is and
has been staying at 55, all winter! Well, she is welcome.
Mr. Cruger has cut a green door into my mother's dining
room, but I do not care." Altogether, she is the queerest
woman I have ever met with. She is now evidently set on
getting possession of her two houses, and manœuvres a
little to obtain her ends. Her face has a bluff water-cure
fullness about it, but her person has lost its symmetry,
and she says she is old. I had a long talk with Cruger last
evening, and mentioned a few things to him that I
thought might be done with propriety, as justice to him.
For instance, she told me that her husband's counsel had
thrown out an imputation of there having been an improper intimacy between her and Mr. Pepper, and that
her counsel had contented himself with saying that the
charge was unjust, and that she defied calumny. Cruger
says there is no truth in either of the statements. His
counsel manifested the greatest delicacy towards her, and
her counsel had nothing to answer.

Your kind and affectionate letter has just reached me, and I feel very grateful for it. But I do not like the English and Philadelphia letters. Open them both, and let me know their contents by return of mail. This was the packet that ought to decide some acceptances, and, while I cannot suppose any thing has gone wrong, the two letters coming together look ominous; let me know, therefore, what I am to expect.

With the truest affection,

Yours,

J. F. C.

FROM S. F. B. MORSE

Locust Grove, Po'keepsie, May 3, 1849

My dear Sir,

I have just been reading your *Sea Lions*, and I write you a hasty line for the double purpose of thanking you for your friendly mention of me in its interesting pages, and to correct an error in the date of my invention which you have inadvertently committed, and which I think is easily accounted for. The *first* idea of my Telegraph I had on board the Ship *Sully* in October, 1832, but as I was intimate at your house after your return, and had many conversations with you on the subject of the Telegraph, as well as on other subjects in our rambles *à la mode de Paris*, in New York, you have undoubtedly blended the Parisian with the New York incidents, and antedated my invention. When did you return? Was it not in the Spring of 1833? I have forgotten, and should be pleased to know.

How do you do, and your family? I am again a married man, as you are doubtless aware, and a happy one I assure you, in the relation. Mrs. Judge Nelson and her

daughter were several weeks with us in the same house at
Washington. I refer you to them for information of
Madame, but hope I shall have the pleasure of a call
from you in some of your journeyings up or down the
river, at least when the Rail Road shall have put me
within two hours of New York. I have a beautiful spot;
one (as "capability Brown" would say) of great capa-
bilities. If the *Pirates* will but cease their piracies, I
should be able to make great improvements, but at present
I can do nothing. My property, being mostly in Telegraph Stock, is rendered insecure by the unprincipled and
reckless mercenary course of the press to a wide extent in
the country. Their motive in their hostility to what they
choose to call my "monopoly" is not even concealed; they
wish to have their despatches at *less cost*, aye, *for nothing*, not perceiving, so blinded are they by prejudice, that
they are killing themselves by the attainment of what
they wish. I speak more particularly of the N. York
city papers, the *Journal of Commerce*, the *Express*, the
Sun, the *Tribune*, and will it not serve them right? Look
at the matter a moment. Let the prices to the press, if
Telegraphing, be *high*, and what is the consequence? The
papers at St. Louis and Buffalo, and New Orleans, will
be able only to give in their columns such a mere abstract
of intelligence from the distant city, as to create a desire
for the New York papers in order to learn the details;
consequently the subscribers of a New York paper in
those distant cities will still require that paper. But now
let the desire to break down these high prices, by encouraging "competition" (which is now the burden of these
papers), and what will be the consequence?—let us suppose a St. Louis paper can get the contents of the *Journal
of Commerce* by Telegraph for nothing, how long will it

be before every subscriber to the *Journal of Commerce* in St. Louis will send to the Editors the expressive notice "Stop my paper"? They will hardly pay full price for a last year's Almanac? It is evident that it is for the interest of the press to keep up the highest prices for telegraphing. But for the public at large I suppose that *low* prices are desirable. With my wish to exercise the largest charity towards that portion of the press I have mentioned, I cannot believe them to be actuated by *motives of an enlarged benevolence*, thus to be willing to *sacrifice themselves* for the public good!! As sure, however, as they attain the end which they seem to have conspired to gain, just so sure they will fall before *"cheap Telegraphing."* Who will take a city paper that brings him only what he has read three days before? The result will be that the New York city papers (*news*papers strictly speaking) will be circumscribed to an area of about 100 miles' radius. I am not prepared to say that such a limitation would not be a public benefit, so far as the papers I have named are concerned. With kindest regards to yourself and respects to Mrs. Cooper and your daughters,

I am as ever truly Yr friend
and Ser^{vt}

Saml F. B. Morse.

J. Fenimore Cooper, Esqr, Cooperstown

TO MRS. COOPER, COOPERSTOWN

Globe, May 7th, 1849

Best Beloved,

Ned came after all and staid two hours with us. We did not go to church, the day being very bad. I gave him Lucy's dress, and arranged for Martha's journey. He told me that the *Independence* was expected at the yard

every day. The late gale is right in her teeth, and so far
fully sustains Sarah. To-day, even, the wind hangs at
the eastward, and it is raw and very unpleasant.

I have just come from 27th Street. The cars took me,
for sixpence, to within a few rods of the door. The house
is decent, three stories, new, but primitive. I was shown
into a parlour and seated myself. A *handsome* boy came
in and took a survey. It flashed on my mind who he was.
"Come this way, sir, if you please—are you Willy De
Lancey?" "Yes, sir." He came up and took my hands.
"And who am I?" "I do not know, sir." "I am your
Uncle Cooper." Away he shot, and his mother soon appeared. Pete is quite ill. Something has broken, and he
spat blood freely. Dr. Brown is absent, and his substitute
hesitates to pronounce. To-morrow, however, there is to
be a consultation, and Mrs. De Lancey will send for me
should there be any occasion. I think she is apprehensive
of the result. She has not yet written to the Bishop.

We have a lady at death's door in this house. She has
a child about three weeks old, and has taken cold. Morris
Robinson died suddenly on Saturday, of a cold across the
chest. Two stories are told about Mr. Powell; one that he
died of Asiatic and the other of common cholera. You
have never mentioned your sister, but Mrs. De Lancey
says she is much better.

Mrs. Washington Carter and family are in this house,
though on the point of leaving. Their daughters, between
the ages of 18 and 9, smoke large strong cigars, and drink
brandy and water. I have not seen this, but hear it from
all around me; quite *à la* Georges Sand. Papa and maman
keep them in countenance.

Ogden's chances are said to revive a little. I have
written to Mr. Meredith in his behalf, but *quien sabe?*

De Kay has gone over to his brother's place in New Jersey, to return this evening.

Tuesday. A ship has just come in to Boston that left the *Independence* at Valparaiso March 2d. This ship has had a run of only 64 days. It has been done in 60. Now, supposing that Shubrick sailed about the 10th, he might very well get *here* by the 15th; unless his delay at Rio was long. His ship is fast, and would make the passage sooner than a merchantman. I shall not wait for him after the 16th. I think it highly probable he is picking up gold, and intends to turn his time to some little account. The *Lexington* is hourly expected here, and will bring the most authentic reports. Motte Middleton, who has come on to join his wife, tells me that he saw a letter from the Commodore to Gen. Hamilton saying he should not get home before the first of June.

I have just had a most extraordinary conversation on the subject of our smoking fairies. Most of it can not be written, but take a specimen of their education: Culver sent up to complain that the young ladies had shut their dog up in a room that did not belong to them: "Tell Mr. Culver to go to Hell," was the reply of the fairy of 16; her mother being present. *He* is drunk most of the time. They are in no society. I question if their relations visit them.

I am trying to sell Tribute Money to Mr. Lenox. He ought to have it, on every account, but is very difficult to approach. He bought Harry Musser's Washington, three or four years since.

Adieu, love, for an hour or two.

There is nothing new. I have not sold the picture, but an opening is made for an arrangement in another quarter. I hope to escape a journey to Philadelphia, and shall be home by the middle of next week, I trust, without fail. If Shubrick come in, this week.

I have been talking with Putnam. He is very encouraging, and has great confidence in the new edition. I am less sanguine, though the trade all talk favourably.

The day is so very bad that no one can do any business, and I am glad to keep the house. De Kay has left me, and his son-in-law was here a few minutes since to look for him. He made the most friendly enquiries, and was eulogistic of Cooperstown.

With best love to all, and most to yourself,

I remain your most tenderly attached

J. F. C.

TO MRS. COOPER, COOPERSTOWN

Globe, Thursday, May 10th, 1849

Dearest Sue,

In the way of table you beat us. I have not seen a good salad this season, nor a radish. The grass is vile. Cruger had it once, but it was good for nothing. I dine there now very seldom, although he has a plate for me every day. His house is full, some six or eight. I keep aloof out of good taste, though constantly invited.

Yesterday I met Mrs. Colden and Wilkes, and had a walk and a talk with them; I must go and see them. To-night, I think, I shall do it.

Pete is better, and Willy dined with me yesterday. He is very like Ned, but better looking, and really a sweet child—quite as much so as Johnny Middleton, who is a wonder. He is rather small, but has time to grow.

I am very glad Charley went to Utica. Mrs. Butler has a competitor in a Miss Somebody, who does very well, they say. There is a McReady riot, and likely to be a fight to-night. As I am not in it, I shall not volunteer a broken head. Some of the *literati* have put themselves forward and won't stand "the hazard of the dye."

I met Morse just now, looking like a bridegroom, and full of law suits. He groans over the press worse than I ever did, and seems to imagine justice deaf as well as blind. Still he is a great man, and will so stand in history; and so deserves to stand.

Afternoon—Morse has just left me. He was friendly and like old times—says he is perfectly happy, hopes to have a house full of children, and is as young as ever.

The important bargains are made; Miss Cruger had the good nature to go as far as Beck and Stewart's with me this morning, and the transaction is closed. She has been laid up with a bad cold, but Mr. Middleton is a water-cure man, and she permitted him to apply an [illegible], and it has cured an inflammation of the throat and chest. So she ventured out to-day. On the subject of the shawl there was very little difficulty. They are scarce just now, but cheap. I paid $7.50, and have got a very suitable one, with a slight exception, perhaps, of a little colour that is too pronounced. It is warm, large, of excellent quality, and in all these respects just what it ought to be. I dare say Sue and Fan will want it.

Friday.

Last evening I passed with Mrs. Colden and Anne Wilkes. Colden went off to back up Mcready, having signed his letter. You will see the account of this miserable affair in the journals. The report in town is that 15 are killed, and 25 wounded. As commonly happens, most of the sufferers had nothing to do with the tumult. I do not think matters will go much further, for the authorities are resolute.

Mrs. Colden read me a letter from Fanny Garnets. The old lady is dead, and the two young ladies are living at Brighton. It seems that Mad. de Penthieu died a few years since, having sunk much of her fortune in an annuity. She left, however, £2,000 to each of the two Miss Garnets, and this has made them quite independent. They have purchased a nice little residence at Brighton, and intend to turn English folk, out and out. The relatives in this country got but little, but enough to give Mrs. Henry near $2,000. The same to each of the brothers. George has two sweet daughters, one like the Kings, and the other like Mrs. Colden. Old Miss Wilkes is well, and 80. I did not see her. The ladies sent many kind messages, and seemed very glad to see me.

No news as yet from Shubrick, although Mr. Middleton told me yesterday he had got a letter from Gen. Hamilton, enclosing one for his son, in which he says that Shubrick had written he would be in about the 7th May.

Mrs. Colden admitted very naïvely that they were sorely disappointed at Mad. de Penthieu's will; though they must have got some $30,000 from her.

While I was there, a message came to George, to go and see old Mrs. Morton. She was standing before the fire in a cotton dress, when it took, and she was burnt from head to foot. Her sufferings were horrible until the doctors reached her. They immediately powdered her with common flour, using a dredging box, when the pain ceased at once. It is necessary to renew the powdering as the flour disappears, until all pain ceases.

It is thought Mrs. Morton must die. Her son Quincy was in a bath, and heard her cries. He ran to her in a dressing-gown, which took fire, and is quite badly burnt himself.

I saw Mrs. Banyer, yesterday. Mrs. Bears was with her. The last asked after Fanny's beau, a widower with six children, etc., etc. She looks very well, but no cubs. Matty came in, looking very pretty and so like her excellent father I could have kissed her.

Most tenderly your own

J. F. C.

Kindest love all round. I put a gold dollar *en dedans*.

TO MRS. COOPER, COOPERSTOWN

American, Richfield, Saturday 3 P. M.,

July 28, 1849

Dearest,

I am very comfortably lodged here, and much better off than when here before. I am not without hopes that the water will do me good. Mr. Newbold thinks he is improving now quite fast, and tells a large story of his trout fishing on his foot for several hours, without any great pain or bad consequences. I find the *long*, *warm* baths very penetrating, and think I shall benefit in the skin if not in the foot.

I was at Cruger's this morning. He had a physician whom I saw, and he thought the case was cholera. Cruger looks much better than when I left him a fortnight ago, and he is quite anxious that I should go with him to Trenton, before his company arrives, which will now be soon. I may go or not, according to circumstances. From his house it can be done easily, and with his horses, in a day and a half.

I stopped at Rose Lawn, passed round by Hall'sville and travelled half a mile on the new plank road. There is a point on the turnpike, as you come here, whence I could see Lakelands, and all the east bank of the lake. The drive is very beautiful, and I must take it with you on my return, if you can stand the tour of the lake.

There must be near a hundred people here, principally of the *hoi polloi.*

Adieu, dearest. God bless you—you must do your own reading for a few days. I may not be back before the end of the week, and Paul must attend to Van Horn.

Love to all—Yours most tenderly,

J. F. C.

FROM H. W. WESSELS

Benicia, Cal., Aug. 28th, 1849

My dear Sir

A few hours' relief from pain this morning, enables me to accomplish in part what I have for some weeks past endeavored to attempt. My superficial knowledge of the country however will not be very satisfactory to you, and my prejudices based upon family afflictions, and great personal inconveniences and annoyances, may perhaps cause me to represent matters and things in a light altogether different from the views entertained by those who have been more fortunate, or who are so strongly operated on by the charm of novelty. The only points of interest presented to me since leaving N. York, are the ports of Rio de Janeiro and Valparaiso, not only because they afforded a grateful relief to the miseries of a sea voyage, but because they possess in themselves merits of no ordinary importance.

The former possesses a harbor of almost unrivaled beauty, and presents an appearance of commercial prosperity, altogether different from what I had supposed could exist in any place under the control of popish influence. Valparaiso on the contrary has but an indifferent harbor, and the town, as seen from the water, offers little else to view than a range of bare hills sloping towards the bay, separated by deep ravines, and presenting the appearance of a succession of small straggling villages. On landing, however, it is found that between the base of these hills and the water, there is an esplanade of level ground, varying in width, and stretching along the shore for more than three miles, densely peopled, and the streets at every turn giving evidence of great commercial enterprise and prosperity; the business seems to be mostly in the hands of foreigners, and their influence is sensibly felt throughout the Nation; in fact the Chileans as a people are more liberal in their republicanism than any other Spanish Colony.

It is an excellent port for supplying ships with fresh provisions; the fruits and vegetables are remarkably fine, and of every variety, and the beef very good, whilst, in addition, the upper classes are hospitable, and the lower ones civil. We would have willingly landed as a garrison for the fort, and left with regret. Monterey, when we arrived, was rather pretty, because the hills were green, and boast of possessing a few trees; the village is insignificant, and possesses neither trade nor commerce, though desirable as a station, because it contains houses. At San Francisco the scene changes and you are suddenly thrown within the blighting influence of gold, a town hurried into existence as it were by a single impulse, where the poor have suddenly become rich, and where labor controls capital. The climate of San Francisco is execrable, a gale of wind is constantly blowing from seaward, and the anchorage of its harbor far from secure; real estate changes hands at the most exorbitant prices, and business is transacted on a scale that would do no discredit

to Pearl St. itself, whilst its Custom house and Post
Office are little inferior to the same establishment in the
City of N. York. Gold in great quantities is constantly
flowing in and coin also seems to be plenty; yet business is
done on credit, and money is loaned on what they call
good security, at the rate of two pr. ct. a month. Neither
the town nor its vicinity produces one single article necessary for the support of its inhabitants (except beef), and
nearly all the meat and vegetables are brought from
Europe or N.York.

The town of Benicia, named from the lady of Gen.
Vallejo, a prominent citizen of California, was started
last winter as the rival of San Francisco, possessing, as
its admirers claim, many important advantages over that
now celebrated place—being as easy of access, having
greater facilities for landing cargoes, safer anchorage,
better climate, superior back country, etc., etc. A grant
of land was made to government for an Army and Navy
depot, and both were ordered to be transferred here. The
town is about thirty miles above San Francisco, on the
northern side, just at the entrance of Suison bay, and
perhaps fifteen miles below the Sacramento and San
Joaquin rivers; the climate is horrible, and the whole
country, as far as the eye can reach, a barren desolate
waste; there is not a drop of fresh water on our reserve,
and not a tree or shrub within three miles. The Strait is
here about two miles wide, and on the opposite side is a
beautiful and productive valley, though small in extent.
At that place we could have made ourselves comparatively comfortable, but the water was said to be too shallow for the easy landing of supplies. I am not familiar
enough with the general character of the country to give
you a correct impression, but after the magnificent scenery

of the table lands of Mexico, it appears to me tame and insipid—the face of the country is generally hilly, but the different ranges are separated by valleys of greater or less extent, quite productive and said to be the most enchanting places in the world. In these valleys alone can agriculture flourish, and it was in such situations that the old Missions were always established—both hill and valley affording pasturage for immense herds of cattle. An enterprising man living (or finding himself) on one of the rivers above, set himself a short time since to mowing grass, and the avails of about six weeks' labor amounted, in the market of San Francisco, to the handsome sum of $24,000. In the Spring, the wild oat appears green and tender, the cattle are fat, and the beef of good flavor. Deer, Elk and Antelope are found in herds, but time is too valuable to waste in hunting. On the whole, it is a country very much overrated both in regard to climate and capacity for producing, and so long as gold is within reach of the poorest laborer, its soil must remain uncultivated. Although gold is so abundant, and apparently inexhaustible, it is obtained only by great labor and great exposure; our Soldiers have all tried their fortunes in that way, but few evince a desire to make the second attempt. For one unaccustomed to labor it would be folly to think of digging, and even those who are able to endure the exposure are scarcely willing to stay in the same place long enough to acquire much, for as soon as a new place is discovered and said to be rich, many of the old ones are abandoned, and they all crowd in, each man hoping to be the lucky one, by falling upon a lump which will make him rich in an instant. Vessels of all sizes are daily passing us, on their way to the upper Settlements, many of them crowded to such an extreme that it is curious to see them. Yankee invention is constantly on the stretch, and we see some strange sights. A few days since, a framed house went by, propelled by steam, and a white hall skiff stopped here for provisions. I saw yesterday three miserable onions sold for 75 cts., and we have not tasted fresh meat for more than ten days. Eggs are unknown, and milk can be bought with great trouble for 75 cts. the quart; butter can be got for one dollar, but very inferior in quality. I have had but a bushel and a half of potatoes since May last, and for them I paid about $8. Before closing I must say that this is the 26th of September, not having been able to finish previous to the last mail. We are in tolerable health, except Henry, who was suddenly seized this evening with the Cholera infantum, but hope it will be slight. We all unite in regards to Mrs. C. and the young ladies, and I regret that I cannot now make myself more interesting.

Yours very truly,

H W Wessels

James Fenimore Cooper, Esq.

FROM S. F. B. MORSE

Irving House, New York, Sept. 5th, 1849

My dear Sir,

I was agreeably surprized this morning in conversing with Prof. Renwick to find that he corroborates the fact you have mentioned in your *Sea Lions*, respecting the earlier conception of my Telegraph by me, than the date I had given, and which goes only so far back in my own recollection as 1832. Prof. Renwick insists that immediately after Prof. Dana's Lectures at the N. York

Athenæum, I consulted with him on the subject of the velocity of electricity, and in such a way as to indicate to him that I was contriving an Electric Telegraph. The consultation I remember, but I did not recollect the time. He will depose that it was before I went to Europe, after those Lectures; now, I went in 1829; this makes it almost certain that the impression you and Mrs. Cooper and your daughter had that I conversed with you on the subject in 1831 after my return from Italy is correct.

If you are still persuaded that this is so, your deposition before the Commission in this city to that fact will render me an incalculable service. I will cheerfully defray your expenses to and from the city if you will meet me here this week or beginning of next.

In haste but with best respects to Mrs. Cooper and family,

I am dear Sir as ever Yr friend and Ser^vt

Saml F. B. Morse.

J. Fenimore Cooper, Esqr

FROM S. B. F. MORSE

Irving House, New York, Sept. 10, 1849

My dear Sir,

Many thanks for your favor of—no date. I hope to visit you next week or the early part of the week after, to take the depositions. I visit Boston this week and will advise you more definitely from that city.

See what I have purchased for myself for the rest of my life, by presuming to invent the Telegraph; litigation, litigation, litigation. I wish I may be able to bear it as bravely and philosophically as you have done.

With kindest regards to Mrs. Cooper and family, and to Judge Nelson and family,

I am as ever

Yr friend and Servt.

Sam. F. B. Morse.

P.S. Such a fine boy I have had presented to me. They call him "Lightning bug." Six weeks old. Weight 13 pounds avoirdupois.

FROM S. B. F. MORSE

New York, Sept. 17, 1849

My dear Sir,

Your Telegraphic despatch from Syracuse did not reach me till this morning, in consequence of my absence in Philadelphia, when it arrived in this city. I am now on the wing to Boston, where I shall be engaged all the week in taking depositions. I shall not trouble you to come to the city, I think, if Judge Nelson is at home. It is possible I may not need your depositions in this case, but would wish them for historical purposes connected with the invention hereafter. Should I visit you for that purpose, I will give you due notice, that your convenience may be consulted.

I am in the midst of the great battle, but I think my forces are so marshalled and so strong that eventual triumph will be mine. The prize it seems is thought *now* both in Europe and this country to be worth contending for, although I have too fresh a recollection of the dispositions manifested to think me insane, by the community generally, while in travail with the invention.

My kindest respects to your family, and believe me

sincerely as ever Yr friend,

S. F. B. Morse.

James Fenimore Cooper, Esqr

TO SUSAN FENIMORE COOPER

Globe, New York, Oct. 23d, 1849

My dear child,

You know all about the death of poor Peter. I heard of it accidentally in the street, and did not get the letter sent to ask me to attend the funeral, until the carriages were gone. I reached 27th Street twenty minutes too late, and that without my breakfast. No arrangements had been made, the letter miscarrying, and the family had to wait until a grave was dug. In addition it rained violently.

My Sunday was spent in attending to poor Ned Myers. He is on his death-bed, beyond a doubt, with enlargement of the heart, and dropsy as a consequence. He may live a month, or may die at any moment. Yesterday I wrote out a will for him, and had it duly signed, an act of great importance to the family. He gives the *use* of his property to his wife for life, and then to go to her children. When I asked him if he wished any distinction made in favour of Lucy, he strenuously opposed. I was quite touched when he asked me to break his state to Martha *tenderly*. This you will do, and the sooner the better.

If Ned should not detain me, I shall leave town to-night, go direct to Geneva, stay one day, and come home. I did intend to go last night, but was unexpectedly detained.

The weather is delightful to-day. Cruger and myself went to see McAllister, a celebrated conjurer, last Friday. In the midst of the entertainment Martha Maitland came running up to me to enquire how I did. The whole family was there. Bob got on the stage twice, and was used in two tricks. He stood it pretty well.

I must tell my news *viva voce.*

Your very affectionate father, with tenderest love to all,

J. F. C.

Po'keepsie, Nov. 20th, 1849

My dear Sir,

Yours of the 17th I have just received. I perceive you are under the widespread erroneous opinion that I am *"very rich."* There is a fallacy in this. If the property invested in Telegraphs were all mine, or even the Patentees' part, I might be considered rich. My interest pecuniarily in the Telegraph is about *one quarter* of the Patent profits, only. The little property in it that remains to me is in *Stock*, mostly as yet unproductive. Out of 18,000 miles of telegraph conductors constructed on my system, I receive dividends only from *725* miles! To this insignificant portion I look for the support of my family, and the payment of my portion of the expenses of a multiplied and protracted litigation. Now although I think I see clear sky ahead, yet the uncertainties of the law keep it yet clouded about me, and I fear on my own family's account to incur expense but for absolute necessaries. I have been in want of many conveniences, especially in buildings about me, and have at this moment builders employed in building for whose services I have been gradually accumulating a little fund sufficient for that purpose. I have not *cash* for the purpose of purchasing pictures of any kind; alas! my dear Sir, the very name of *pictures* produces a sadness of heart I cannot describe. Painting has been a smiling mistress to many, but she has been a cruel jilt to me. I did not abandon her; she abandoned me. I have taken scarcely any interest in paintings for many years. Will you believe it, when last in Paris in 1845, I did not go into the Louvre, nor did I visit a single picture gallery. I sometimes indulge a vague dream that I may paint again. It is rather the memory of past pleasures when hope was enticing me onward, only to deceive me at last. Except some family portraits, valuable to me from their likenesses only, I could wish that every picture I ever painted was destroyed. I have no wish to be remembered as a painter, for I never was a painter; my ideal of that profession *was* perhaps too exalted; I may say, *is* too exalted. I leave it to others, more worthy to fill the niches of Art.

Excuse my prosing. I mean only to show you that I am in no condition at present either to purchase or enjoy pictures. I may be in New York about the time you are there, and shall be glad to see and talk with you on the subject. I am generally at the Irving House.

By the by, before closing, let me explain in one word, why we did not take your deposition. My counsel thought it hardly worth while to trouble you, since we had direct evidence in abundance of the strongest kind to maintain my position, and for all purposes of the trial it was sufficient without yours.

With sincere regard
Truly Yours
Saml F. B. Morse.

J. Fenimore Cooper, Esqr

TO MRS. COOPER, COOPERSTOWN

[New York], Thursday, [December] 6th, 1849
Best Beloved,

I begin to grope my way through present difficulties,

and this by disposing of literary property. As yet nothing else has offered. I hope to get through next week.

Last evening I passed with Miss Eliza Cruger, on a visit to little Saidee. I have not seen my neighbors very lately.

Archy Kearny sat half an hour with me this morning, and I broached the affair of Phil and Di. He was not explicit, and I fancy, while there is no separation, there is not much harmony. She has gone to pass a *year* with her mother. Now, we old folk would not quite like that. I asked Archy if she were not attached to Phil, and he evaded an answer by telling me what queer people the western world contained. Things are not right, while they might be worse. I am afraid there is too much of Uncle John in his distinguished grandson.

Called to-day on Mrs. Laight, and was not admitted. Met a Mr. and Mrs. Izard at the door. He knew me and spoke to me. Who could he have been? A tall, genteel, handsome young man, a son of the general's perhaps!

I hear nothing new. The town seems dull, in the way of entertainments. I was quite touched when I heard Mrs. Macomb's child christened Susan. It recalled my two Susies, each of whom is so very dear to me. I like to meet the name among your connections.

I have not seen Mrs. Maitland, but hope to, to-night. God bless you. Be of good heart, for I think all will go well.

Most tenderly yours,

J. F. C.

Saidee sends her regards to you all, as does Miss Eliza Cruger, whom I met in the street one hour since.

TO MRS. COOPER, COOPERSTOWN

Tuesday, Dec. 9th [11th?], 1849

A Count Gurowski, a Pole who came to see us in
Paris, a one eyed man, is in the house, and spoke to me
this morning. Bearnatzki is still living, but Louis Plater
is dead. Michiewitz invented a religion, but submitted to
Pius IX. He is still flourishing. Janski is connected with
the press, etc., etc.

Keep up your heart, my well beloved; we have seen
darker hours, and are in merciful hands. My tenderest
love to all—

TO MRS. COOPER, COOPERSTOWN

Globe, Dec. 14th, 1849

My dearest wife,

If it were not for Susy's little matters I should leave
town with this letter, and be with you to-morrow. As it is
I expect to be home Tuesday the 18th, which will be
three days later. I am through myself, or essentially so,
for I am waiting for a letter from Philadelphia, containing a note that had given me much anxiety, but which is
now *paid*, and with my own money. But dear little Susy,
meek little Susy, must not be forgotten. With Putnam I
have arranged for her, and the contract [for *Rural
Hours*] is to be signed this forenoon, on the following
terms: viz.,

Copy Right and *Plates* to be hers.

Putnam to sell for 5 years.

One thousand copies to go free to pay for plates, which
will scarcely do it.

After 1000 copies sold 12½ per cent to go to author.
This on 3000 or 4000 copies will make a reasonable com-

pensation, and at all events she will have the plates. Appleton has not yet given an answer. It is he who detains me.

Yesterday, I dined with Mrs. Banyer, Wm. John, Mrs. John, Eliza and Matilda at table. To-day I take my last dinner with Cruger, and in the evening his sister and a Mrs. King of Charleston go to the opera—Cruger and myself are not of the party. *We* talk of the circus. Colden is better; out of all danger.

I am packing up, and clearing out—sending off papers, manuscripts, etc., right and left.

Night before last I was at a literary *soirée*. Bryant, Willis, Gliddon, Dr. Robinson, etc., were there. I was glad to see the two last, whom I had not met for twenty years. I staid until eleven o'clock.

I have several visits of digestion to make, and shall be busy every evening I remain in town. Mrs. Baker has sent a bundle for Anne.

There has been a great sale of Cashmere shawls. The dearest sold for $800, the cheapest $15. Five went into one family.

Adieu, my love. Keep me nearest your heart.

J. F. C.

TO CAROLINE DE LANCEY

Hall, Cooperstown, Dec. 20th, 1849

My dear Caroline,

I find some brandy fruit, here, sent by *you* to *me*. This little proof of regard has made me very grateful, and in a degree duly proportioned to the meanness of another person, whom I will not name, but who, no doubt, has guzzled all her share in order to keep the flesh on ribs

that can no more be seen than poor Mrs Costar's beauty.
Well; we are not all self denying, and humble, and of
moderate appetites, as we should be. Gluttony is a great
affliction, and I pity those who are its *victims*, meaning
in this instance myself, as another such a jar would have
made a beautiful pendant to that you have so kindly sent
me. I know how to deny my longings, however, and to be
grateful for what I have, as I am most sincerely to *you*.

I was at the christening of Mrs. Macomb's child. Its
name is Sue. Think if I did not admire it.

Phil and Di have got an arrangement by which she
goes to St. Louis and lives with her mother, while he goes
where he pleases. He allows her $3000 per annum, and
she takes all the children. He no longer talks of quitting
the army, but told me that he thought of joining his troop
in California, or somewhere on that line of communication. I do not understand that there is a permanent separation, but one so far as the present time is concerned.
Two high and independent tempers are at the bottom—
Archy would say no more than that "Western women are
queer"—"not like eastern women"—"wouldn't have one
for a gift," etc., etc.

Rosy Bayley [Roosevelt Bayley, later Archbishop of
Baltimore] came to see me—a good-looking priest. He
will be a bishop some day. What do you think of Forbes?
There will be a mutiny among the women if the priests
all renounce matrimony. Bishop Ives is in a dilemma. A
poor business, Cally dear—a very poor business. Don't
tell this to Pink.

So Mag is engaged. Well, it now remains to make the
best of it. He may do better than he promises—No one
can say. All matrimony is a lottery, and prizes are scarce.
Is Street married? If not let him beware of Pinky.

Morse is a papa, and very happy.

M^rs Wm. Cooper is lost, so far as I am concerned. I can not learn anything of her, and have not seen her these four years. She appears to have withdrawn from the world.

All here send love. Adieu, dear Cally—every thing that is kind to you, but to that t'other woman, war and bloodshed, the glutton! Adieu.

J. Fenimore Cooper.

Tell Pinky I forgive her, and wish you all a

MERRY CHRISTMAS

TO "SAIDEE"

Hall, Cooperstown, Dec. 20th, 1849

My Dainty Little Saidee,

I am a scamp, an unmitigated, shameless, truth-despising fellow! What, when pledged to Saidee, betrothed, as it were, to come and see her, to let a little water float in the way! I feel not only shame, but contrition. But I had my punishment on the spot, and you your revenge. I waded across the street to 55, got a cup of tea, when, instead of my usual entertainment of a nap with Harry, or a pantomime with Miss Nina, her can full of high Dutch, who should come in but Garry Van Waggenen (Low Dutch). On this apparition the lady abandoned even Suabia to play the amiable to her guest, and I had to entertain T. and be entertained by him. Now, you little crocodile, I could a tale unfold, etc.,—Hamlet— but I will not. Cousin Nina gave me some awful glances, and I left town, I fear, under her high displeasure. Never mind, she is gentleness and forgiveness itself, and will get over her displeasure by February, when I hope to be restored to favour. By the way, the two *Dutchies* must have set her ears ringing. Now, don't you tell her any of this.

I went to the opera, Saidee, and to Bentoni, and talked of going to see the clown, and you were not with me at either—no, not even at the last. This must not be, in future.

By the way, did Aunt Nancy expect me? If so, tell her of the tempest that alone kept me from 9th Street. I do not like such a numeral—utterly without poetry and musick. We will call it *Strada Saidee*, henceforth, and make some rhymes on it, hereafter.

Pray, did you ever read a Chinese novel? Three or four have been translated, and curious things they are. All the plots and scenes are alike—"taking a few *cups*" of wine, not tea, and "making a few verses" is the never failing announcement of the hero and heroine. The great thing is for the hero to marry *two* heroines—polygamy is allowed—who like each other, and who can hold forth a reasonable prospect of happiness in that duplicate state. Then you see it requires twice as much love to render matrimony secure, in China, as it requires in America. Here, if a man love a woman, and vice versa, the household may rest in peace; but, at Nankin and Pekin, the man must love *two* women, and what is still more difficult of achievement, these women must love each other! Now, imagine how much finesse is necessary to get along with a work of fiction, on "them principles."

Well, Saidee dear, we went to the opera. There sat Mrs. King, in her love of a cloak, Cousin Nina in her no love of a cloak, and Mrs. C. in the back ground. T. looked like a Margrave, on the other side of the theatre.

We, Harry and I, were looked down upon, and recognised by our *bald* heads. This was the compliment we received from sitting in the pit. If there were no wig in the case, the Margrave need not go into the pit, in order *not* to be recognized. To think of a woman's giving herself airs on the strength of a scratch. If it were the *"old scratch,"* one might understand it—many a person does *that*—but the scratch is *new*, nicely curled, and every way suited to the occasion.

By the way, Saidee, I lent Cousin N. a copy of Irving's *Life of Mahomet*. She will soon demolish that Turk, and do you get the book and read it, for my sake.

Here, we are well. A little snow, but, as yet, a mild winter. One of our neighbors, a Judge Morehouse of the Supreme Court, is just dead of apoplexy, which is an event for a village, but this is all our news.

As I shall not send my letter for a few days, I shall put it aside, for another sitting.

Saturday 22d—I have "killed," which in farming parlance means that sundry porkers garnish my larder, spare ribs, tender-loins, roasting pieces and sausage abound. Without letting the right hand know too much of the left, dear Saidee, I may tell you that we keep up the good old rites of the season. We burn the Christmas yule in a happy spirit. Most of us worship God devoutly—alas! that I should be an exception—and every body is the better for the festival.

Sue is full of her Christ Church Charity House. The dear creature is all charity. She has persevered in this thing with a steadiness and constancy that have awakened the interest of her friends, and money comes to her right and left. Under judicious management it will do a great deal of good. How I love that child! Her countenance is that of a sister [Hannah Cooper] I lost by a fall from a horse, half a century since, and her character is very much the same. They were, and are, as perfect as it falls to the lot of humanity to be. I am in love with Sue, and have told her so fifty times. She refuses me, but promises to live on in gentle friendship, and, my passion not being at all turbulent, I do not see but this may do.

Give my kindest regards to Doreen, and tell her I acknowledge myself to be a scamp. Tell her also to drink up all the cider, to the last drop. I am unworthy of its juice. Cousin Henry has some stuff he calls cider, but it is nothing but damaged champagne. It is good enough for a scamp.

Now, Saidee, I have a little secret to tell you. Mrs. Laight is worried at receiving visits when she does not want to see any body. I was in town three weeks, called several times, and she would not see me at all. Since then she has written apology after apology, but always expressing her aversion to seeing any one. She speaks of the kindness of her friends, Doreen among others, but wishes, just at this season, to be alone. Mrs. Yates is almost the only relative she sees.

If you ever see aunt-cousin Louisa, pray give my regards, as also to Mrs. O. I send nothing to Cousin Nina, who is so much under High Dutch influence that she speaks English with an accent. She is now exercising herself in the use of the word "*Ja*," which she will one day utter, as she does all things, gracefully, in the most lady-like manner, and truthfully. These are qualities I cannot deny her, even while I dispute her taste. Don't tell her the last, for the world.

I hope to kiss t'other cheek, in February, until which time and forever afterwards, my dear child, I commend

you to God's Holy keeping. Merry Christmas, the blessing of 75 can do you no harm.

                                        J. Fenimore Cooper.

"Saidee" was a young niece of H. N. Cruger's.

TO MRS. COOPER, COOPERSTOWN

                                Globe, Jan. 24th, 1850

Dearest Sue,

I wrote hastily yesterday, and shall not finish this until
to-morrow, though I may put a good deal in it to-day.

In the first place Ben is to be tried, and Shubrick will
probably be the president of his court. I have written to
him to come to this house, where we can keep old-maid's
hall together.

Talking of that interesting class, I passed last evening
with Anne Maria Clarkson. She was as gay and talkative
as ever, and told me lots of things of old friends. Among
other things she said that she had recently been to pass
an evening with Mary Prime's daughters, the oldest a
young woman of twenty!

One of the Miss Rays is to be married, but, for the life
of me, I cannot remember to whom. Perhaps I shall recall
the name before I get through.

Mrs. Macomb invited me to a small party last evening, but I did not go.

Friday morning.

Last evening I went to 55, and found Saidee, her
elder sister, Rentley Hassle, and the lady of the house.
Cruger is still at Albany, Trapmann, I believe I told
you, gone to Charleston. I gleaned some gossip, which I
shall try to repeat, though my "thick of the leg" really
pained me so much I came away early, and was not fit to

648 CORRESPONDENCE OF [1850

be in society. I gave it a good rubbing, and this morning I am very much better.

In the first place the gentleman who married Miss Ray is Capt. Schuyler Hamilton, a son of John's, and the young warrior who was run through with a lance in one of the Mexican skirmishes.

Miss Alice Jones—one of the Calfards—is to marry a Mr. Howard James, of the Albany family. This is Mrs. Woodbury Langdon's sister, and Woodbury is reported to have said "Howard, you may as well give up. You'll have to marry Alice. Her mother has got her hand on you."

"Mammon and Gammon" have come to an issue. He has given up the ghost, and gone to Havanna, they say. Which is the cause, "mammon" or "gammon," I do not know.

Broadway is wonderfully improved. Getting to be almost European. City Hotel stores are up, and look nobly.

A few days since Mrs. John Stevens bought fifty tickets for Burton's, asked as many friends to accompany her, and wound up with a supper, returning home a little before the cock crew. It rained cats and dogs and many of the ladies got their feet wet. All Mrs. Stevens' shoes and stockings were put in requisition, but nothing would fit. The stockings would not keep their places, and shoes were all down at the heels.

Saidee told me she heard that Paul was engaged to a Miss Barrows. Miss Bailey was her informant.

McCracken has printed a few copies of a play, which I intend to obtain if he will give it to me.

I have not yet seen Putnam, nor done more than enquire.

To-day it rains, and I shall begin work.
God bless you all, and Caroline in particular.
Most tenderly your own
J. F. C.

Washington 25ᵗʰ Jany. 1850
My dear Cooper
I wrote to you the day before yesterday on the subject of your letter received this morning but my letter was directed to Cooperstown.—On inquiry at the Department, a few moments since, I am informed that the time fixed for convening the court for the trial of poor Ben is 14ᵗʰ Feby., the pressure of business at the Department having prevented the preparation of the papers for an earlier day.—The court is to be a full one. Stewart to preside—Morris—Downes, Read—Kearney—Perry—and myself—and Captains in addition to make the 13.—The charge is prepared. I have not seen it—but the Secretary said in conversation with me, that although *"other matters"* had reached his ears, he should confine the charge to the single offence of "leaving his station before regularly relieved"—he considers the case the more important as it is the first that has occurred in our service. —The bringing the ship home, the largest in the squadron, is an ugly feature in the business—for "though the Commodore may have been condemned by medical survey—I suppose the Doctors did not survey the ship." An officer writing from the station says, that although the Commodore will find it hard to excuse his return those who sent him there to command deserve punishment much more than he does.—It was one of Mʳ Masons mistakes, of which he made many.

I am sorry you came down from Cooperstown so soon —for I fear you may finish your business before I get on—you must spin it out—and remain to see us—me I mean—and help poor Ben.—I understand the Surgeon, who would be a principal witness in his case, has gone back to the coast of Africa in the ship—his official reports are in the Department, but it will, I suppose, be for the accused to say whether he will rest his defence on them or not.—

I will write if any thing more turns up.—

We are all well—the ladies send kind regards—

as ever

W Branford Shubrick

J Fenimore Cooper Esqre

TO. MRS. COOPER, COOPERSTOWN

Monday, Jan. 28th, 1850

The first thing I do this morning, my blessed Sue, is to congratulate you. I hope this same thing will be repeated about twenty times, and then you will not be as old as Mrs. Yates, who walked to church with me yesterday, as active as you are now yourself. Her tumble seems to have done her good. I dined with her, and passed the evening up town. On coming home, between nine and ten, the street was covered with promenaders by moonlight, as in May. Yesterday and Saturday were fine days indeed—May days.

Cruger got back Saturday evening, victorious. It seems that Douglas refused point blank to pay the $5000. ordered in the decree. An application was made to arrest him for contempt, but the judge held the case for advisement, until the result of his motion to set aside her appeal was known. This has now been done. Her appeal has been set aside as premature, and the court distinctly said that the order to pay the money must be obeyed. Cruger told me yesterday that his wife snapped her fingers at the court, and is resolved not to pay. If she can persuade her brother to go to gaol, and hold out, it will be a beautiful scene.

This last decision puts Cruger on firm ground. Before he got it, he offered to take $6000 a year for life, to accept $20,000 for the arrears, instead of about $37,000, to which he is entitled, *after allowing for all that has been received by him from Lewis*, about $3000, on account of the mortgage, and to make peace. She refused his terms, and now, he says, proposals must come from them. Miss C. is very well, and gave me a seat yesterday morning in her pew, as did Mrs. Neil in the afternoon. By the way, do you know that Mrs. Yates is reformed Dutch? We dropped her there, and went on to Dr. Hawks' ourselves. Little De Lançey was with us, and went out only once, to get a drink of water.

McCracken has been writing a play, has given me a copy, and I send it to the girls. Anything will do for the country.

By the way, Cruger tells me that Duncan Pell got as far as Congress Hall, on his way to London, when sober Dick got at him, and persuaded him to return. Can this be so? The eldest daughter of Ned Prime, mother a Miss Band, was married to a musick master last Saturday morning.

Everybody says I am getting delicate, and among others poor Ben Cooper, who is still so weak he barely walks from the fire to his bed. Shubrick has written to tell me he is to be tried, and that the department attaches great importance to the case, the first that ever occurred in our service. The court is to convene here on the 14th Feb., and is to be composed of thirteen members—Stewart, Morris, Read, Shubrick, Kearney and Perry, and seven captains. Poor Ben is shivering. He is not fit to meet a court, and it would be the height of cruelty to bring him before one, just yet. This I shall write to Shubrick to-day.

Ben was very glad to see me, and very willingly listened to my advice. His face does not look amiss, but he tells me he is nothing but nerves. Ben Cooper still, full of fun and joke. Little does he anticipate the blow that is pending over him. I make very little doubt of his being cashiered, though he may be restored to rank but never to command. Putnam tells me very little can be expected from the other side. They are determined, by combination, to force us into a reciprocal law. I fear I shall have to take Bentley's offer. Of course I shall write no more in this form.

I hear that Christine is very thin, so much so as to occasion remarks. Sam Neil is my informant, but thin she is. Yesterday, when Mrs. Yates asked me what Mrs. Cruger's income might be, and I told her about $12,000. per annum, she answered à la Astor—"That all!—I thought it had been much more considerable!"

I have called on Mrs. Laight, without success. Saw her at church, but, as usual, could not catch her eye.

By the way, talked a little with Mrs. Neil about Phil and Di. She thinks there is an implied separation. Says that Di had been suspected of interested motives in marrying, and had a reputation that way early. Thinks there is disappointment. But this is mean.

As yet, nothing offers. "Patience," my good mother used to say, "Patience is what you all want, learn to be patient." I am busy with the work *en attendant*.

Adieu—with my tenderest regards, and another special benediction for Caroline.

Yours most affectionately as ever,

J. F. C.

TO MRS. COOPER, COOPERSTOWN

Globe, Wednesday, Jan. 30th, 1850

Best Beloved,

All your letters have arrived safe. I have been a good deal occupied with Ben Cooper's affairs, the last few days. His family seem to lean on me for assistance, and I give all I can very cheerfully.

To-day I walked all the way to Miss Munro's, to see the Bishop *et Uxor*, but they had gone to pass the day with Harry, who lives in Brooklyn. Ned is here, and Peggy told me he and Joey were to come down and live with her. I took an occasion to tell her how much respect her course had obtained for her, and how generally it was approved of. She seemed gratified, but merely observed how much better it was than to be dependent.

I am likely to fall in the way of invitations again, which by the way I do not want. I have been at Maitland's, but they were out. To-night I shall go up town, though where, I have not exactly decided.

Everybody exclaims at my healthy and youthful appearance. De Kay was here yesterday, and I dined with him. He compliments me highly. He is now quite at his ease, has $3000 a year, and his place on the Island. This is the result of the decision made by Nelson. George's debts exceed $100,000, but his widow has a little left her by old Mrs. Eckford.

The Dr. enquired kindly after you all, particularly Sister Sue. I have a likelihood of getting a small price in England, though a very small one.

This house is nearly empty, and I have it almost to myself.

Tell Sue, Putnam does not cling to his title, but submits to her better judgment.

Yesterday I went through the market, and a sight it was. One man had several thousand dollars' worth of poultry. The beef, best pieces, is only eighteen pence, but very fine beef it is.

I postpone the rest until to-morrow, and shall probably pick up something to tell you this evening.

It seems Miss Prime *would* marry the German, who by the way was not so much enamoured that he could not drive a bargain.

I have gained great renown. We tried the twenty guesses, three gentlemen answering my question. At the twentieth guess I said "It was the suspension Bridge at Niagara." "It was!"

I passed last evening with Mrs. Colden, etc. Tried Mrs. Watts and Mrs. Delafield *en route*, but could not get in.

Did I ever tell you that Mad. de Ponthieu left the Garnetts $20,000, quite unexpectedly to everybody? The Wilkes' got $5000. each, including Mrs. Henry. I do not think there has been any reconciliation, as between the men.

Miss Prime's marriage makes a good deal of talk. "He didn't want to marry her," said George Wilkes' youngest. "Why did he marry her then?" I asked. "She *would* have him." This, I believe, is the true state of the case.

I am to try another literary *soirée* this evening, *chez* Professor Robinson of Eastern memory. He sailed for Europe in the *Don Quixote*, the day we sailed in the *Hudson*. That was nearly a quarter of a century since, my love!

I got a letter from Dickenson this morning, forwarded by you. It is on Ned Myers' affair. I shall send McCracken's play to-day.

There is a little brighter speck for the sale of the new book in England, though it will not amount to much.

I met Cruger in the street yesterday, and he told me Madam and Parson Pepper had come to swords' points. O'Conner has left her case, for she won't pay, and the upshot will be she will return to her husband—in my opinion. He looks as satisfied, however, as if he contemplated no such calamity.

God Bless you all, with tenderest affection.

J. F. C.

FROM WILLIAM CULLEN BRYANT

January 31, 1850

Dear Sir

I am sorry not to find you in this morning, as I went to ask you to go to Mr. Leupp's to-morrow evening, No. 66 Amity Street, where the Sketch Club meet, and where you will probably find some of the members of the old Lunch, Mr. Verplanck, Mr. Durand, and myself certainly, with several others of your acquaintance.

Each member has the right to take any stranger who may be in town, and Mr. Leupp I know would be offended with me if he knew I had seen or written to you, and did not ask you. I hope you will do us all the favour to come.

Yrs truly
W. C. Bryant

J. Fenimore Cooper, Esq.

Globe, Monday, Feb. 4th, 1850

Dearest,

Eighteen or Fifty-eight, it's all the same to me, whereby you see your letter has been received.

To-day, in walking up Broadway, for exercise, I met, very high up, Susan De Lancey going down to Mrs. Laight's. I gave her my arm, and we paid the visit in company. I was let in, and found Mrs. L. in pretty good spirits. I sat an hour with her. The Bishop had called but did not see her.

To-day I had a visit from Gen. Scott and Phil Kearny. They want me to write the life of Stephen. Scott conversed very freely about Mexico.

Yesterday I went to Trinity, and sat with Gil Verplanck. Sam came home with me to dinner. He and Gil live with the two Hobarts. Mary and Walton are in the country.

I heard the whole affair of Greene and his wife from a Rhode Islander last evening. He was too poor to bring her with him, when he came away, but at the revolution he mustered all he could, and sent it to her. Her sister wrote him back that she was dead. It seems, however, that the Pope granted a dispensation, as Greene was a foreigner, and she had married again. Greene put on mourning, and was quite disconsolate, when the consul informed him of the fact.

My fall was this. In passing a new house, coming home from Miss Clarkson's, I put my foot on the edge of a plank, it slipped, and my whole weight came down on the foot sideways. It hurt me excessively, but I hobbled along as far as Cruger's door and went in. They were all out, but I sat there a long time, and then got across to the Globe. I fully expected a sprained ankle. Next day, however, my ankle and foot were well, and have been ever since, while I found I had sprained a muscle in the hip. The last is now well however.

A curious thing has just occurred in connection with Ben Cooper's affair. Shubrick wrote to me that the Secretary was displeased with the last letter he had received from Ben's son, George. George wrote to know in what he had offended, and they sent him an extract from his letter, and one from their letter, to which his own was an answer. He says that he never received one, nor wrote the other! There is a George W. Cooper in Brooklyn, whose letters have come to Geo. H., and it is possible that this Geo. W. has got the letter and answered it—this answer being very much such an one as a man would write who knew nothing about a subject. We shall know in a day or two.

Shubrick will certainly come on. The court is to meet on the 14th. He will stay but a few days, however, I imagine.

You have seen the account of the terrible accident by the explosion of a boiler. I was at the place yesterday (Monday), but we were all kept at a great distance.

To-day (Tuesday) I am to dine with Alfred Pell. This will be my third dinner out, two with Cruger, so you see I am very temperate. The cold weather sets me up. Ben and his wife say I am much thinner than I was, so much so as to strike them both very much. I am thinner, but quite stout enough. I never felt better in my life. Heel quite well, and no more headaches.

Poor Abraham Schermerhorn is dead. He had all sorts of maladies. One lung indurated, asthma, gout, and everything of that nature. His sufferings were hardly to be borne.

The feeling that I anticipated is coming over this market, and we shall see its point, in prices, I think, ere long. There is a menacing cloud over the country, yet most persons look on with indifference.

I must now go and return visits, of which I have a dozen or more to discharge.

With tenderest love to all, and my special blessing to Caroline, I remain just as much yours as when you were sweet eighteen.

J. F. C.

TO MRS. COOPER, COOPERSTOWN

Globe, New York, Feb. 8th, 1850

My dearest Sue,

What has become of you? Your last was dated on the 31st, and this is all I have got for more than a week. Scott wrote to me on the 4th, and I suppose it would have been mentioned had anything occurred. To-day I fully expected one of your kind, warm-hearted letters, but none came.

The Bishop sat with me an hour, yesterday. He does not believe in Jim's drinking. He wishes Paul to take charge of Angevine, and sees no difficulty in making the transfer without expense, except this little stranger might create one. The best way will be to apply to the court.

The Brevoorts gave a farewell ball last night—a fare-well to the house, which has been sold to De Kham.

I have received a very good offer for a new work, and am inclined to accept it, as I should like to write it, and it is quite in my way. The only difficulty is in the mode of payment, which promises to be too distant and insecure, as respects most of the consideration. Still something may come out of it, and it would not materially interfere with other views.

Yesterday I devoted several hours to calls. I saw Mrs. Baker, the Gays, Mr. Van Buren, Bancroft, the Pells, Capt. and Mrs. Breese and various others.

On Saturday I am to dine with Mrs. Brodie, but, on the whole, I have been very moderate in my way of living. I find that wine affects my cheek, and I drink very little, and shall be glad to get back to your unwearied care and the Sarsaparilla. I dined with Alfred Pell on Mon-day, and that is all the out-of-the-house eating I have done in more than a week.

Mr. Russell has been to see me, as have a good many chaps, who are glad to rest their legs in my room. Tom Rochester has been among them. He says it is a slack time with the doctors. Even the itch has given out.

Tuesday.

Thank heaven your letter of Wednesday arrived this morning.

My coming home before March is highly improbable. Apart from the £100 I am now earning, and my engage-ment with Putnam, and thus far with the Robbinses, which may lead to something very useful, there is Ben Cooper's trial on my hands. He looks to me for support and countenance, and I can not fail him. Then Shubrick will pass a week or ten days with me, and we shall have several good tavern dinners together.

Poor Cruger is very much dejected. These Douglases require to be driven into everything that is done. He has been compelled to have a bench warrant issued to commit Wm. D. for refusing to obey the order of the Court, and this he has done with the greatest reluctance. There is also an affair that occupies much of his own and his sister's time, connected with a relative. They are both up-town much of the time, and I see much less of them than formerly. I am not in the secret of the up-town matter, though I suspect its character from Cruger's language.

To-day I dine with the Brodies. Poor Mrs. William-hees is a widow. Her husband died in December, and the news has just reached here. There is romance in real life, for you!

As for my looks and health, there is every reason to be grateful. My feet are nearly well, and I no longer suffer from the easterly winds.

As for my letters, love, I write twice a week, and a little more. You do but half as well.

I had a talk with Mrs. Baker. She says Cally beats Christine all hollow. The last she describes as a bunch of bones—a pretty big bunch, I ween. I called yesterday on Mrs. Watts, but did not get in.

With tenderest love and renewed blessings, I am, as ever,

Most aff. yours,

J. F. C.

Fancy Shubrick and myself running about town at sixty! Hope on—God bless you.

Globe, N. Y., Thursday, Feb. 14th, 1850

My beloved Sue,

Tuesday evening I went to see Mrs. Norris. She was glad to see me, well, and just as formerly, but desperately deaf. Mrs. Henry looks very pretty and Henry thin.

Yesterday Shubrick, Norris, and Stewart all came upon me in a body, and we have scarce separated a moment, except to sleep. In a few minutes we go to the yard. Ben is too ill to be tried, but the court will be detained until next week. Last night we had a naval levee, officers calling on Stewart. Kearny, Byrne, and Breese sat with us until eleven. On Saturday, Shubrick and I dine with Breese, and to-morrow I rather expect with Col. Murray. To-day I think we shall have an *omnium gatherum* here. We are like a parcel of boys, and one laugh succeeds another, one story its predecessor. Ned keeps me in a roar, with a description of African life. He described a public dinner, at which an English officer gave as a toast, "The *fair* sex of Liberia," at which the niggers were infinitely pleased.

Shubrick looks well, is stouter than I am, and is in excellent spirits. Nothing but good will prevails. Norris looks better than I have seen him in years. Poor Dan. I am now going to the yard, write in a great hurry, and will finish on my return.

2 o'clock. Just returned, in a rain storm, from the Navy Yard. We went in a carriage, however, from this house. A very fair court, and every man well known to me. In consequence of Ben's non-appearance, there was a long discussion, which terminated in an adjournment until to-morrow, to enable Ben to put in proof of the state of his health. I shall have to attend, as a matter of course.

The Court will then report to the secretary, and the court will probably adjourn *sine die*. This court will be a good one for Ben, and I regret he cannot be tried by it, for tried he must be, and I am not without apprehensions of the result.

We all dine here, again, to-day, but to-morrow, I think we shall have some invitation to take us out.

Shubrick sends his kindest regards to you all. He looks very well, and is in perfect health. The kindest feeling towards Ben prevails, but—the absurd mistake of the secretary about the letters acts in his favour, though it is a very unpleasant affair altogether.

I have not been surprised at Mrs. Clark's death! her sending for the parson was a proof of failing faculties. Poor woman—her hope is truly in the mediation.

Shall I put a crape on my hat? Dick and his brothers and sister might like it, and it is for the living, and not for the dead, that we do these things.

Give my tenderest love as usual. Tell Susy she shall not be neglected. The proofs will soon come, and the work will be published at the appointed time. My own book moves rather slowly, on account of the interruption. It will be finished, however, in about a fortnight.

Believe me, my darling Sue, as ever yours most truly,

J. F. C.

TO MRS. COOPER, COOPERSTOWN

Globe, N. York, Sunday, Feb. 17th, 1850

My Best Beloved Sue, though the other is very, very much beloved, too—

I dined last evening with Breese. At table was Cunard, who told me that your old friend, Mrs. Murphy, left

Halifax, about ten days since, with a son of some ten or twelve years, in a coaster—that the vessel was wrecked, and both mother and son were drowned, less than a week since. The vessel was lost near Sandy Hook. There is no mistake in the matter, two or three gentlemen at table vouching for the fact.

We had a very pleasant dinner, with a bottle of noble Lachryma Christi. I asked Sam how many I might expect to meet. "Less than the Muses and more than the Graces—let me see—one, two, three, four, five, and you three from the Globe (Morris, Shubrick and myself); yes, you come as the Graces!"

Ben Cooper's matter must lie over. After church, Shubrick and I are to go and see him. Shubrick will remain here some ten days longer. As for myself, I have the book to finish, three weeks' work, and a bargain with the Hartford men on the tapis.

2 o'clock.

Heard Dr. Haight preach a sermon on the respect due the parsons. Last Sunday, it was the respect due the building! So the world wags. After church Shubrick and I went to see Ben. Found him worse than I have yet seen him. Made a call or two on sailor men, and have just got back.

The walk has done me good, for I have eaten too much since our mess was gathered together. To-day, we shall be more moderate.

I have sent half of the new book [*The Ways of the Hour*] to Bentley, submitting to the loss. The Hartford affair, if it come to anything, and I have just got a rather promising letter on the subject, will give a good, old fashioned price at home, and give me time to look about me. As yet, no other opening has offered, though this is the place to cut in when occasions offer. The good time will come.

I saw Mrs. Cruger yesterday. She was quite gracious, as was William, who was with her. I see very little of my neighbours just now, for two reasons, the season, she being of the starving kind, and my companions, who take up all my spare time. Yesterday, however, I was in C.'s office, when young Kane came in. He opened by saying that his mother had been to Park Place, where there had been a great family "Donnybrook." For some time I did not know what he meant, but at last I found out that among these amiable persons, a royal quarrel is termed a "Donnybrook," from the doings of the Irish Fair of that name. It seems that Douglas was so abusive that Mrs. Kane announced her intention never again to enter his house.

As for Cruger, Douglas has appealed from his arrest, and the thing is to be settled to-morrow. I have little doubt that the appeal will be dismissed, when Douglas must pay or go to gaol. He will hardly submit to the last. This matter occupies Cruger so much, I scarce see him, unless for a few minutes in his office.

I am invited to a party at a Mrs. Curtiss', Washington Place, on Tuesday, but can not go (of which I am glad), as Shubrick is not asked. We have agreed to refuse all single invitations.

The weather, under the lee of the houses, is delightful. The sun is bright most of the time, and it really seems like Spring.

Putnam tells me there has been a warm controversy in the English papers touching Copy Rights, in which my name has been freely used. I have not seen it, but shall endeavor to get a sight of it.

Adieu, my excellent Sue. Do not worry. Trust in your

great protector, who will take care of you, and of all that belong to you. Of my tenderest affection you ought to be well assured by this time. When they write to Paul, send him my love, and tell him to visit.

J. F. C.

TO MRS. COOPER, COOPERSTOWN

Globe, N. Y., Feb. 20th, 1850

My dearest Wife,

Your letter of Sunday has just reached me. Better late than never.

Yesterday, Morris, Shubrick and myself dined at an oyster house, and passed the evening quietly in my room, though invited to a ball up town. We pass most of our evenings at home. Shubrick, who has a great deal of wool drawn over his eyes, talks every day at dinner of going to see Christine, and every day *after* dinner is too lazy to budge. He lies down on my sofa and snores like a troop of horse. When he wakes up, however, he is excellent company, and so like himself; and so like old times!

I see the end of my book [*The Ways of the Hour*], thank heaven, and am driving a bargain with my Hartford men. It may, or it may not, end in a contract. If it do, it will be a very good thing. I have sent the sheets of the novel to Bentley, after all.

To-day, Gen. Scott, Com'dr Morris and Shubrick, Judge Oakley and myself dine with Cruger. Since the arrival of Shubrick I have hardly been in the house, this week not once, yet he gives this dinner in compliment to my friends. To-morrow *we* dine with Col. Craven on codfish, in Brooklyn. After that I believe we have no engagement of any sort, and I cannot say I am sorry, for I want to return to my old simple diet. I never was better, and have quite forgotten my heel. Rens. Nelson is below, and I postpone the rest until to-morrow. I suppose the gentleman will bring back from the yard the secretary's decision in Ben's case. They are now trying a sailor for mutiny—an affair of life and death.

Thursday. Our dinner went off well. Scott was prosy and over minute, as usual, but good natured. He is the toughest man in society I have ever encountered. Morris and Shubrick set off the Navy to great advantage. One is constantly tempted to compare Scott's *great* deeds to his *small* talk. His wife was not mentioned. We played bak until eleven, the General appearing quite willing to remain.

Shubrick tells me Augustus Jay has purchased a house in Washington and is living there very prettily. His wife is considered a superior young woman.

Nothing has yet been decided in Ben's case. He is in a bad way, and it is thought very questionable whether he ever gets out.

I shall see Mrs. Myers, and settle that affair myself.

I am deep in the Hartford negotiations, but the result is quite uncertain. I ask $3,000, prompt pay, in addition to some future rights. They do not object to the prompt pay, and are prepared for a liberal price. I have not yet heard how they take the precise sum, which was named only yesterday. It will be a prodigious accession.

I get no news from Paul. Tell him to write to me when his money is out. I trust you will do the same. I have gold enough to carry your hoard to $100 and mine too. That is as much as we ought to keep. But gold is very abundant. One sees it in great quantities toted about.

I have been so much with Shubrick, have seen so little of any one else, the Crugers included, that I have heard nothing new. That unhappy affair of poor Mrs. Murphy is all. The match between young James and Miss Jones is said to be off, and there are difficulties about settlements in the case of her sister and Mr. Fairish. This last is a nephew of Lewis Rogers, and was at Henderson last Summer. He is a Virginian and a tobacco merchant, in a very fair way. I get all this from Cruger.

No decision yet about William Douglas and the gaol.

Old Taylor says that "he don't know the way for states to go out of the Union, but he does know the way to keep them in." They say the old man is very resolute.

Rens. Nelson came to see me yesterday. I suspect he is here on a frolick. He looks thin. There is to be an extra session in April, May, and June, and Mrs. Nelson is to go to Washington.

They call out for breakfast, and as I am caterer, I must go. I trust it's all over by this time, and that your anxiety is removed. God bless you, my Sue, with the same to the children. Tell Susy she shall soon get her proofs.

Adieu, my dearest love. Ever yours,

J. F. C.

TO MRS. COOPER, COOPERSTOWN

Globe Hotel, New York, Feb. 23rd, 1850

My excellent, much beloved Grand *ma*tie

Your letter has just reached me, and I send you back congratulations by the quantity. Give my tenderest love to the mother, and tell her that her conduct does credit to her training. I owe you, my dearest wife, more than I can ever repay you for the care you have bestowed on all our dear children.

Well—you will be grand-*ma*tie, in future, instead of

*mat*ie. It is time we had a lift. My hair grows gray so fast I can see the change.

I believe I forgot to mention the grapes in either of my letters. They are a fresh importation here, coming from Almeria, the port in Spain where I first tasted the delicious fruit. I was there in the *Sterling*.

Shubrick quits me next week, and I am getting to be homesick. I cannot return, however, until *Ways of the Hour* is ready. Putnam wishes to publish by the last of March, and this could not be done through our post office. I must see it out, now I am in for it.

Of course Uncle Paul has been duly notified of his dignity. Give my kindest love to Aunt Susy, and Aunt Impudence, and Aunt Fanny, and congratulate each and all. I write to Fred direct.

The name is an awful consideration. I think the father's the best the child can have, but that is their affair, not ours.

I am sorry to say the Hartford negotiation has fallen through. The money down is the obstacle. I could not undertake what they asked without good assurance of the honorarium. Something else will turn up, though nothing has as yet. I wait for occasions. Heaven be praised—I can make them, if they do not offer.

Shubrick and myself were to have dined with Col. Murray to-day, but he has been called into the country, and begs off until next week. Thursday we dined with Col. Craven, who lives with his son, which son is married to a sister of the young Schermerhorn whom we saw in Paris. The dinner was a good one. Prairie fowls, wild turkey, and venison abound, by means of the rail-roads, and we see them on every table.

There was a very great wedding in the Ascension yesterday. Miss McEvers to a Mr. Tho. Whitlock. I do not know the groom, but the bride is a daughter of Beche McEvers.

Mrs. Brodie told me yesterday that a Mrs. Wetmore appeared at Mrs. Curtiss' party, where I did not go, in a dress that cost, including jewels, $30,000—pretty well for New York. Mrs. Philip Rensselaer comes out this winter in great beauty and great magnificence. In a word, the town is a great arena for the women to show off their fine feathers in.

Mrs. Brodie told me that she was about to move, when she expected a visit from Mrs. Pell. We are to have *the* Brodie again, next summer.

The three letters arrived, and they gave me a terrible fright. One I thought was Dick's hand-writing, and the two others I fancied might be Johnson's or Thrall's. I was so much scared I did not see the "Globe Hotel" on them, in your own dear well known hand. Dick's turned out to be a letter from Nelson, all about the troubles at Washington. Another was to send me a puff, and the third was from an old class-mate to enquire after "Old Rudd."

You may as well open my letters, and see if they are worth paying postage twice. As yet, I have had very few.

With my renewed blessings and most tender felicitations to you all, the mother in particular, I remain

As ever yours,

J. F. C.

TO MRS. COOPER, COOPERSTOWN

Globe, Feb. 24th [25th?], 1850

Both your welcome letters have reached me, dearest

Sue, and glad enough was I to get them. Yesterday, Shubrick and I went to Trinity, and Mrs. Heyward's pew having some interlopers, I put the Commodore in it, and went on to Mrs Laight, to the perfect astonishment of all near her. It was amusing to see the curiosity excited by my being received in her pew. Several spoke to me about it afterwards, saying I was the only person who had been seen in it since her re-appearance at Trinity. After service we put our heads together, and had a little talk, still more to the admiration of the observers, for she has been in the practice of entering and quitting the church without even looking on her old acquaintances. She told me she had heard from Charlotte, and seemed to take an interest in the events.

Morris (the Commodore) told me yesterday that he had seen the proceedings in the Middleton case, for a divorce, and that it was a pretty clear affair. It is now said that the lady's mama was a kept mistress when Middleton married her, and that he was warned of 'er, but married with his eyes open. It is supposed there must be a duel, when the legal proceedings are terminated.

Bishop Hopkins was at Trinity, yesterday, morning and evening, but he did not preach.

I am getting to be homesick, but cannot quit until I have finished and sent off the book. I am now writing the last chapter but three and hope to have the book done next week. When done I may possibly leave it to be finished through the post office, though it will be hazardous and might produce a mistake that would cost me a hundred pounds. On the whole, it will be best to make an end of all I can here.

I am sorry the Hartford affair has fallen through, but it would have been very useless and unwise for me to have given six months of severe labour with an uncertainty of remuneration. I keep an anxious eye about me, but nothing offers as yet. In the good time, I trust we shall not be overlooked. I dare not write as freely as I wish to, on account of the publicity you give my letters.

I crossed yesterday, between churches, with Shubrick to see Ben. He is about the same, relieved from arrest, but, if he gets well, he will doubtless yet be tried. I do not think he appreciates his own danger, either physically or morally. His wife seems an excellent woman, with a good deal of good sense. The children, too, appear very well, and one of the daughters is a very pretty little creature. There is a simplicity about them all that renders them respectable.

Capt. Breese has been here, and I have taken a short walk with him on the battery. I feel all the better for it, and make no doubt that I shall be quite well again, by observing a little moderation in my diet.

Give my kindest love to Caroline, and thank her for the little boy, who, I dare say, will be a great pet.

By the way, open my letters, and see if they are worth sending. As yet, I have received but one, this way, that might not have been spared.

I am pressed with proof sheets, and must conclude with love and blessings to all at home.

Yours most affectionately,
J. F. C.

TO SUSAN FENIMORE COOPER, COOPERSTOWN

Globe, Feb. 28th, 1850

My dear Sue,

I cannot let the occasion pass without expressing to you the great satisfaction I have had in reading the sheets

[*Rural Hours*]. So far from finding them disjointed and tame, they carried me along with the interest of a tale. The purity of mind, the simplicity, elegance, and knowledge they manifest, must, I think, produce a strong feeling in your favor with all the pure and good. I have now very little doubt of its ultimate success, though at first the American world will hesitate to decide.

I shall see that the sheets are sent to England, where I should think its success would be marked. The unfortunate state of the copy right law may prevent your receiving much remuneration, though it must produce something.

Tell your mother I am much better, and begin to feel strong again. I hope to be home in a fortnight, at the farthest—perhaps sooner. My commodores quit me to-morrow. Shubrick has sent a very pretty little present to Master Phinney—*via* his mamma. In return I have sent "Miss May" a small gold pencil, and given the Commodore himself a port-monnaie. The present in my hands consists of a case containing a spoon, knife, and fork, all of silver—the cost $9. The articles are about dessert size. I shall keep them, I think, until I go home.

I have read the sheets twice, and with real pleasure. You have picked up a great deal of information, and imparted it in a very pleasant, polished way.

Adieu, my beloved child—the success of your book is much nearer my heart than that of my own, and I own I am not without hopes for you, while I have little or none for myself.

Give my tenderest regards to your sisters—as for Ma-tie, I shall tell her my own story.

Yours very affectionately,
J. Fenimore Cooper.

Sunday, March 3d, 1850

Beloved,

The bells are tolling for church; Miss Arch. C., or
the "ninety gun ship," as Shubrick and I profanely style
her, has rolled past, on her way to Trinity; little Miss C.,
my *vis-à-vis*, has glided past, on the same journey, and
I—shall stay at home. The wind is east, it snows, and I
am slightly affected in the old way—very slightly, however—my heel and that affection being sensibly better,
by means of the gloves and the sponge. Both are again in
requisition.

I am on the 29th chapter of my book, thank heaven—
that is, in writing—on the 22d in printing. I shall hardly
stay here to finish it.

I was getting homesick when Shubrick arrived. His
presence changed everything, and for sixteen days I had
a very pleasant time of it. We dined out but four times—
twice with Cruger, once with Breese, with Craven. Shubrick dined with Murray, but I was under the weather,
and could not go. Indeed, I go out very little now-a-days,
working in the evenings as well as in the day, in order to
get on. Our mess was very agreeable, and everybody
seemed to enjoy it.

I sent the Commodore's present by express, thinking
it might amuse dear Caroline to see it. I trust you will get
it safe. As the young gentleman is eleven days old to-day,
I presume he makes himself heard.

I have written to Sue to say how much I am pleased
with her book. It is not strong perhaps, but is so pure, and
so elegant, so very feminine and charming, that I do not
doubt, now, of its eventual success—I say *eventual*, for,
at first, the world will not know what to make of it. I

shall do all I can in England, but we cannot expect much there, for any thing, just now. We shall get something, I make no doubt. Let her be at ease—I shall do all I can for her. She has struggled nobly, and deserves success. At any rate she has pleased us, and that is a great deal for so dear a child.

Ask her if I may show some of the sheets to Mrs. Laight. I should like to ascertain their effect.

By all I can learn, Phil and Di's separation is a pretty serious affair.

The Middleton business is going into testimony, and is serious too. Shubrick says that Ingersoll is very cool to Master Harry. I make no doubt it will breed trouble all round, though she still manifests great forbearance and good sense. Young people should not quarrel, they have so much before them—as for old people, they must be fools to allow of any such nonsense. Whom do you think I saw yesterday? Mrs. Wm. Cooper [the widow of Fenimore Cooper's eldest brother]. It was on Trinity Church walk. She either avoided me, or did not see me. I think the first. She turned aside, and got into an omnibus. She looked pretty well; her dress was a rustyish black, but not very bad. Her face very little changed. For a woman of sixty she is well preserved. I did not see her in time to speak to her—nor could I well quit my companions, a party of navy men. I have taken into my head that Lawrence Kearny means to get married again. There is Bolton's widow, the child of his first love; let him lay siege to her, though they do say that a lieutenant is already in the field. Lieutenants are no longer boys. Shubrick says that the Secretary appointed the youngest captain, Long, to a steamer, thinking it might be well to give him employment. Soon after, he was told his young captain had called to pay his respects. He turned out to be a gray-headed old man. Shubrick is very little gray, and except a certain rotundity about the bread basket, I see very little change. He is of about my dimensions, I think. Mary, the chambermaid, protests she likes him vastly, "he is so like me"!

Morris gave me his history one evening that we passed alone together. In 1802, he was put on midshipman's half pay, nine and a half a month. He thought too the navy would be reduced, and felt the necessity of doing something. He kept school within six miles of Coopers-town, on the Burlington road, whipping the cat, just as young Munro did!

There is a good deal of uneasiness felt concerning political affairs, and many think the Union is in danger. If slavery is to be accepted as a regular principle in the constitution, that is to colour everything, I would prefer a peaceable separation were it possible—but it is not possible. The Mississippi is there to prevent it. *Nous verrons*.

Adieu, my best love—my best beloved, though the children are very close on your heels. Supply Paul with money, if he want it. I would send him some, but don't know where to find him.

God bless you all. I must seal my letter to save the mail.

TO MRS. COOPER, COOPERSTOWN

Globe, Saturday, March 9th, 1850

Dearest,

If you want to see me one half as much as I wish to see you all, we shall soon have a happy meeting. I am on the wing for Philadelphia, whither I have sent all my manuscripts—to be home this day week—making an absence of near eight weeks.

I am to dine with Cadwalader on Tuesday, and Geo. Ingersoll and Mary Wilcocks are asked to meet me. Barton too.

Yesterday I dined with Thorn. All very glad to see me—Angeline, Mrs. Thorn, two young daughters and Miss Morris—Mrs. Hamilton's sister.

The dinner was a French Service, on a French table. Every thing excellent, and on a great scale. Two footmen, neither in livery, but both in white gloves. Service quiet, and dinner excellent.

I dined with Dr. Wainwright the day before, marrowbones in Lent. Good dinner.

Bancroft came for me, again, but there are all my dissipations. I have not dined with Cruger lately—only four times in five weeks—and two of those times were with Shubrick.

They are actually ripping up and tearing to pieces this house. I shall not quit it this visit, but, after this, I suppose I must go somewhere else.

Wiley has failed. It is said that Putnam's rivalry has done him much harm. I never was better.—Adieu.—I long to fold you in my arms—and to have a game of chess.

TO MRS. COOPER, COOPERSTOWN

Broadway House, May 22d, 1850

Yesterday, I read the comedy [*Upside Down*] to Burton, the manager, who professed to like it—made very fair suggestions, and accepted it, to be played in about ten days. We have not made any bargain, but he offered me his cheque for $500, with future emoluments contingent on success, if I would let it be announced with my name. He, and not Hackett, is to play Lovel, and he can do it quite as well, if not better.

I am now correcting.

In the sale of my old books, I have as yet done nothing. Stringer evidently wants them, but does not wish to pay my price. I offer them at $3500, but I fancy he hopes to get them for a thousand less. Under other circumstances I should ask $5000, and they are well worth it. I shall do something.

Ogden says he cannot go this Spring, and I must get the cause put off again. As they did this last autumn, I may do it this Spring. I am not sorry, not being in funds for the campaign. I shall have to go to Michigan, notwithstanding, to look after my lots.

Cruger and his wife have compromised. He accepts $20,000 and pays the debts of his relatives with the arrears, receives $1000 quarterly for life, and gives up both houses. He has taken his brother Lewis' house at Saugerties. for the next year, takes his leave of Herkimer next week, and quits the town house by the 1st July. She has had an account published in the *Express*, which is filled with misstatements, as usual. I have not seen Cruger since, but fancy him savage enough.

Mr. Bancroft invited me to dinner yesterday, but I was too busy with Burton to go. I hear from other quarters that My Lord is very desirous of seeing me. David White told Hackett this. I must try and see him to-day. I rather think he dined with Bancroft yesterday. I shirk for my meals, and live rather economically, scarce spending ten dollars a week.

Broadway House, May 26th, 1850

My dear wife,

Ketchum came to see me a day or two since, and was in the midst of some explanations that I fancy he intended should bear on my claims, when My Lord Bishop was announced. I was compelled to beg off for the moment, and to defer the explanations to another time.

The Bishop is very like his father: a small, feeble man, but with the countenance, and particularly with the voice of William Spencer. It seems there are two bishops, brothers, one of Madras, now retired, and this of Jamaica. When we were in Paris this man was a clergyman in Bermuda. He offered to remain there if they would make it an archdeaconry, which was done. Then he was made bishop of Newfoundland, and subsequently of Jamaica. He tells me they talk of making him Archbishop of the Antilles, but he opposes it, as he prefers being in the province of Canterbury, as he now is. He seemed very glad to see me, begged me to call on his wife, and I saw him to a mitred barouche at the door. He means to go to Saratoga, to get his liver rectified.

Burton has not re-appeared. He took the comedy and vanished. I rather think he is getting ready.

I have been to see poor Ben Cooper. He is in his bed, and I should think cannot survive a month. The doctor has told the family to be prepared for the worst. To add to his cares, the Secretary has most thoughtlessly, if not maliciously, put him on furlough, thereby reducing his income one half. She behaves admirably, and I should think has no hope. I have written to the secretary.

You will see by the papers that Cruger and his wife

have compromised. He pays his brother's debts, gives up
the houses, and receives $6000. a year, and a balance of
arrears, amounting to $20,000. Although it was solemnly
agreed, and in fact so entered in the decree, that she was
not to get Henderson until the 10th June, she had some
articles published in the newspapers, as I believe, for they
bear the impress of her veracity, and setting at naught her
own bargain, made only three days before, she appeared
suddenly at Henderson, and demanded admission on the
strength of this decree. John Simpson stood out, and refused to give up without orders. I did not see Cruger
yesterday, but I understood him the day before that he
intends going up to-night, in which case they will meet on
the debatable ground!

The weather is as bad as can be. Three evenings have I
passed with the Delafields, and each has been a storm. I
dine at Taylor's, near Franklin Street, and run down to
Joe's for my cup of tea. The Hosacks live opposite, and
I get a chance at two or three houses in that neighborhood.

The Bishop was to preach in Calvary to-day, but his
congregation will be very small. It is now raining quite
hard. I am afraid, love, it may be snow with you.

I am afraid your eyes are not well, as I have had but
two short notes from you in ten days. Tell Paul to write,
and let me know how Champenois is getting on. I may be
detained here two weeks yet, as I must provide funds.
This week will be the trial week. By the way, there is a
faint hope for the picture, though very, very faint.

They are waiting for my letter, and I conclude with
blessings and the most tender love. I miss our little
morning readings.

TO MRS. COOPER, COOPERSTOWN

Broadway House, May 30th, 1850

My Blessed Sue,

Burton was with me yesterday. He is confident of the success of the comedy, but there is another play in its way, just now. He has had it copied over, and has curtailed according to his own notions. I am to see what he has done to-day.

Ways of the Hour has a curious fate. Many people like it, exceedingly, though it is not a general favorite. The objection is anti-Americanism!

Most tenderly yours,

J. F. C.

TO MRS. COOPER, COOPERSTOWN

New York, June 3d, 1850

My best beloved,

I am now on my way to poor Ben Cooper's funeral. He died early on Saturday, perfectly calm, and conscious of his state, and able to converse. He sent for his old friend Capt. Stringham, on whose arrival he stretched out his hand and said—"I'm dying, Stringham—God bless you." In five minutes he was dead. He is to be buried at three at Greenwood, with military honors. I am asked to attend, as a relative. I have no doubt that the secretary's inconsiderate conduct had a great influence on his fate.

I am negotiating about the books, and about the comedy. Nothing done as yet, but something in view. I scarce know how it will terminate. I am now near three weeks from home, and nothing, or very little done. I could do my part of all I have to do in one day, but others must be got up to the striking point. I hope for the best. After a storm there must be a calm.

Cruger has resigned Henderson. His wife behaved like a crazy woman—broke into the house—cut all sorts of capers—until he appeared, when she shrank into her shell, leaving him to regulate everything. Mrs. Hamilton is here, looking ill, they tell me, for I have not been there since her arrival.

Last evening I passed with A. Pell and his Scotch wife, and the evening before at the Bakers'. Christine is in Kentucky.

I shall send you a copy of the *Herald*, containing the case of Mrs. Sallie Lawrence, who is the lady that her husband advertised. Old Kentuck took fire at the indignity, and a law was passed that came quite near "enacting" a separation, as Lovel would say.

Sue is going the rounds of the papers, taken from Bentley's advertisement, but it is of no consequence, as the authorship could not be concealed. Putnam's whisper to the auctioneer let the cat out of the bag. My play has got out, in the same manner.

Be of good cheer, my beloved Sue. Ever most sincerely and gratefully yours,

J. F. C.

FROM W. E. BURTON

June 5, 1850

Dear Sir,

As it seems impossible for me to hit the moment of your leisure, owing to the occupation of every hour of my time (being my own stage manager, and having all the out of-doors business to attend to), I trouble you with this letter, to settle if possible the two points mentioned in your note.

I assure you I did not mention the possession of your comedy to any one. I believe Mr. R. Griswold spoke of it in the presence of Mr. Fuller, of the *Evening Mirror*, who gave the first public notice of the fact. I promised you that I would not mention it, and I kept my word.

I have been in the habit of paying by the night for all new pieces played at my theatre, and will do so now, if you prefer it. But I am inclined to be more liberal to you than to any other author who has yet favored me, as I hope to receive a 5 act comedy from your pen for the next season. Please to bear in mind that our prices of admission are but half of the old Park Standard, and that actors' salaries are higher than ever, making a manager's expenses more and his receipts less. Nevertheless, I propose for you to draw upon me for two hundred and fifty dollars when you please, leaving further payments to be determined by its rate of success.

I have employed Mr. C. Bass, a sterling actor, for the part of M'Social, and believe him capable of doing all we can desire with it. I purpose producing the comedy on Thursday, 13th June—to-morrow week, positively.

What shall we call it? *Upside Down?*

I am, my dear Sir,

Yours, very truly

W. E. Burton

J. F. Cooper, Esq.

FROM JAMES H. HACKETT

14 Wall St., N. York, June 28, 1850

My dear Mr. Cooper

You did not ask me (nor perhaps do you expect me) to report to you the reception by the Audience of yr. comedy. Briefly then, I was at Burton's its first night and saw the whole (from the rising of the Curtain to the going down of the same upon the 3d act) of the play. The first act told exceedingly well, the second began pretty well but grew heavy towards the close, and the third act dragged very heavily until the *dénouement* at the conclusion surprised the attentive into warm applause, which awoke and carried along with them in expression, those who had lapsed into indifference respecting the result.

The dialogue was as effective and smart as I can remember, but I will not go into detail now;—referring you to the *Albion* of last Saturday (22d), which gives a very fair report of its reception, and also reasons for its not proving more decidedly successful, wherein I concur generally. If you do not take, nor can find *The Albion* in your vicinity, and will so advise me, I will get it for you and transmit.

The theatre was only moderately filled the first night, implying a want of curiosity in the Public which surprised me; especially as I thought that the things which had preceded it were so many times repeated, they must have become stale and *novelty* be relished. I was well pleased with yr. essay, and Burton said, though yr. piece had not proved attractive, he did not regret the bargain, which made him Yr. acquaintance and notable as a manager "encouraging *Amer*. Dramatic productions." He observed that he withdrew it after the 3d (or 4th) night, because his "receipts dropped down to under $100—less than half his average before and after the event."

Your piece was exceedingly well acted as well as suitably cast.

In haste, but Yrs. faithfully,
Jas. H. Hackett.

P.S. The enclosed was cut from the *Express*, the only paper, besides the *Albion*, which said as much concerning it.

Enclosure.

Burton's—A new American Comedy, written by a popular author, called *Upside Down, or Philosophy in Petticoats*, was produced last night. It shows up Socialism beautifully. Horace Greeley will of course not like it. The Social lecturer (Bass) and the Social female philosopher (Mrs. Hughes) are great characters. Burton, who as Richard Love, is the antidote to the poison, is capital. He is the grand exponent of the humbug. There is a scene in which he is wooed by a she-Socialist that is screamingly delectable. The piece is altogether well cast and played. It possesses many tit-bits that bring down the applause in shouts, and its only fault is being upon the whole a little too conventional or closetty, a fault that will be corrected by judicious curtailment tonight, and then the comedy of *Upside Down* will be right side up.

TO AN UNKNOWN PERSON

Hall, Cooperstown, August 21st, 1850

Sir,

Never having seen the publication of Mr. Barnum, to which you allude, I can give no opinion of its accuracy.

I know nothing of such a man as Enoch Crosby, never having heard his name, until I saw it coupled with the character of the Spy, after my return from Europe.

The history of the book is given in the preface of Putnam's edition, where you will probably find all you desire to know.

Respectfully yours,

J. Fenimore Cooper.

The original of this letter is attached to a little book entitled *The Spy Unmasked, or Memoirs of Enoch Crosby, alias Harvey Birch, The Hero of Mr. Cooper's Tale of the Neutral Ground* (Second Edition, 1831), edited by H. L. Barnum, and was evidently written in answer to an inquiry from the owner of the book.

TO MRS. COOPER, COOPERSTOWN

Broadway House, Sept. 14th, 1850

My Dearest Sue,

I have seen Putnam. He says everybody praises *R. H.* [*Rural Hours*] and that cordially. Alfred Pell told me that he attributed a remark of mine, made last winter, that it was one of the sweetest books ever printed, to a father's weakness, but he now admitted the truth of what I then said. Bryant, he added, was of the same opinion.

The fine edition is not *yet published*. It is so nearly sold *to the trade*, however, that Putnam admitted to me that he should have to print another edition, say by next month. The small edition is selling well, and will be reprinted in about a month. The sale is quiet, not with any rush, but very even and good. This is what the trade tells me, too. The sale is likely to continue for years.

I shall write to Graham to offer him the autobiography. My price will be $50. If he decline, I shall then offer it to the rival magazine, Sartain's.

I saw Stevenson, who insists that he has not got my letter. He was glad to see me. He had a plate for me one day, and the governor another. Cruger called and seemed disappointed at not finding me.

I met Amariah this morning, and he had been at the fair too. He says Mrs. G. told him A. was resolved to marry S. If such is her determination, the sooner they are married the better.

I have been amused with one circumstance touching "Jenny" [Jenny Lind]. Her original bargain was to stay a year. Within a few days of *her arrival* it was changed so that she might return to Europe whenever she pleases. Out of all doubt, her heart failed her, after seeing the sort of persons who crowded around her! She is very much liked, nevertheless.

I think, my love, you need give yourself no concern about the S. & T. affair, which I shall get settled in some form or other, next week. I have seen Worth, and he is content.

I suppose the all important organ will be with you about the time you answer this. Do not forget to let me know how it is received. It will be your Jenny Lind.

By the way, A. Pell tells me the prices here are the common London prices. He paid two guineas a seat when last abroad.

My love to all, keeping a large slice for yourself.

Most tenderly your h——

J. F. C.

TO MRS. COOPER, COOPERSTOWN

Broadway Hotel, Sept. 19th, 1850

My beloved Sue,

Right and left I hear of *Rural Hours*. I am stopped in the street a dozen times a day to congratulate me. The price of the fine edition is $7, Putnam making from one to two dollars a set at retail, and from three to four at wholesale. It will be the presentation volume of the season. I can see that Putnam expects to sell some eight hundred or a thousand of them.

I went to see Mrs. Morris last night. She was well,

and had just returned from a wedding at the Sheriff's old place, at which the clan Morris was assembled. One of the Zabriskies marries Wm. Morris' last daughter. Henry told me they had sold about two fifths of the Commodore's farm for one hundred thousand dollars, enough in hand to secure the purchase. The farm altogether will bring double that sum, making the two sons independent without counting their mother's property. The improvements here are wonderful. They build chiefly brown free stone, and noble edifices of five and six stories, with a good deal of ornamental pretension.

The town is beginning to fill. Bessie Middleton quit Saugerties Monday, I heard last evening, and after passing two or three weeks at Flatbush, I fancy, goes to Newport for the Winter, her husband proceeding south, to look after the rice. I hear she takes all Cruger's servants, from which I infer he will go into lodgings for the Winter, and his sister will go with Mrs. Hamilton. I may run up and see them for one day, Cruger being much disappointed at not meeting me at Albany. This is not a settled thing, however, my business just now being to look after the main chance.

I sat five times for lithographs, yesterday, and with vastly better success than before. The pictures are all very like, and very pleasing. I am to have one, which will fall to your lot, as a matter of course.

Stewart is making a palace of a store. He takes in the whole front of the block on Broadway, with fifteen windows in front, and all of marble.

With tenderest regards to all, I remain as ever

Yours most tenderly,

J. F. C.

Broadway Hotel, Sept. 22nd, 1850

My dearest Wife,

Last evening I passed with the Hosacks. Mrs. Phil Church is staying with her daughter, and we had a long chat. Now, what do you think she told me?—

Mrs. Romayne had so often enquired after Peter Cruger that it reached his ears. Thereupon he wrote to her. She answered kindly, and invited him to come to England. He answered that he had not the means. She replied by sending him a remittance. All this he told John, his son, who gave him the needful, and off he went. It seems that Mrs. Romayne has some $3000 a year, and, in *her* opinion, on this they ought to be able to live. The upshot is that Peter Cruger and Mrs. Romayne are married—he, at the ripe age of seventy-six, and she some seventy or more. "Isn't it shocking!" exclaimed Mrs. Laight to me, after church yesterday. "No, it's only ridiculous." I hear that they are to come home, though she is undecided whether it shall be now or in the spring. She has very few left to come to.

I am going to Cruger's for one day. I can do nothing here until after Friday next, and he has written me such a letter that I cannot well avoid the visit. On Thursday I shall be back here. I hope to return home early next week.

I sat with the judge an hour yesterday, and found John there. "An old A—— is a hog," is a byeword among us. We laughed a great deal.

Of course you will hear that I have sent Sue $50 for her article. It has been at very good interest for the last three years.

I have just seen a very favourable notice of Sue, in a

magazine called *The Lady's Companion*. It says that she fills a niche of her own, and ranks already with the Haworths, etc.

Phil Church is losing his memory, De Zeng tells me. She seems quite as gay as ever, though every trace of beauty is gone. Her daughter is quite pretty.

My French letter was from Michiewitz. He tells me that Mad. Marlay is just dead—that he often heard of us through her—*how*, I cannot say. His object was to get my interest in favour of a German artist, as he says, of uncommon merit.

½ past 2 P. M. I have just been to see Mrs. Laight, to whom I took one of the fine copies, just to look at. I was induced to accept her $7 for it, and I have handed the money to Putnam. The last tells me that he shall publish in ten days. His principal clerk told me to-day that the book was selling steadily, and he seemed to think more had been sold than I had supposed. The demand continues, at all events, and thousands will sell as the book becomes known. I have seen two or three English notices, and I send you an extract from one, though I fancy you have seen it. *Bentley's Miscellany* has a very good notice.

Mrs. Laight thinks Mad. de Gourlay is at the bottom of this marriage. She saw Mrs. Romayne at Bath, and the General is very intimate with old Peter. Mrs. L. spoke of Mad. de G. in language that surprised me. Called her "that woman" and says she had not been near *her* these four years.

I have not seen Fred, and have been a little disappointed at not hearing from you to-day. I daresay all is right, however, and I send love as usual.

Most tenderly yours,

To *you*.   J. F. no Old Bo.

TO MRS. COOPER, COOPERSTOWN

New York, Sept. 30, 1850

It is amazing how people spend their money. Twenty or thirty dollars to hear Jenny are paid by those who live from hand to mouth.

Michiewitz speaks of Mad. Marlay's death.

FROM WASHINGTON IRVING

Putnam's Desk, N. Y., Nov. 11th, 1850

My dear Sir,

I had hoped to send you by this time Mr. Crisp's book, as Mr. Putnam had undertaken to write to Messrs. Ballard, Lee & Co. on the subject. He forgot his promise, however, until reminded of it this morning. He has just written a letter in my presence, and I trust the books will arrive in due season; when I will see that they are forwarded to their respective destinations.

Permit me to congratulate you on the great and well merited success of your daughter's delightful work. I hope it will encourage her to the further exercise of her pen.

yours very respectfully

Washington Irving

J. Fenimore Cooper, Esq.

TO MRS. COOPER, COOPERSTOWN

Broadway Hotel, Friday, Nov. 15th, 1850

My dearest wife,

I have been obliged to come to this house, *faute de mieux*. I left Paul well, *tant soit peux* melancholy, I thought, for the want of tobacco, but in good heart, and every way equal to his work. I have no concern on his account.

Julia and Miss Thomas came down with me, to hear Jenny Lind. "Have you heard Jenny Lind?" "How do you like Jenny Lind?" are the questions that supplant "Fine weather to-day" and other similar comprehensive remarks.

I am patiently waiting for the *Lake Gun*.

This morning I met Tom Shankland. He told me that Isaac [Isaac William] died about a year since. He did not know what had become of his family. They had lived quite near him, but have disappeared. I suspect this is true, as it accounts for my not hearing from him for so long a time. This closes the history of William's children!

Ned is well. De Zeng is still here. Old Peter is not yet married, but the affair is postponed until Spring, when the bride and groom will return to America. They wish to prolong the delightful delusions of courtship. I hope they may be as happy as we have been, and love each other as much forty—days, after their union, as we do forty years. God bless you, my love.

J. F. C.

TO MRS. COOPER, COOPERSTOWN

Broadway Hotel, Friday, Nov. 22nd, 1850

Dearest,

We had a very agreeable party yesterday, Bryant, Dr. Bethune, Prof. Anderson, Alfred Pell, and myself.

The Pells went out in twenty-two days, and he will be back about the last of next month. Bethune has just returned, having been at Berlin, Vienna, Paris, Dublin, etc., etc., within the last three months!

I have not heard Jenny, and to-night is her last. Mrs. Field has sent me an At Home for to-morrow, to meet Jenny, but I do not think I shall go. The furore increases and she is said to grow better and better. Many, however, express themselves disappointed.

Beresford and I breakfast together, he occupying the next room to mine. McIntosh has had another operation without success. Beresford's sister was operated on yesterday for cataract, and can see. Dr. Elliott, however, was not the man. So long as you can read without spectacles, my love, it will be hardly worth while for you to undergo the pain and anxiety of an operation.

Great news from Unadilla! Harry Munro, who is dealing in Westchester lands, tells me that so great is the rise that Angevine will be dog cheap at $6,000. He thinks it can be made to bring $9,000. That building sites are up, and going up, is true, but that we shall reach the latter figure is not very probable. Still, it is worth the trial, and I shall give this matter my attention.

I wish you could have heard Bryant last night on *R. H.* "Yes," said I, "it is a nice book." "Pooh!" he answered—"it is a *great* book—the greatest of the season, and a credit to the country!" Was not my heart glad!

My fingers are the same, but I use them without much difficulty. In other respects, well. I lay in a warm bath an hour yesterday, thinking it might warm my fingers, but they were cold, even in the bath. The feet begin to sympathize, but walking keeps them in friction, and sometimes they are in a glow. I wear cotton as yet, but use thick boots.

As for returning, I have done nothing as yet. I may come home for ten days and return here, to conclude. Putnam has asked me down to Staten Island to pass the night and then I shall have the best opportunity for making my bargain. He told me yesterday he had sold about 500 of the fine edition, and expected to sell 1000 by Christmas.

I hear surprisingly little about a Bishop. I lean towards Wainwright, who will be decided enough when he is made Sixtus.

As for Paul, give him health, and he will do well enough.

Doubt seems to exist about old Peter and Mary of the haystack. Her friends evidently hope it will not come to pass—she has about $3,000 a year in rents, with reversion to her heir, settled by her father. So Peter must take good care of her.

The Germans are driving the Irish from the field. Even the groceries are passing into the hands of the Germans and beer is supplanting whiskey.

The growth of the town is incredible. Brooklyn has 120,000 souls; Williamsburg 30,000 and Manhattan 550,000, it is said.

As for Harry, I shall get along with him, well enough, I doubt not. I can toss him as high as any one, and tumble him about as hard. I am glad you have him to console you in my absence.

With tenderest love to all,

Ever your,
J. F. C.

TO MRS. COOPER, COOPERSTOWN

Monday, Nov. 25th, 1850

My precious Sue,

I fully intended writing yesterday, but I rose late, and Frank March came to take me to Church, while I was at breakfast. We went to hear Hawks. When up town, they made me dine there, and I took the opportunity in the evening of visiting Georgianne and Susan De Lancey (who are neighbors). It was near eleven when I got home.

This afternoon I go with Putnam to Staten Island, to return in the morning, to-morrow I dine with Leupp, Gideon Lee's son-in-law, and next day, high ho, for a new bishop. Many of us will go for Wainwright. We hope to defeat Seabury, at least.

Susan says that Powell's estate will bring more than $100,000. She and her sister sold for $300 land that has now sold for $30,000.

I am finishing off the *Lake Gun*, which earns the $100 that lies untouched in my trunk. I should like to work at this rate the year round. I believe this miscellaneous writing pays the best, just now.

Mrs. Field gave a great party on Saturday, at which Jenny Lind was present. I was asked, but did not choose to go five miles into the country, of a cold evening, in order to look at a singer of no personal charms.

I am told all our Cooperstown folk are in raptures. I cannot consent to pay $30 for a concert, and they are welcome to their ecstatics.

I dined with Dr. Wainwright on Saturday, when important matters were settled. To-day I met Joe White, on his way to see Sir Henry Bulwer, whom he had invited me to meet on Staten Island on Wednesday. I cannot go.

Constance Brevoort is to be married to-morrow. Everybody is going to her reception. I have not yet seen Christine, and think Mr. Griffin might come to see me.

Balch has resigned his church, and goes to Philadelphia, where he is to be some sort of professor.

Georgy says Hal is a very fine boy—and cousin The says he is the first child he ever called on formally. As for his Schottishes and Polkas, let him practice them well, as I shall certainly expect him to exhibit for my amusement. I shall pay him high honours; sharpen my razor well, go over my face twice, and kiss as gently as I know how—pretty rough at best.

Susan says the Dicky Haight who is making such a figure with his travelled wife is a Rye man, and an old admirer of Caroline's. Do you know any thing of such a person?

I must get ready for the island. Tenderest love to all—a kiss for Harry, regards to Fred, and what is to be done with his $8?

Very tenderly yours,

J. F. C.

TO MRS. COOPER, COOPERSTOWN

Saturday evening, Nov. 30th, 1850

Thank Heaven, my dearest Sue, I can now sit down and write you a good long letter. After seven ballotings and two conferences, the Convention adjourned, *sine die*, without doing anything. This movement was unnecessary, and came from Trinity, which was afraid that Wainwright would succeed; and he would, had we taken two more ballots. Spencer, who is another Trinity in his way, was bent on Williams. The mistake was in putting the matter in the hands of men who were carried away by faction. Well, the struggle is over, having cost me three days, and almost as many nights.

I have made my proposals to Putnam, and Monday we shall conclude. I gain something for Sue, but not as much as I could wish. Still her two books will bring her a handsome sum. I sell the new one for three years—at least that is my proposal, though Putnam thinks, if he pays for the plates, and gives them up, that he ought to have their use for five years. We think of making the book a

.75 book, and of giving the author 12½%. This would make copy money to the amount of a little more than nine cents a copy. 5000 copies would give more than $500. Then there would be the plates, and all the subsequent sales.

My own matters will be more simple, and will yield better. So would Sue's, if she could work up her subject to a dollar book.

I saw Mrs. Maitland and the finery to-day. Everything is ready, and Fan will scarce know herself, she will be so fine. The silk dress is really rich, and the other extremely genteel. The hat will give every possible chance to Fan's nose. I have changed the boots—shall get the gloves, and order the oysters on Monday.

Mr. Battin, in common with all the clergy of the North, has been detained over Sunday. We voted 177 parishes at the last vote. In our former struggles we voted only 80 or 90.

Harry Jones was in Convention, looking fat and well. He seemed pleased at my praise of his son, De Lancey.

I went to see Mrs. Yates to-day, and Josy, Peggy Munro, etc. Josy calls herself well, but to me she looked ill. Will was there, just as laughing a rogue as ever.

I think, should the weather be cold, it may be well for John Collar to kill the porkers at the farm, the old hog excepted. This might be done Tuesday or Wednesday, so that I might get some of the tender loin, etc. Should I be detained, however, later in the week, do not give away plucks, livers, and tender loins. I do not intend this year to take out more than half of the spare ribs, leaving the rest in to be cut up with the pork, which is sweetest next the ribs. Perhaps Wood might be consulted. Let him cure *two* sides of one of our pigs, in bacon.

Sunday morning.

On the whole let the pigs live until my return.

There is an expectation of trouble at the South this Winter; I am not afraid of it. Uncle Sam has a long arm and a strong grip, and an exhibition of his power may be necessary to make certain persons respect him.

Tenderest regards to all—spank Harry for me.

Yours most affectionately,

J. F. C.

I am going to Trinity and shall see Mrs. Laight.

FROM W. B. SHUBRICK

Court Room, Washington Navy Yard,

4th Jny., 1851

My dear Cooper—

Your letter with the disjunctv. dates of 3d and 25th of December of the last year, was received last week, and I take the first moment of leisure from business and frolicking to offer to you and yours the good wishes of the season—from the bottom of my heart I desire for each and every one of you all that can contribute to your happiness here and hereafter. I am much concerned at the account you give of your health; you have, no doubt, the best medical advice, and it would be presumptive in me to offer any, but I may *suggest* that as much exercise as you can take *without fatigue*, with moderate feeding and a glass of brandy and water at dinner, might be found the best treatment in your case—ask your Doctor.

We are deep in Jones's case—the charge for executing the two men in California was thrown out by the court, on the ground that the civil laws of the U. S. not having been extended over California, the court martial was rightfully held, and besides if it should be found that the court erred in coming to this conclusion and the men were hung without authority of law, it would make a case which would not come before a court martial but would belong rightfully to the civil courts. The case is bad enough without that, but we are not yet through with the testimony on the part of the prosecution—we have had nothing yet on the part of the defense.—I am not among those who have had fear of a dissolution of the Union in consequence of the agitation of the slavery question—what could South Carolina and Mississippi, or a half a dozen states combined, do against the other States? The North will have to execute the fugitive slave law *in good faith*, and the South must take care to keep as many of their darkies at home as possible. The North cannot do without the South, the South cannot do without the North—they must kiss and make friends. Holmes told me when he came on that he considered the people in Charleston (the majority) mad, but he had just lost his election, for coming out as a Taylor democrat, he said the life of no man was safe who showed himself a friend of the Union in Charleston, and that he had thought of writing an address to his fellow citizens on the subject before he left home, but he feared it might be attributed to pique at the loss of his election.—He intends to seek his fortune in California.

Mary has been writing to Charlotte and was charged with all our congratulations and good wishes to Fanny. I renew to her mine separately—may she be as happy as she deserves. Could I say more?

You don't know what you say when you talk of comparing your grandson with our May—why, *she* is the wonder of Washington, and we talk of sending her to the World's fair in London—her grandparents, who of course are the most impartial judges in the case, are firmly of opinion that there can be nothing like her in this or any other country—so you must give up.

W. B. Shubrick

TO "SAIDEE"

Hall, Cooperstown, January 18th, 1851

Glad enough was I to receive your letter, my dear Sayd, since it let me know that you were all well and disposed to be happy. I did think of writing to you at the commencement of the year, but I have not been well, my child, and have been trying to get things right again. I am just fit to go to Mrs. Hake's party, if Hake be her name—Heaven bless the woman—the gentility of my shape enabling me to thread a crowd as you would a needle. I have lost twenty-two pounds, and some persons think it an advantage. I can see the old countenance returning, by means of the glass. It looks like the face of an old acquaintance, set off with gray hairs! For the last, there is no help. You can not imagine how intellectual I look. All the burly character of the face is gone, and I come out a poet once more.

I was shocked to learn the deaths of Messrs. Bandy and Kearny—They were related to my wife, and married relatives, and at one period of my life I lived in great intimacy with the last, as a country neighbour and connection. Until I got your note, I did not know what had taken him off. It was so recently that I saw both, and that together too, that I was shocked when I learned the facts.

Sunday, and a clear, cold day.

Last night I got a letter from Cousin Henry, who sends me lots of cancans from town. A skrimmage between *The*

Bristeds. Why, what does the man mean? His mamma flogged her second husband after forty-two rounds. He—old Bristed—failed to come to time for the reason that his neck was under a window sash, while she "fibbed" him to her heart's content, using one of his crutches. I believe that the particular punishment she inflicted is termed, in the language of the ring, a "cross"—but cousin Henry will explain it all to you if you ask him. "Patty cake, patty cake" and "pick it and pick it" and "toss it in the oven, etc." But Doreen is looking grave, and here is her health in hard cider. And now that the fun of the piece is over, let us turn to the sentiment.

So Woodbury Langdon has been stabbed? What does the lady who was about ready to give up the ghost say to this? A woman whose husband has been stabbed by a jealous Italian has a right to live, and will live, and her looks belie her. Old Astor too, instead of a library, should have endowed a "Cock-pit" and a "hospital" attached.

My daughter staid but a very short time in town. I believe she saw no one but a few relations, some very old friends, and half a dozen pals. It is odd, but she had Jenny Lind's parlour, and was directly *vis-à-vis* to cousin Nina. Fan is again absent with her husband, having gone with him into Columbia County for a fortnight. She seems very happy, and that is all I care for. Seven children, to be sure, is a large allowance to begin with, but she has ever loved them and treated them as her own.

Little Jane, one of Dick's daughters, is now staying with me. I told her last evening that this marriage made a change in our position. Formerly she was my great niece, but now my daughter had married her father it altered the affinity altogether. "What am I then?" said Jenny, half ready to cry. "An esteemed friend, my dear; that is your

name in future, in this family." Jenny protested, but I
maintained my ground. Shortly after, Willie Cooper,
seven years old, pointed to his sister's profile, thrown by
the lamp on the wall, and said, "There's the esteemed
friend's picture."

My grandson is a prodigy. He passes two or three
hours here every morning, and I could no more think of
quitting home while he remains than you would think of
marrying young Bristed.

In the first place, he manifests the love for music that
distinguishes his father's family. He cannot stand alone—
eleven months to-morrow—but put him on a chair, with
a hold of the back, and play a lively tune, and he will
dance minutes at a time. He commences slowly at first,
with a single bending of the knees, moving up and down.
Then his feet move until he jumps and laughs and squeals
with all his heart and soul. Stop the lively air, and he
stops dancing—change the tune to a song, and begin to
sing, he tries to sing too, standing still the while. His delight in the dancing reminds me of the niggers, and I am
sometimes afraid he will be taken up for a fugitive. Alas,
my dear Saidee, what are we all coming to? Hamilton
advises a southern convention, and then to come and fight
us. Will is a moderate man. Separate we cannot, yield so
far as to make any new bargain with guarantees for slavery we will not, and fights must come. Which will get the
best of it, think you? We shall know, after the war. I
can tell you who it will not be—not the chap with his
neck under the window sash.

This marrying does leave sad vacancies at the table
and around the hearth. Paul has flitted, leaving only four
of us, at a table where the same seven faces had been so
long seen. I am horribly afraid for Bend Seathee. She is so

pretty, and good, and engaging, and all that, I fear some fellow will be after her. There is no one here *she* would marry, but they send her documents from the Smithsonian Institution, franked by M. C.'s, and make so much fuss about her, I expect a special ambassador every day.

I hope you are passing your time pleasantly. Tell Doreen to tap the other barrel, as I shall not be in town in time to help. I am not certain I shall ever see New York again. There is no place for me to stay, now. Above Chamber I will not come, below there is no room. I have a great mind—by the way, Sayd, I have got an invitation to a party. Mrs. Norrie, my old friend Mrs. Norrie, has sent me a card. I dare say Anne Margaret Van Horn is at the bottom. If she be, what a long way down it must be! I may attend that party, as an acknowledgment of the civility.

Do not expect a valentine from me. My heart is as cold as my feet. I am not gouty, can walk, run, jump, do anything that men at my time of life can do with their feet, but warm them. Depend on it, my dear, I am not a thousand leagues from the land of spirits. How long shall I be remembered after my name is called? My children will never forget me, nor my wife, but little Harry will, most other persons will. You will, I am afraid; that old Saidee will come along, and then you will forget all your flirtations, sentimental, experimental, and ail-imental. Ours is ail-imental, which is the reason I give you my pulse to feel. To think of that fellow Bristed's cuffing his wife! Cuffs are in fashion, but the women use them.

Well, my dear, I have used up all my paper, all my sentiment, all of your patience, and no small share of my wit. Everything, indeed, but my regard for you, of which

there is enough still to make a railroad from here to California, were it of iron. Being of something more precious
we will keep it between us, each using it as may be convenient, and see which will come to the bottom first. I'll
engage it will not be I.

Adieu, my dear, with regards in Clinton Place and
elsewhere. Twenty guesses. You burn—you are right—
I mean Miss Louisa Sayd.

Yours very affectionately,
J. Fenimore Cooper.

FROM W. B. SHUBRICK

Washington, 17th March, 1851

My dear Cooper

Soon after my last letter to you, I was called suddenly
to Charleston by the alarming illness of my sister M^{rs}
Henry. I left this on the day after the termination of
Jones's trial, and the accounts that I had received had
been such that I had little expectation of finding my
sister alive. She was better however when I reached her
house, and when I left Charleston on the 26th ul^{to} her
physician was of opinion that she was slowly but surely
recovering, and I have had good accounts since.

You have seen the result of Jones's trial and his address "to the public," in the *Union.* He has done himself
no good by the course he has taken: much sympathy was
felt for him at first, but now the opinion, in private cir-
cles as much as in the Navy, seems to be that he did not
get more than he deserved—he takes the whole matter, as
well he may, much to heart and threatens [to withdraw?]
from the public stare.

I cannot learn what it is the intention of the Department to do in the case of Vorhees; it will be very extraor-

dinary if they should allow him to go unnoticed after convening a court for the trial of Ben Cooper for the same offense. Vorhees left his command without permission; his excuse, I understand, is sickness, but it could not have been extreme, for he was in Washington during my absence, looking *"pretty good for him."* I have heard, but not from a source in which I could place much reliance, that the Secretary is hesitating whether he shall bring him to trial or dismiss him without trial. I hope this is not true; no officer should be dismissed without trial, except for conduct combining great *moral* with military delinquency—in such a case public opinion would bear the execution out, but not otherwise.

There is a deep feeling of disaffection to the Union in South Carolina, and it is strongest in the most influential class, the wealthy planters. I was in Charleston when the election took place for members to the State Convention which is to assemble in 1852, to settle the question *finally*. The result was mortifying to the democrats—the city, which has upwards of 3000 voters, polled only about 800, and some men who are not ultra in their sentiments were elected—they were much pleased with an extract, published in their papers, from your answer to the New York invitation.

Stewart, Morris, Perry, Breese and myself are still at work on the revision of the Laws, Rules and Regulations, etc., etc., for the Government of the Navy—I think we shall be able to mend matters a little if Congress can be prevailed upon to carry out what we recommend, but it is difficult to get that *enlightened* and *patriotic* body to attend to any thing but the dirty *logrolling* necessary to carry on the business of President making. My new house is getting on well. I shall begin to plaster next week, and

I hope to get into it early in July—every one tells me
that I have done well in building it—it is 46 feet front
by 42 feet deep—not of course to compare to "the Hall,"
but a respectable house for a city and for a poor man.

We are well—my wife for the last fortnight in Baltimore, and Dr. Aymer in Pennsylvania—Mrs. Aymer
keeping house for me.

I have sent you recently the new Army and Navy
Registers—we are now at 5 P. M. in the midst of a N. E.
snow storm which commenced some time in the last
night.—Mary unites with me in love to all with you.

as ever
W. B. Shubrick

Tell me, *when you write, particularly* how you are.

TO MRS. COOPER, COOPERSTOWN

Albany, 12M., 19th March, 1851

My dearest Sue,

The ride to the Mohawk was comfortable enough, the
waiting for the cars irksome, and the cars the easiest I
ever rode in. Paul was at the station, and I went up to
Congress Hall in the carriage. At nine I supped, and
ten retired. Paul gave me his bed and room, and here
comes a great secret that I must now reveal.

Charley Clark [Charles C. Clark, at one time treas-
urer of the New York Central Railroad] has had the
small pox, of the confluent sort. He has been ill two
months. Of course he was removed, to a house not far
distant, and these two months Paul has slept in his room,
to take care of him at night. He describes the case as very
grave at one time, and says he never saw such an object
as Charley presented for about a week. Still he is not

much pitted, and is so far recovered as to talk of returning to the tavern in a few days.

I had the room to myself, and slept in Paul's bed. His
affinity to bed clothes just suited me, and I have not had
so good a night in months.

The air and exercise agree with me. I am at Stevenson's, where I dine, and to-night I shall go down. I find
care very necessary, though I stand exercise and the open
air well. My feet and legs are better.

Pell came to see me. Is in good spirits—hears from
Anne once a week, and goes across early in May. I am
about to telegraph the College Hotel for a room. It can
do no harm and may succeed. With the deepest regard,
yours most tenderly and devotedly,

J. F. C.

Remember me to the rats, do. Fan, Dick, Jenny, and
Willy.

TO MRS. COOPER, COOPERSTOWN

New York, College Hotel, March 21st, 1851

Dearest,

Paul saw me to the boat, last evening, and took care
of everything. He was very attentive and kind to me.
Gansevoort dined with us, Stevenson, Paul and I, and sat
until past seven. James says Mrs. Barnard is getting
more reconciled to her honours, and will probably remain
abroad some time.

Wm. Bayard and Dr. Cox were on board the boat,
and I had much chat. The Dr. was fresh from Buffalo,
where he had been lecturing, anti nigger.

I telegraphed to know if I could have a room. In about
two hours I got an answer "yes." My question went out
in radii, of course, and complimentary messages were sent

in to me, immediately, while I was in the office—*printed* messages. Utica said: "Our compliments to J. F. C., and hope he is as much pleased with what we write, as we have been with what he has written."

I passed a good night in the boat, though it was, and still is, very cold. On reaching the tavern, about eight, I found a small parlor, with a very good bed room ready for me. They are in the fourth story, and it tires my legs to mount, but Saunderson hopes to move me in a few days. The rooms are well enough, and I have both a rocking chair and a sofa. Some things are wanting but many comforts are here.

Putnam is in Philadelphia, and I have not yet seen him. In his store I met Tupper and, contrary to my wishes, was introduced to him. His first question was whether he was to have the pleasure of seeing me at dinner at Mr. Astor's to-day? I had not the honor of visiting Mr. Astor. Here was bathos. His manner is English, flippant, and by all I can hear much like James. I am very sorry I was introduced, but my apologies of ill health will probably lead him not to expect a call.

I went to Cruger's office, and sat an hour. He gave me quantities of gossip. Mrs. Haight, after giving her party, has let her house for three years, flowers and all, and gone first to Cuba—eventually to South America, I believe. Cruger swears all Dick has to live on is the picture of the spread eagle that you see in the bottom of our hats.

Mr. and Mrs. Bristed are off for Europe; Mrs. Sedgwick has their house.

All the Cruger race is as usual, including the lady. He says, when the thermometer was below zero she dragged her brother up to Henderson to collect her rents—that the consequence has been almost a revolution, that some of her stoutest partisans have left the place, and she is now laid up with the cold taken in the excursion.

I sat an hour chatting with Cruger, who says I look now wonderfully like Bonaparte again. Jack Hamilton, they are afraid, has the consumption. His mother and sister are still at Newport, Middleton is on his plantation, and Lewis is at Washington seeking employment.

On leaving Cruger I bought my silver. I then came home, took some soup, and a nap. It was so unpleasant I would not go out again, but have remained at home since two o'clock. I have not touched my dinner, and took only half a cup of tea at seven.

This house is not on the Globe plan at all. It has an ordinary, and that on so small a scale as to be of the most unpleasant character. Saunderson, however, is very attentive, as are the servants, and there are no loungers, smokers, tobacco chewers, or other monstrosities.
Saturday morning.

I had a good night—my feet and knees do not much trouble now in bed. I pile on clothes, and manage to sleep warm. Towards morning I get cold, and have to parliamenteer, as old Johnny Hatfield used to call it, in order to recover the warmth again.

Cruger has just left me. He came to renew offers of his services, manifesting a good deal of concern in my condition.

I shall now go and give the orders to send off Fan's tea-set. I like it, but she may think it too small. For half a dozen people, it is sufficient—besides she can skimp, as the Yankees call it, in the milk.

It is a beautiful day, and I intend to pass most of the morning in the air.

Adieu, my excellent wife. God forever bless you and

have you in his goodly keeping, and I pray the same for all our dear children.

J. F. C.

College Hotel, New York, Saturday,
March 29th, 1851

Best Beloved,

Night before last I passed the evening at Mr. Norries,' and got lots of gossip. The Misses Clarksons go up town. So do the Norries. Anne Margaret says that when her father was dying Susy Chacomb sent for her aunt, who did not go, and that Susy had not visited her aunt since. This is bad for people so near their grave. Archy was here to-day, and I probed him a little, but he was vague in his answers, as he generally is. He admitted however that something was *wrong*. "Never marry a western woman," concluded Archy. "She'll paint, and spend your money, and like as not run away from you."

The Major is in California, safe and sound—though he had been very ill at Panama, and again at Benicia.

Last night I was actually dissipated. Lewis came for me in a carriage, and carried me off almost by force, two miles to Dr. Bellows', where I met the Sketch Club, some forty people, many of whom I know. I staid until past ten, ate a water ice, talked a great deal, returned, went to bed fatigued, but slept it all off. I sleep well, invariably. Some of my naps are delicious.

My friends are very attentive to me. They all seemed glad to see me, and all think I am improving, as I certainly am.

To-day Willie has paid me a long visit. I sent him to the museum. He has gone to dine with Aunt Peggy.

Amariah says he has some segars for Dick. Johnnie was with him, looking like a new sixpence.

I shall come home shortly. The Philadelphia business may detain me a little, but not much. I want to be in my garden. Then I wish to be in your dear hands, love, for though you know nothing you do a great deal that is right.

Last evening I passed with Charlotte Maillard, who wanted to take me home to nurse me.

There is no chance of seeing Shubrick.

Adieu, my love—God forever bless you.

My blessing on the girls, all four of them, and dear Paul too.

J. F. C.

TO MARIA FRANCES COOPER

March 31st, 1851

My dear child,

I spent Saturday evening with Charlotte M. and dined with Peggy Munro yesterday. On the whole I rather improve, though my case did not reach its worst point until I got to town.

Tupper proves a tramp. He drinks freely at dinner, and talks like a fool. "Thackeray is coming out here, with evil intent, but I will keep an eye on him." Abused the Corimans to Dr. Beltour, and says he may have to die at the stake, yet! Meaning Cardinal Wiseman to blow the fire. I call him Mr. Twopence (Tuppence), for he is about as big as a new three cent piece.

God bless you, child.

My regards to Jenny, and the b'hoys.

Your affectionate Father,

J. Fenimore Cooper

FROM WILLIAM COOPER

Keokuk, Lee County, Iowa, April 7th, 1851

Dear Uncle,

I wrote to you some eighteen months since, and have not recd an answer. I once more take my pen in hand to inform you of my whereabouts, and my prospects. In the first place, I must inform you, that I have been to California. I left the Missouri River at Council Bluffs on the 7th of May last in company with three of my wifes brothers. We started with nine horses, and two waggons. On the 28th of the same month, arrived at Ft. Laramie. We passed through the Omahaws, Pawnees and Sioux nations; and found them friendly, but thievish. The country is not susceptible of cultivation. For two hundred miles of the distance there was not a tree to be seen, and in fact there is no timber, except a few small cotton-woods on the Platte River; which River we camped on nearly every night. Platte River is as wide or wider than the Mississippi, but very shallow, with quick sand bed. Ft. Laramie is situated in the forks of the River. It was formerly an old French trading post, and is now nothing but a garrison. Government has one horse power saw mill, and they raft their small pine logs down the Laramie fork. They were erecting several fine frame buildings. One of the officers told me, that they could not raise any vegetables, except a few radishes and lettuce, by highly manuring. We left Ft. Laramie the same day and arrived at Salt Lake on the 21st of June, making one thousand and ten miles from the Missouri. The route we found circuitous; crossing several rapid streams, with but a very little grass. I may as well say a barren dessolate country, for where we did not find mountains of granite, we found a perpetual desert; with a little grass on the borders of the streams. We found it necessary to keep a close watch on our horses, that they did not drink Alkali, which had evaporated, and left black salts six inches thick, we used it, and found it to answer as a substitute for Salaratus. What was more remarkable, we found in a desert, under a broiling sun, about six inches from the surface, a large bed of pure ice, about three feet thick. We went through the S. W. pass of the rocky mountains, and would not have known it, had it not been for our guide book; for the ascent had been gradual for about a weeks travel. The wind river mountain showed its lofty snow capped peak far above the clouds, and about 80 miles to our right. We passed through the Crow nation, but did not see any of them. At Ft. Bridger, a french trading post, about 180m east of Salt Lake we saw large bodies of the snake indians; they were very friendly. In the whole distance from ft. Laramie to Salt Lake, I could not select five hundred acres of arable land, put it all together, and no timber to fence it. Salt Lake City lies at the foot of a snow capped mountain, in the Utah valley, and the foot of Salt Lake. The City is laid out in square form, each lot containing one acre and one quarter of ground. The houses are built of Adobes or sun burnt brick. Their principle crop is wheat, which grows to perfection; averageing fifty bushels to the acre, and they had in twelve thousand acres. They are obliged to irrigate their land, but being situated so close at the foot of the mountain, they have water running through every street, and on both sides. Fencing with them, is a serious difficulty; as they are obliged to go into the mountains, and cut spruce poles; and often the cattle, waggon poles and all come tumbling down. The lake is said to be the saltest water known. In the Autumn, they go and shovel up waggon loads of salt.

There is also in the vicinity, several mineral springs. Some of them hot enough to boil an egg. We traded part of our horses for cattle; being out of flour, we jerked six hundred weight of beef, traded some coffee dried fruit and sugar (at the rate of two pounds of one or·the other, for three pounds of flour) on the 27th of the same month hitched our cattle to the waggon (having left one on sweet water river) we started for California, and arrived at Hangtown or Placerville on the 5th. of August. Desolation and the destruction of property stared us in the face the whole way. Hundreds with nothing to eat, but dead horses and mules, we gave them such as we had when they asked for it. As for bread; we only made it twice. We would hang our camp kettle over the fire, part full of water; cut our beef into small pieces, and put them in, and then stir in a handful of flour. Such was our living for eleven hundred miles, with the exception of tea and coffee. Our fuel was sage brush the whole of the way, until we got to the Sierra Nevada mountains. When we struck the head of the Humboldt River, we crossed it and followed it down to its sink, which was over three hundred miles. The river was up, and the grass eat off, consequently we had to swim it, and cut grass for our stock; and a precious little we got at that. At the sink or big meadow we cut grass for crossing the desert. We had to wade in the water half a mile knee deep; and then found the finest clover I ever saw. We rested two days, and then struck a cross the desert, traveling day and night until we struck Carson River. I had the diarrhoea, and walked the whole way on two buiscuts, and half a pint of water, my sickness was caused by drinking Alkali water, and it finally compelled me to leave California. We followed up Carson river to the head, at the foot of the Sierra Nevada. Carson valley is a beautiful place, covered with clover, red top, and several other kinds of grass. It is about forty miles long and seven wide. The only land between Salt Lake and the West side the Sierra Nevada that is susceptible of cultivation. Now we come to mountains. Yes, mountain upon mountain; and the only timber I had seen for seventeen hundred miles;—and such timber; I measured pine trees that were thirty-six feet in circumference. I can't describe the mountains, they are beyond one's imagination. We crossed the highest peak in the afternoon in the last of July, over fifty feet of snow. We took only two horses over the mountains, having lost two, traded one off in Carson valley for five pounds of flour; and bought fifteen pounds more at one dollar a pound. I found Isaac on the middle fork of American River, engaged in damming. I worked in his old lead about ten days, and made three hundred dollars. Isaac then started for home, and I took his place in the River. It proved a failure. Working in the water irritated my disease, and the Doctor told me I had better leave for home. I took his advice, and twenty days after I got on ship board, I got well and have gained forty pounds, and at this time enjoy better health than I have since I had the small pox. Isaac made three thousand, and I lost about three hundred. One of my wifes brothers came home with me. He started back last Tuesday. I could have made money had I kept my health, and it was my intention to have given you a call on my return. You probably hear the great excitement about a rail road to California. Set it down as the greatest humbug of the age. I left San Francisco on the 3rd of last October in a schooner. Thirty one days out we put into Acapulco for water. Our Capt. owned the vessel; and for his misconduct, we took it from him, put him on shore, and made the mate captain. We were fifteen days to Realijo, where a party of us left her, and crossed through Nicaragua to St. Juan on the Atlantic. Nicaragua is a beautiful country. We traveled as far as the City of Grenada in ox carts, and then took a small boat across the lake and down the St. Juan River to the Atlantic. On the 15th of December embarked on board of a Dutch Barque and arrived at New Orleans on the 10th of January, and on the 27th arrived at my wifes fathers, which is four miles from Keokuk, and two from the Mississippi, where I shall remain this summer. All his boys being in California, he was anxious for me to stay with him. I have been ploughing all this week for planting corn. Isaac and I will sell this summer if we can and buy in this section. I have a daughter seventeen months old, and tell Fanny she has a namesake. I came part of the way home in company with William Spafard. He had done tolerably well, but his health was poor. Who falls heir to three mile point. If it is me, I would like to have the title if there is any title to be transfered. I would like very much to hear from you soon. Give my love to all.

Your Affectionate Nephew
William Cooper

J. Fenimore Cooper, Esq., Cooperstown

FROM W. B. SHUBRICK

Washington, D. C., 2nd May, 1851

My dear Cooper

I was much relieved by your letter of the 13th with Charlotte's to Mary and myself, and I feel much assured that as the spring advances and you are able to take exercise out of doors, you will be all yourself again. I have taken it into my head that Cooperstown is a bad place for you to spend the winter. You are too much in the house—too much in your arm chair. You should come to Washington where every day something would occur to excite your attention. My house will be finished by August at the latest; it is large enough to accommodate all of us. It has four rooms on the first floor, four chambers with two dressing rooms on the second floor, and six rooms on the third story; what more do we want for the accommodation of your family and mine? We are about a mile from the Capitol, a pleasant *daily* walk for an *elderly* gentleman—think of this. I mean what I say; we should be delighted if you would come and spend all winter with us.

You have seen by the papers that I have been turned over to the Treasury Department. Congress passed a law at the last session authorizing the appointment of a Board to consist of two Navy officers of high rank—two Engineer officers and a scientific civilian—to examine all the Lighthouses, Light Boats, Beacons, etc., of the U. S., to report on their condition, ascertain where new ones are wanted, and if any now existing can be dispensed with; and to digest a general plan for the construction and management of Lighthouses in future. This you will perceive is not a small business. The Board consists of myself and DuPont of the Navy, Totten and James Kearney of Engineer, and Bache of the Coast Survey, with a Lieutenant of the Navy (Jenkins) as Secretary. We are to convene on the 20th of this month in this City, where we are to receive special instructions from the Secretary of the Treasury—I presume we shall go on the Eastern coast this summer, visit the Gulf of Mexico in the winter and, take the Lakes in the next summer. Now can you by any ingenuity make it appear that a Lighthouse is needed

on Otsego? If you can, send your petition to the Board
and we will come and examine the ground, or rather the
water, and there is no telling how far a good chowder at
the "three mile point" might go to establish that as the
most eligible spot for a Light. We shall have a steamer
for the coast duty—why not go with us when we go into
the gulf? After a spell of very pleasant weather we have
it quite cold to-day and frost last night—still spring is
much advanced; we have asparagus in market in abundance at 12½ cents a bunch—two bunches making a good
sized dish.

I have little Navy news to give you. Vorhees has been
let off—though there was not half the justification for his
coming home that there was in poor Ben's case, political
influence has done it—I never expect to see a fair and
impartial administration of the Department—is it impossible under our institutions? if it is, the institutions are
defective. Well, we are to have Stockton in the Senate—
he is on the Naval Committee, and I am told talks large
about what he intends to do. He is full of wild schemes,
such as doing away with necessary ships and recruiting
officers. His plan is, that when a Captain is appointed to
a ship he shall recruit his own crew, and they shall not be
transferable—could any scheme be more destructive to
the Navy? The next step would be the selection by the
crew of their own officers—but I think the Commodore
will make a small figure in the Senate, though his money
will tell *over there.*

Morris is as well as he has been for years, and I have
reason to think will take charge again of the Bureau of
Construction, etc., as Skinner talks of retiring—he thinks
his health is giving way under the sedentary duties of the
office. Comm^d Barrie's death brings up two hard cases for

promotion—Dale and Rhodes, both of whom would be utterly useless in the work to which they severally claim to be advanced. I understand the President talks of having a regular court of inquiry in each case—I think they would pass over Rhodes without much difficulty, but there is a feeling for the son of Commodore Dale which makes his case more difficult. The result in my opinion will be that both will be promoted, nor do I see how it can be avoided, as within the last month, two officers (one a Lieu^t in the Navy, the other in the Marines) have been cashiered for drunkenness by sentence of a court martial and both *immediately* restored on twelve months' suspension. The Lieutenant ꞏof the Navy is a pet or protégé in some way of Mr Webster, and the Marine was let off for the sake of appearances.

Jones complains bitterly of his sentence and is preparing, so I understand, to make an appeal to Congress, though I do not see how Congress can meddle in the matter.

We are all well, and unite in love to all.

As ever
W. B. Shubrick

J. Fenimore Cooper, Esqr

FROM CHARLES B. TAYLER

Otley Rectory, Ipswich, July 26, 1851

My dear Sir

I am a stranger to you, and yet no stranger, for you know no greater admirer either on this, or your, side of the Atlantic. I always admired your fine conception and personification of truth in the character of Leatherstocking, one of the most beautiful and simple characters that

was ever drawn by a master's hand. I am not a novel
reader, but have made your volumes an exception, and
one of your works which I last read delighted me more
than any of them—I allude to *The Bee Hunter*—for it
was evident from the pages of that book, that its author
was an enlightened and godly man. I had before been
satisfied with admiring you as an author, but I have since
wished to express to you how sincerely I rejoiced to find
that you had become the earnest and powerful advocate
not only of truth and uprightness, but of the only source
from whence such principles and such conduct proceed,
vital and spiritual religion.—You sent me a kind message by a kind friend of mine, Miss Lippitt, one of your
country women, who just became acquainted with me,
through my books, and I have begged my dear young
friend Mr. Low, who is about to sail for America, to be
the bearer to you of two of my volumes which his excellent Father has published—I hope he may be able to see
you, and I assure you, he is a superior young man, with
whom I think you will be pleased. He is visiting America
on account of his health; having been a great sufferer;
but his sufferings have been sanctified to him, and he can
say, from his heart, "It is good for me that I have been
afflicted."—I wish I could visit your country, for I feel
it is our second home, and I look upon you all as our
brethren, and repudiate the bad spirit of those who would
sow dissention between us—I am aware, however, from
your own observations, of many of the evils which now
prevail in your states, and sincerely deplore them. I have
been lately charmed by the poetry of Longfellow, whom
we can scarcely rival in this country at present, and have
long been delighted with the prose of W. Irving, whom
I used to meet at the Williams's some thirty years ago,

when I had just left college. You have a successful imi-
tator in Myers, one of whose books I have read.—I do
not ask you to write to me, but I wish you would send
me one of your books, with my name, written by your
hand, in it—my especial favourites are *The Bee Hunter*,
The Wept of Wishton Will [*sic*],—I am always puz-
zled by that title—and *The Last of the Mohicans*. We
shall probably never meet in this world—but as a Minister of that gracious Lord, whom we both love, and in
whom *alone* we trust for pardon and for grace, I hope
we shall both be found in Him, and among those, who
are *"with* Him"—and *"called*, and *chosen*, and faith-
ful"—having deemed the knowledge of Him, our cruci-
fied and risen Lord, the one thing needful, and having
chosen *that good part* which shall not be taken away from
us.—
     I remain, my dear Sir,
               faithfully, and with high esteem, yours,
                                   Charles B. Tayler
J. Fenimore Cooper, Esq.

   Charles Benjamin Tayler (1797-1875) was an English clergyman who wrote many books, mainly for the young. He was
educated at Trinity College, Cambridge, and was Rector at Otley
in Suffolk County.

                    FROM WILLIAM JAY
                         Bedford, 3rd Sept., 1851
Dear Cooper
   The public Journals give, I trust, exaggerated accounts
of the state of your health; yet I have reason to believe
you are labouring under severe illness. I am unacquainted
with the particulars of your sickness, but I know it must

occasion discomfort to yourself and anxiety to your family. I think of and sympathize with both. Time is passing rapidly away, and with you and me it will soon be no more.

A bright and unfading inheritance is offered to us in a better world on conditions which we both understand. God give us grace to accept the conditions, and grant that should we see each other no more in the flesh, we may meet in bliss and glory.

May you be filled with joy and peace in believing, and abound in hope through the power of the Holy Ghost.

Your friend,
William Jay.

James Fenimore Cooper, Esq., Cooperstown

This letter closes the friendship of a life-time, begun at the school of Reverend Thomas Ellison, Rector of St. Peter's Church, Albany, where William Jay, the poet Hillhouse, and James Cooper were fellow students in 1800.

On the back of the letter is written, in the handwriting of Susan Fenimore Cooper, "One of the last letters received by my dearest Father and which I read to him as he lay in his bed."

James Fenimore Cooper died at his home, Otsego Hall, in Cooperstown, New York, September 14, 1851. His wife survived him a little over four months. She died January 20, 1852.

The following note on her father's death was written by Susan Augusta Fenimore Cooper, his eldest and perhaps favorite child. It was found among her papers after her death.

Monday, Sep. 15th: His birth-day. He would have been 62. Charlotte and I sat up with his dear remains! His face very noble, and calm. Dear Mother went in with us to see him; kneeling and praying beside him. She is very calm, though grieved to the heart.

He is to be laid in his grave, Wednesday, at 5 o'clock, just one week after his darling grandchild.

I go in very often to see him, and kiss him. His face seems just as dear to me in death as in life. I could sit by him, and caress him all the time. Never before have I *loved* the face of death, it has always hitherto been painful to look on the dead countenance of one I had known alive. Even with dear little Hal it distressed me, there was an effort, it was a relief to turn my eyes away, the darling child was so altered. But it is not so *now*. There is a comfort, a blessedness in these last looks of the beloved dead. O my darling, darling Father!

Going in to the room once, I found Mr. Scott and Mr. Battin there, both in tears.

Sitting with dear Mother while the rest of the family are engaged with the necessary details, she lets me talk about him. Speaking of their reading the Bible together, she says it was on his birth-day, about five or six years since that they began to read it together, regularly; not by chapters but a hundred verses every morning before breakfast, unless the close of a chapter occurred to break or prolong the reading. He admired the Psalms inexpressibly. The Book of Job also. The prophesies of Isaiah, and the Epistles to the Hebrews struck him very forcibly. He admired the Epistle of St. James very much, calling it a beautiful pastoral letter. He told Mother once, "I used to think a great deal of St. James when I was a boy." He was deeply impressed with the book of Revelations. The allusions to Melchisedec always interested him particularly. He said, speaking of the definition of faith by St. Paul: "Faith is the substance of things hoped for, the evidence of things not seen," that it was so noble, so comprehensive, so just, so full, that the words themselves seemed to have been sent directly from Heaven.

Speaking of the admiration he had always felt for the Liturgy, dear Mother mentioned his most deep sense of the excellence of the Lord's Prayer. He loved particularly the anthem, "God be merciful unto us, etc., etc." "The Liturgy was a blessed service to him," I observed. "Oh," cried dear Mother, "Blessed indeed! He *lived* on the Collects for the last few months!" They were in the habit of saying together every morning for years "Direct us O Lord, etc., etc."

They knelt together, Father's arms about Mother; when he grew feeble she knelt, and he leaned his head on her shoulder.

On the morning of his death dear Mother kneeled at the bedside and said the prayers they had been accustomed to use together. He seemed to understand, and follow, though with effort—partially conscious to the very last hour.

For many years before separating, for even a short business absence of dear Father's, they always said together the prayer in the Marriage Service. Dear Mother added this prayer to others the last morning of his life. He seemed to understand but could not speak. The morning of his death when I came into the room dear Mother said, "Here is Susie, come to kiss you!" He partly opened his eyes, made an effort to smile, and put up his lips to kiss me—but his voice was gone.

APPENDIX

A Journal kept by James Fenimore-Cooper, January-May, 1848, in a Daily Memorandum Book, for 1848, published annually by Francis & Loutrel, Manufacturing Stationers, 77 Maiden Lane, New York.

1848.

January.

1. Saturday. Read St. John. No church. Weather very mild, though snow fell in the night. Walking very bad and I paid no visits out of my immediate connection. Had Dick Cooper, Alice, Georgeanne Woolson, Platt and Charley Foot at dinner. A very merry evening with the young people. Played chess with my wife. Wrote a little to-day in *Oak Openings*, to begin the year well.

2. Sunday. Went to church in the sleigh, but the streets were all mud. Weather quite mild. All the ice disappeared. Dick dined here with his two eldest sons. After dinner he went to Hyde, taking Alice and Georgeanne with him, who return to school. Dick and Gold staid with us. Grew cooler towards evening. Read in St. John in the morning.

3. Monday. Weather a little cooler, though still very pleasant. Write in *Openings*, and drove wife to the Chalet, but sleighing execrable. On my return read in St. John. Worked on the *Openings*, as usual, evening, played chess with wife, who beat me, though she was not very well. Young Dick and Gold still here.

4. Tuesday. St. John. Paid Harry Clark and Fish & Payne. Worked on *Openings*. No snow and weather quite mild, though it grew colder towards night. Dick and Gold left us. Paul told me he was going to Utica. Wrote to Capt. Wessels and sent him an Army list. Chess in the

evening with wife. Read the papers to her. Frank and Morris Foot dined here, but were so noisy that I sent them home immediately after dinner.

5. Wednesday. Paul went early. St. John, two of the doctrinal chapters. Weather pleasant but cooler. Began to read Siborn's *Waterloo* again. Find in it less impartiality than I at first supposed. Chess with wife. Worked on *Openings*, which gets on slowly. It tries to snow, and ice begins to make a little in the lake, but on the whole the weather pleasant.

6. Thursday. Weather still pleasant. Ice about a mile up the lake. Went to-day to the farm, but found the sleighing execrable. St. John in the morning. Chess with wife in the evening. Still pleasant, with occasional spitting of snow. Dick came down from Hyde, after having taken Alice and Georgie to Albany.

7. Friday. Weather much the same, but moderating and growing cooler by turns. Towards evening getting quite cool. St. John. Work on *Openings*. Dick got back from Albany on Wednesday, and reappeared here at dinner yesterday. To-day he took Jenny back to Hyde, and did not dine with us. Began to snow in the evening. Chess with wife as usual. Grows colder.

8. Saturday. Some little snow had fallen. St. John. Work on *Openings*. Took wife to Chalet, but found the sleighing very poor—better, however, than the last time. Went through the woods, where we did pretty well. Lippet had taken away the big cow, for which he is to pay me $40. Chess in the evening. Weather moderating, and more like snow.

9. Sunday. Snowed in the night. Finished St. John. Went to church in the sleigh. About six inches of snow,

but so light that the runners still cut through. Getting packed, however, and hope sleighing will be pretty good to-morrow. Parson preached in behalf of foreign missions, but post-poned the collection till next Sunday. Snowing at times throughout the day.

10. Monday. Began the Acts. Last night was severely cold, as has been to-day. Thermometer in cold places below zero all day. Went with wife to Chalet, but were nearly frozen. Caught a turkey and killed it myself, and bought a keg of oysters on my way back. Sleighing tolerable, but not as good as we are accustomed to at this season. Paul returned. Chess with wife, she beating outrageously. No more ice.

11. Tuesday. Last night a tickler. Acts. An oyster breakfast, with thermometer at 40 in the hall. Lake frozen as far as we can see. As the wind has changed, I think it will moderate. I find the thermometer stood before sunrise at $25°$, $26°$, and $27°$, below zero. This is within four or five degrees of our coldest weather. Moderates sensibly, some thermometers ranging as high as $15°$ above zero.

12. Wednesday. John Morris arrived last evening. He reports his Uncle John as failing daily. Acts. The weather much milder. Worked on *Openings*, and drove wife to Chalet, and afterwards around Great Lazy Man.* Marmaduke came back to school this morning.

* "Great Lazy Man" was the walk or drive around the part of the village of Cooperstown which lies south of Main Street: down River Street, around to Chestnut, thence to Main Street, and back to the corner of River Street. The origin of the name is evident: a long walk for a lazy man. It is possible that the walk around the north part of the village, a much shorter distance, was known as The Lazy Man or The Small Lazy Man.

Dick dined here. Chess with wife, she beat, handsomely. Weather much milder; hardly down to freezing at 3 P. M.

13. Thursday. Weather still mild, but clouded. Acts. Worked at *Openings*. This book is more than a fourth done. Dick brought Willy and Jenny down from Hyde, this morning. This afternoon a tea-party, and a dance in the hall after the piano. Jane Morris, Mrs. Henry Van Rensselaer, John Morris, Cally Foot, Mary Farmer, Platt and Charley, Kate Prentiss, etc., etc. No chess this evening. My big cow weighed 834 lbs. dead.

14. Friday. Thawing. Acts; martyrdom of Stephen. Lent John the sleigh, and did not go to Chalet. Work at *Openings*. Took a walk, but walking bad. The wind has got round to the westward, but still very mild. John Morris left us to-day. Dick dined here. In the evening all the children went out, leaving me alone with my wife. Chess, at which I beat three games.

15. Saturday. Rained in the night, and continues mild. Snow going fast. Acts. Wrote letters to-day. Dick did not come down from Hyde. Rained most of the day. Chess in evening, wife beat grievously and neatly, two check mates, with half the pieces on the board. The third time I beat, but a mere hammering game.

16. Sunday. A little cooler in the night, and sun rose clear. A lovely day. Acts. Was unwell, and did not go to church. Dick brought Jenny down, about noon. Reports roads good, and thawing in the sun. No change in the weather all this day. No one at dinner. Nothing new in the papers, congress quarrelling about the war, one side endeavoring to make capital out of it, and the other the reverse.

17. Monday. Beautiful day. Begin to think the predicted comet may influence the weather. Acts. *Openings*. Took a long walk on the planks, where wife joined me. Dick down to take leave before going below. Paid girls $10 each, of allowance. Company in the evening. Chess, I beating, all hollow. Fine weather continues.

18. Tuesday. Acts. Had a bad night, from eating Boston biscuits. Nothing Yankee agrees with me. Better in the morning. Flurries of snow, but not enough to cover the bare spots. Took a long walk on the plank. *Openings*, finished 10th Chap. Chess with wife in the evening, I beat. Wife nervous. She grows fatter, but wants air and exercise. Out of Carter potatoes to my regret.

19. Wednesday. Grew much colder in the night, but no snow. Wheeling good, but not a bit of sleighing. Acts. Reviewing *Openings*. Thaws in warm places, but a fair winter day. House very comfortable. Franklin in our room has not been lighted this winter. Took a long walk, wife with me part of the time. She wants air very much, and we miss our sleighing. Chess, both beat. I lost queen early, and at end had a castle and two pawnes against a queen! Beat handsomely.

20. Thursday. Still pleasant, though cool. Acts. Took a very long walk, weather charming, though freezing a very little in the shade. Wind at S. W. and mild. No sign of snow, and wheeling capital. Chess in the evening. I beat altogether. Began to revise *Openings* to-day, of which ten chapters are done. Congress making a fool of itself by betraying its utter ignorance of the Constitution.

21. Friday. Weather still more moderate, and an April day. Acts. After breakfast drove wife to farm, on wheels, roads capital. Did no work to-day. Congress does not

seem to be aware it can not order the Constitutional Commander in Chief to send a regiment anywhere. Chess. Wife gave me two out and out check mates.

22. Saturday. Acts. Another fine day, but cooler than yesterday. Drove wife to farm on wheels. Cattle doing well on this weather. Steers improve, and store cattle in good health. Feeding out the English potatoes, which turn out indifferent. The Carters are decidedly our best potatoes. Got no New York mail this evening. Chess. Wife beat me two games ignominiously, check mated both times with nearly all the pieces on the board.

23. Sunday. Acts. Another charming day, cool, but clear and pleasant. Mr. Hall preached. Brewer was married in church, just before the sermon, and Dolphin the brewer was buried in our church yard, though the service was at the Methodist building. Dick and Gold, who came up from school on Friday, went back this afternoon.

24. Monday. Finished Acts. Another glorious day. *Openings*. Drove wife to farm. This afternoon walked on the planks until after sunset. The evening a very little cool, but delightful. Chess, wife beat me two games infamously, fairly *walloped* me. I got the third game. Wife plays much better than she did. Practise makes perfect.

25. Tuesday. Began Romans. Another mild day, but not so pleasant as yesterday. *Openings*. Drove wife as far as Myrtle Grove, by the new road, which is a very pretty drive, and a great addition to our outlets. But the Grove is spoiled. This place is a monument of the "people's" honesty, and appreciation of liberty! I know them and would as soon confide in convicts. Chess.

26. Wednesday. Romans. Weather still mild, but not pleasant enough to ride out. Rained a little indeed.

Openings. In evening, chess. Wife gave me another of her quick check-mates, terrible defeats these. I beat her two games, afterwards, however. The Whigs at Washington seem about to cut their own throats again, on the question of War. Does Mr. Clay understand the Constitution, or is it ignorance?

27. Thursday. Romans. Rained in the night, and all the forenoon. Wind north east. Sent 10 chapters of *Openings* to Fagan, by Express. Got a letter from him in the afternoon. All right as to *Jack Tier*. Chess, wife beat one of her slapping games, again, but I beat her two afterwards. One of these beats puts her in good spirits for a whole evening, and I delight to see it.

28. Friday. More mild weather, with a little rain. Romans. A little but very little snow fell in the night. Dick got back, demurrer not reached. Chess, I beat this evening, altogether. Wrote to Fagan and enclosed a bill on Bentley for 100 pounds Sterling. With this bill he is to meet my note to him for *Crater*, and remit to me the balance.

29. Saturday. Romans. Weather still mild, and a very little more snow. The thaw has cut up the mud in the road, which prevents the sleigh from running. *Openings* again. I have been reading D'Israeli's *Curiosities of Literature*, a curious work, but of less interest than I had supposed. Chess. Wife check mated in her slapping way, but I beat her atrociously in a second game.

30. Sunday. Romans. Still fine weather, though a little cooler. No sleighing. Thaws freely in the sun. Was not well enough to quit the house. This evening received a letter from Commodore Shubrick, dated Monterey, Oct. 2d., '47. He was about to sail on an expedition to capture

Guaymos, Mazatlán and Acapulco. The two first our advices overland tell us have been taken.

31. Monday. Romans. Another beautiful day. Such a winter as this, thus far, has scarce been ever seen in this region. It is as mild as a Philadelphia winter certainly; and in some respects, milder. Went to farm in wagon, met a team that ran against us and broke both my shafts. Horse began to plunge, and I told wife to jump. She did so, without injury. The horse plunged for a short distance, when I turned him into the upper ditch, where he stopped. It was a marvellous escape. Wife had to walk a mile in the mud.

This month, generally, has been one of the pleasantest ever known in these mountains. On two occasions it has been cold, but only for short periods, and most of the time the weather has been quite mild and clear. I have remarked that the sun has had more power than is usual in January, many days having been hot.

Congress has been out-doing its own out-doings this month. Talk, talk, talk, the President asked for ten new regiments to carry on the war, and Congress has been talking on the subject until some of the patriots have come out with a declaration it is now too late to raise the men, as the sickly season would overtake them!

February.

1. Tuesday. Finished Romans. It snowed in the night, but the foundation for sleighing is not good. Could not persuade wife to venture out. Grew mild as the day advanced, and the road soon got bad. Chess. Wife beating terribly at times. Commenced on new part of *Openings*,

and wrote moderately, but not *con amore*. This book is not a labour of love, but a labour.

2. Wednesday. Corinthians. A little colder in the night, nay a cold night, but a charming day. Drove out Cally Foot in the cutter. Wife being still too skittish to venture. Road very indifferent. Chess, both beating, I most however. There were some young folk this evening, and a good deal of laughing, and chatting as is usual with them.

3. Thursday. Corinthians. Another cold night. Wife went with me to farm to-day. Did pretty well by keeping on the side of the road. Fortunately Pumpkin was not at all frightened the other day, and behaves as well as ever, which is not particularly well. Chess, both beat. Wife certainly plays this game much better than she did thirty years ago. Paul's birthday.

4. Friday. Corinthians. It was a very mild night, and to-day it thaws freely. Went on the plank walk, and shovelled off the snow myself. Afterwards walked there more than an hour. Half sold my hop-poles while there. Chess, as usual, both beating. I have been astounded by a published letter of Judge McLean. He affirms the right in Congress to control the movements of the army, among other monstrosities.

5. Saturday. Corinthians. It snowed in the night, leaving about seven inches on the ground. The roads were not in the best condition for it, but on the whole the sleighing is good. Went to farm with Sue, who is getting over her alarm. Wm. is drawing wood, and we are likely to get through the winter comfortably. Chess, five games. Wife beat two slappingly, and I beat three. A little side talk lost me one. Fen and John came up this afternoon.

6. Sunday. Corinthians. Snowed a little, but always mild, almost thawing, and quite so whenever the sun appears. A good deal of snow fell in the course of the day, and the weather is somewhat colder. No more thaw. Dick, his two eldest sons and Jenny with us to-day. Went to the rectory, which is a hospital. The old lady very well, but all the rest with colds. Looks like more snow.

7. Monday. Corinthians. Not cold at all, but a feathery snow falling throughout much of the day. Drove wife out, but did not go to farm. Plenty of snow, a foot or more, and sleighing will be good as soon as the roads are beaten. Chess. Wife beat *awfully* first game, but I retaliated the next. Children in high glee around the fire when I went to bed.

8. Tuesday. Finished 1st. Corinthians. Grew cold in the night. Joe Tom brought in a report that Union Factory was burned down in the night. Drove to the Chalet, sleighing good. The cattle look well, and are evidently improving. The young oxen grow and are getting heavier. Got the first proof sheet of *Openings* this evening. Chess, Wife beating two games smashingly. She certainly improves.

9. Wednesday. 2nd. Corinthians. A cold clear morning. Worked as usual, and drove wife to Chalet. Pleasanter than yesterday, and sleighing royal. Carried some meat up to the poultry. Butcher told me it was a piece of Hobley! Chess, four games; wife beating three and I one. All these games were played rapidly, and my beat, and her first beat, did not take half an hour for the two.

10. Thursday. Corinthians. Much more moderate, and looks like snow. Began to snow in the forenoon and two or three inches were added to our supply. Did not drive

out on account of weather. Chess. Beat and Beat. More news from Shubrick, who is very down-hearted in consequence of having asked his recall. We hear, however, that he has taken Guaymos and Mazatlán.

11. Friday. Corinthians. A very fine day and sleighing glib. Getting ice to-day and yesterday. It is better than I expected to see. Pack away this year forty loads, which I think must hold out. I have got rectory ice-house as well as my own. Chess, wife rather on stilts. The weather is more mild, but still cold. Thermometer has been at zero several times this week.

12. Saturday. Corinthians. Still milder. Went to Chalet, capital sleighing. Hens begin to lay, though a little snubbed by the cold weather. We have had about a hundred eggs since January, which is much better than last winter. A little party in the evening, including a Miss Dering from Utica, Nicoll's daughter. No Chess.

13. Sunday. Finished Corinthians, Milder. Church in forenoon. Congregation about 100, which is now our usual number. All the parsons in Cooperstown, Campbell excepted, want to depart, I hear. Nay, two have gone *faute de viande*. Dick got back two or three days since, and was down to-day, but would not dine. Congress acting like intrinsic knaves, which a good many are.

14. Monday. Galatians. Much milder. Until to-day I have found the hall at 38° every morning for a week, notwithstanding the fires have been kept up. To-day it was at 42, and soon rose to temperate. Went to Chalet, and killed a turkey. Got but one more on the eating list, and not many poulets. Chess. Wife beat two, right off the reel. Then I beat two, all quick games.

15. Tuesday. Galatians. Much more moderate. Thermometer at 50° in the hall when I came out. Drove to Chalet, and found sleighing tolerable. Chess in the evening, one game, I beating, rather magnificently. Miss Beebe passed the evening with us, to take leave of us. At 8 o'c this evening Mrs. Crippen was brought to bed of a girl. Doing well. Letters from Morris Cooper announcing his marriage.

16. Wednesday. Finished Galatians. 5th a noble chapter. Another fine day, and mild. Took a good long walk, and was about a good deal in the air this morning. No one seemed disposed to drive out. It is cooler than I had thought, though clear and a bright day. Thaws in the sun, but no where else. Chess. I beat once, wife beat awfully, and I beat again. One game pretty long.

17. Thursday. Ephesians. Weather colder; so much so as to cover the windows with frost. Most of the ice-houses are now filled. I wrote at *Openings* steadily. Sold my hop-poles this morning. Went to Chalet. Weather quite mild, but sleighing going as a matter of course. A great "ride" this afternoon. Paul goes, but no one else from the hall. Chess, both beating. Miss M. Bowers and Mrs. Collins sat an hour with us.

18. Friday. Ephesians. Still another bright day. Drove wife to Chalet across the lake. Went on at foot of West Street and off at two Mile Point. Found Dick's track, who has now been up and down three times. Some one followed us, and the road is made. Chess, wife made a tremendous hit, quite ashamed of myself. I beat next game. Young Dick and Gold came up from Hartwick.

19. Saturday. Finished Ephesians. Of all these epistles I like those to the Corinthians the least. A part of Ephe-

sians is wonderfully comprehensive and fine. Weather
clear and a little cold, but not enough to prevent thawing
in the sun. For six weeks, unless when it has snowed we
have had clear bright weather. This is the best February I
have ever known at this place. Chess. Wife gave a slash-
ing beat, but I got my revenge.

20. Sunday. Philippians. It thawed in the night and
snow seems to be going. Unless it change the road will
break up. Read service to wife and Sue at home, we three
not liking to encounter the bad weather. Dick and Gold
went back to school shortly after dinner. Mr. Ames
Beach preached, our parson relieving guard. In the evening looked over Eusebius, which strikes me as a singular
book. Must read it altogether and closely.

21. Monday. Finished Philippians. Still very mild but
no rain. Wind got up, and got round to the west, but
continues mild. Took long walks on the planks, forenoon
and afternoon, and found it delightful. Five of the ladies
joined me in the afternoon. Chess. Wife not well, and I
beat one game somewhat easily. She played no more and
I read Eusebius, an author not much to my taste.

22. Tuesday. All of Colossians. Still mild. Stiffened a
little in the night, but scarcely froze. There were beautiful rose coloured northern lights last evening, which I
forgot to mention. Very fine, though I have seen finer. It
tried to snow to-day, with wind easterly, but could not
succeed. The little fell melted immediately. Chess. Wife
gave one terrible beat. I retaliated. Then came the con-
queror, which got to be king and castle on each side. I beat
finally by an oversight of Sue's.

23. Wednesday. First of Thessalonians. Still mild. A
very little snow in the night, but scarcely enough to

whiten the roofs. It has been a very beautiful day, and I have had two long walks on the planks. About two it was as warm as April. I have no recollection of so mild a winter in this climate, and particularly of so much sunshine. Chess. Wife beat twice; both times slappingly, but I got the third game almost as triumphantly. One of my beats was shameful.

24. Thursday. 2nd Thessalonians. Weather not bright, but still mild. Tries to snow, but there does not seem to be any humidity in the atmosphere to congeal. Had northern lights, last evening. News from Mexico very pacific. The projet of a treaty, indeed, is said to be in Washington. Old Quincy Adams dead. He died in harness, falling in a fit in his place, in Congress. Chess was terrible. Two beats slap bang.

25. Friday. 1st Timothy. Grew colder in the night. Paul came in from a supper at Roselawn, having driven down the lake, at midnight. To-day clear and cold. We hear that Quincy Adams is still living, but unable to be removed from the capitol. I got a good walk on the planks to-day, and good thrashing at Chess, in the evening; two ignominious beats. A third game I beat, though nothing brilliant.

26th. Saturday. 2nd Timothy. Clear but chilling weather. The sun has great power. I paid John Clayton $100 to-day, the first cent he has asked for though he and his wife have now lived with us nearly ten months, at $100 per annum. Small pox in town, some say varioloid. No chess, having a nervous attack. The mail brought the news of Mr. Adams' decease. He literally died in the capitol, never having been removed from the speaker's room.

27. Sunday. Titus—Philemon. Much milder, and looks like snow. Not well enough to go to church in the forenoon. Wife went, however. The peace news increases in intensity. I have thought these six months that peace must follow our successes if the Whigs will allow it to come. Tries, but cannot snow. News from Washington not quite so pacific this evening. Some doubts about the treaty being accepted.

28. Monday. Hebrews. Much colder to-day. A cold night in fact. Hannah came over with several letters fi ɪm Wessels. He writes in pretty good spirits. Wound quite healed, and he amusing himself with looking at the different fields of battle. His wife read us the reports in which her husband is commended. Capt. Casey, in particular, speaks of Wessels in very favourable terms. Chess. Two ignominious defeats, and one rather clever victory.

29. Tuesday. Hebrews. This book is much superior to most of the writings attributed to St. Paul, though passages in the other books are very admirable. A little snow in the night, and cold to-day. I think a sleigh might run tolerably well. Small pox, or varioloid increases. Calvin Graves has it, now, though no bad case, except one of Adict, a blacksmith, is very serious. There must be six or eight cases in the village.

This month has been unusually fine. The brightness of the days has been its most remarkable feature. I finished ms. of *Oak Openings* to-day. And in the evening got a long letter from Mrs. Pomeroy. Chess. Two infernal beats again, slap bang, and one victory. Well, this delights my wife and so I care not. I *can* beat, if I try.

March.

1. Wednesday. Hebrews. This book is so much superior to the rest of Paul's epistles that I must think some one wrote it for him. The allusion to Melchisedec is most extraordinary and I scarce know what to make of it. Calvin Graves is now said not to have the small pox. Weather windy but not cold. Snows at times. Chess. A most degrading defeat. I grow quite ashamed of myself and must be getting old. *Ætatis suæ* 59th.

2. Thursday. Finished Hebrews and all of James. I like this last apostle. In my childhood he appeared to be a sort of relation, on account of his name. Day clear, but pretty cold. Chess as usual. Wife beat me again with a *dig!* I can only say that I play somewhat carelessly, for I dislike plodding over the board. Then Susy is so inwardly delighted to beat, while I care nothing about a defeat. *"So besser."*

3. Friday. First of Peter. Easterly weather and snow. March is likely to turn out a sleighing month. Old Adams is buried, and a good deal of old Adam with him, notwithstanding all their eulogies. He was a learned man, but his mind wanted a balance wheel. His father was much the abler man of the two. Chess, and I beat twice. Rather rappingly.

4. Saturday. Second of Peter. A good plain book. Weather clear and coldish, though not very cold. No frost on the windows. The wind blew fiercely in the night. The day has not been cold and the sleighing is good. The treaty is said to encounter difficulties in the Senate. I think we are now sure of Mexico's coming in, as deputies are said to be at Washington, to urge an ad-

mission into the Union, for three of the northern provinces. If so, the central government must come to.

5. Sunday. The three epistles of St. John, and that of St. Jude. The celebrated passage touching the divinity of Christ is so embedded in similar doctrine that it strikes me the whole chapter must go if those two verses go. But is not the entire new testament full of this doctrine? The pride of man makes him cavil at that which he cannot comprehend, while every thing he sees has a mystery in it! Church to-day in the forenoon.

6. Monday. Revelations. Milder, and snowing at intervals. The snow did not amount to much, but the weather is unpleasant. Chess. I beat twice rappingly, wife once, and one drawn game. Of course we played very fast, at which sport I usually get the best of it. One more bad case of small pox, Susan Brimmer the mantua-maker, a grand-daughter of my father's old gardener.

7. Tuesday. Revelations. Day clear and reasonably cold. Grew milder, and drove wife to Chalet. Pumpkin quite lame. The wind has got to the south, and promises a thaw. Town meeting to-day. It is a sad commentary on human wisdom that men quarrel just as much about these town offices as for those of the state, *giving the same reasons for it!* Chess and I beat.

8. Wednesday. Revelations. Ash Wednesday. Went to church. Uncommonly soft, spring-like weather. The snow goes very fast. Sleighing indeed gone. Looks like rain. No New York mail to-night, probably on account of the ice's moving at Albany. Received a copy of the report of Commissioners to revise practice of the courts. Many things in it that are good, and some that will never, never do!

9. Thursday. Revelations. Snowed in the night. Snowing more or less all day. Susan Brimmer is dead of the small pox, a most malignant case, the pustules filling with blood. She was vaccinated a few days before she was taken ill, and the pustule actually formed well, but it also filled with blood. Chess, mama beat.

10. Friday. Finished Revelations, a most extraordinary book. It is genuine beyond a question, from internal evidence, if from no other. Snowed a good deal to-day, and grew a little colder towards night. One or two more cases of small pox, but none very bad, now Adict, who has been at death's door, is recovering. Chess, I beat out and out. I think success depends on the humour.

11. Saturday. Genesis 5 chapters. A strange account! Yet much profound understanding of the subject in it. The weather is milder, and looks like a thaw. Went to the Chalet, not an egg. Stock doing so so, except Wm., our cow, which is sick. Four rapping games of chess. Two beat, two got beat. All played quickly. Wife is plucking up spirit, and often beats me when I little expect it.

12. Sunday. Genesis. A cold night. No church to-day, and read service at home. It grew milder towards noon, and began to rain in the evening. The accounts by to-day's mail say that the Senate has approved of the First treaty, with certain exceptions. Begins to rain, and threatens a thaw, and a break up. Mr. Van Schoak's letter came in Home Journal.

13. Monday. Genesis. Grew colder in the night, and has been all day, a most unpleasant chilling day, snowing a little. This month is very reluctant and cold, without being very cold. It is better for us, however, than warm weather. No papers to-night. Chess, beat and beat. A

long talk in the evening with Paul about Junius. He reasons well, and laughs at the notion of Horace Walpole having been Junius.

14. Tuesday. Genesis. A cold, disagreeably wintry day. The weather has now been good January weather for nearly the whole month. Went to the Chalet but got only three eggs. Found all my cattle eating *straw*, and my mans shut up, well supplied with the best of my hay! So the world wags. Chess, wifey rather walloped me. She enjoys success so much, I like to see her beat.

15 Wednesday. Genesis. A cold, cold night. The thermometer must have been down to something like ten above. Making ready to go to town. How wonderful is the sacrifice of Isaac by Abraham. Wife says the *place* is thought to be Calvary. Thermometer was *below* zero, this morning! Chess, both beating. Cold enough this evening.

16. Thursday. Genesis. What an extraordinary history! It is impossible for us to appreciate conduct, when a power like that of God is directly brought to bear on it. Obedience to him is our first law. Thermometer only 16° below zero this morning. Weather grows milder, however, this has been the coldest March I have ever known. Chess. Wifey gave an awful check-mate, then a drawn game, then I won the laurel.

17. Friday. Genesis—extraordinary! Extraordinary! Night not quite so cold as the last, but very wintry. Day clear, and sun has power. Thaws fast in the sun. I have postponed going below to next week. Nelson has got home, full of Washington news. 8° below zero this morning! Went to Chalet on the ice, cool ride.

18. Saturday. Genesis. The more I read of this book the more I feel convinced that sin is "transgression against the Law," and nothing else. Much milder. Thermometer at 20° *above*, at day-light, and thawing, though cloudy all day. Wind still at east. Chess, one game, I beat, when Judge Nelson came in, and sat until near ten. He is full of Washington news.

19. Sunday. Genesis. The history of Joseph. A colder night than the last, though not very cold. Day clear and bright, not a robin has yet made its appearance. The astounding news of a revolution in France has just reached us. I have always thought that Louis Philippe would have to decamp, and I expect yet to see the Duc de Bordeaux on the Throne. The rumor is that a republic is set up.

20. Monday. Finished Genesis. Much milder to-day, but drove wife to Chalet *via* the lake. Sleighing good on the lake, bad on the land. Preparing to go to town. Gave my orders on the farm and returned home to get ready for my journey. The papers continue to give us more tidings from France, all showing that the revolution is through. Chess, as usual, both beating.

21. Tuesday. This morning rose early, breakfasted and left home for town. Went in open wagon, with four horses. Roads not very bad, but covered with a light mud that spattered us all famously. Saved the cars by two hours. Reached Albany in good season, and went to Delavan House. The ice not started, but a steam-boat only five miles from Albany. Saw the Fishes.

22. Wednesday. Went to the capitol this morning, and examined documents in the library. Paid visits to my nieces, Alice and Georgeanne, promising to take them

home with me on my return. Met Maj. Douglas, and had a long talk with him. It is a pity so able a man should not have a permanent situation. Passed the evening with Stevenson, Mrs. Barnard and the Fishes, with lots of children being there. The ice moved off this morning, quietly and without damage.

23. Thursday. Went to see Barnard this morning. Said that he had seen J. Q. Adams last spring, at Washington. He then said our union would last about 8 years, "I shall not see it, but you may." On Barnard's telling him how well he looked, he answered, "Yes, I am pretty well now; but I shall die in about a year." He did die in about a year! Left Albany this afternoon in the steam boat.

24. Friday. Reached town in good season, and went to the Globe. Town dirty, dirty, dirty. Globe nearly empty. Distributed my papers, etc., and set about my affairs. Saw Griswold in the streets, who came home with me. *Jack Tier* is doing well; better than common. I went to see no one, where my business did not call me. In the afternoon left for Philadelphia, arriving at nine.

25. Saturday. Saw Fagan, who promised to let me off early in the week. Got all ready for operations. In the evening went to Charles Ingersoll's. Made a few other calls but found no one at home. Old Mrs. Cadwalader is dead, as is one of the Miss McCalls her sister. I do not think the country is much in advance of New York, or New York as much as usual in advance of Otsego. Sold bills to Fagan.

26. Sunday. I did not go to church to-day, but read in my room. Took a long walk before dinner, as far as Schuylkill, and meeting Mr. Timberlake, returned as far as the Delaware, thus crossing the peninsula twice, mak-

ing near five miles altogether. Went to see Dr. Hare in the evening. His children have all flitted and left him and his wife alone. They were in good spirits. Prime is at Naples.

27. Monday. Getting on rapidly with the volume, and shall be off to-morrow. Passed the day at home working, and the evening with Mutter. Met Mrs. McEwan for the first time, and her son. Passed a very pleasant evening. Mutter is well, and his wife grown into a very fine woman. Clever she always was, and will be. We had much amusing chat.

28. Tuesday. Finished off to-day, and got ready for a departure in the morning. I have made mistakes in en-tries, visiting Ingersoll Sunday, Hare Monday, and Mutter to-night. They all asked me to dine, but I excused myself on the plea of going away. No one seems to have much confidence in the immortality of the French repub-lic. Clark Hare visited me this morning.

29. Wednesday. Breakfasted, and was off at nine. Reached New York at one. Found letters, etc., and made my arrangements for leaving town to-morrow so as to get home on Friday or Saturday if the girls go up. This kept me busy making purchases and transacting business. It has been a working day with me, and I have got through with a great deal.

30. Thursday. This morning received letters which will compel me to remain here until Monday evening. Tire-some enough, but no help for it. Went to see Mrs. Ellet, found her in, and a nice little woman. Talked a great deal of her book. Then finished my purchases, and put my papers into John Jay's hands for preparation. He is to make a motion in court for me.

31. Friday. Loafing about. Met Capt. Breese, and went to look at some new steamers with him, the *United States* and the *Southerner*. Both fine vessels; particularly the first. Had another but a very short interview with Mrs. Ellet. Dined with Cruger nearly every day I have been here. His brother, Lewis, and sister, Caroline, are with him. Went to see Christie's minstrels this evening, with Cruger, and his two cousins.

April.

1. Saturday. Still loafing. This town is getting to be large. Last night I walked to twenty third street, with Miss Cruger and Miss Oakley, a distance of near three miles from the Globe. What is more we walked back again. This afternoon did almost as much more, with Cruger. We supported nature by ices and Roman punch, by the way. Every where I see signs of rapid growth, and of an improving taste.

2. Sunday. Went to Trinity this morning, and heard Dr. Haight. Sat in the Crugers' pew. Mrs. Heyward was third. Dined with Cruger. Peter Cruger, his sister Mrs. Heyward, Lewis Cruger, and myself were the guests. As usual, a good dinner, and a good glass of wine. Staid until nine, went home, and went to bed. Cruger and I took a long walk this forenoon, and afternoon; between 4 and 5.

3. Monday. To-day gave myself up to the business in court. It detained me until one. Then I got ready and packed up. Ran over to say good bye to the Crugers, and left the Globe at 5. Went on board *Isaac Newton*. Bought three noble shad. Found Roy Keese on board, who goes up before his parents, in order to get Edgewater in readiness.

4. Tuesday. Reached Albany early in the morning. Roy took charge of the shad and went on, while I repaired to the Delavan. Passed the day with Ned, and Major Douglas, paying a visit to the girls to let them know when to be ready. Stevenson has gone to Charleston, and when he is absent I find little to do in Albany. Saw Mrs. Fish and Mrs. Collins in the former's carriage.

5. Wednesday. Left Albany with Alice and Georgeanne at ½ past 7. Reached Fort Plain by 11, but could not get off until nearly 12. Went off in hired wagon, but met the stage on the hill. Changed passengers, and came wallowing on for nine mortal hours, to get through twenty two miles. I never knew the roads much worse. Reached Cooperstown at ½ past nine P. M.

6. Thursday. Tired enough to-day. Scarcely left the house. Distributed presents, however, and settled the quarter with my children. The spring is fairly opening. Find I have two calves, and all looking well. This evening the Keeses arrived, getting in about the same hour we did. Paul talks of venturing down.

7. Friday. Pleasant weather, and roads drying fast. To every body's astonishment mail came in at seven this evening. The improvement in the roads almost miraculous. I am preparing hot-beds, etc., and have set Collar fairly at work to make garden, certainly three weeks earlier than we were last year, hot beds excepted. Chess, as usual, both beating.

8. Saturday. This morning Paul was off. No doubt he got down in good season, as the mail was in before dark last night. At work in the garden. William was down yesterday and to-day to haul manure for the hot-beds. Got

most of them ready, and intend to get in many seeds next week. Chess, not much difference in the play.

9. Sunday. Exodus. Went to church this morning. One of the loveliest days of the season. Ice nearly gone, floating about in large cakes, but of no consistency. No snow worth mentioning any where to be seen, and every sign of an early spring. Mail in by four o'clock this afternoon. A change of five hours in four days!

10. Monday. Exodus. Another lovely day, even milder than that of yesterday. The ice has altogether disappeared, and we have the lake clear again. John at work with his hot-beds. Got in melons and various other seeds. Went to Chalet with wife, where the farm is getting a spring look. Joe Tom bought and took away the boar. Chess, each beat, and that ignominiously.

11. Tuesday. Another charming spring day. Exodus. Bill Collar came to work to-day, and we are making great progress with the garden. More news of revolutions in Europe. Austria is among the constitutional countries. All this is well, as the people must gain by publicity, and by having a voice in taxing. Chess. Both beat. We play very rapidly, and not very well.

12. Wednesday. Exodus. Another delightful day, though it rained towards ten at night. The grass on the lawn is starting, and a week will make us green. Still at the garden. Got asparagus beds spaded and cleaned, and put in divers early seeds. It may be too soon for their own good. Chess, both beat as usual.

13. Thursday. Exodus. Weather cooler, and a good deal of snow fell. At one time it looked like having a coat of white, but it soon disappeared. Salted my asparagus beds,

but no one worked in garden. It has not been a working day to-day, in any form. Papers still full of the late news. The king of Prussia seems to be playing a great game. A German nation is a great and useful idea! Chess.

14. Friday. Exodus. More snow, but does not whiten the ground. The earth must have been too warm for that. Collar and his son repairing fences. I had brine put on two of the asparagus beds this morning.

May.

13. Saturday. Numbers. Weather cool, and more rain towards evening. My planting gets on but slowly. Drove wife to Chalet, however, and went up to the new corn-field and so down the cliff, across the new meadow. The grass all looked unusually well. Towards evening it rained smartly, with a promise of its continuing all night. Chess. Only one game, which I got. No news this evening. Mexican treaty still in doubt.

14. Sunday. Numbers. Raining and cool. Most of us went to church, notwithstanding. About seventy persons attended. The Judge was there, having got home last evening. In the afternoon I read the service for my wife, who did not like to risk the weather. About five the wind went down, and it cleared. It seems as if all the clouds that passed in the last easterly storm, have been driven back by this from the west.

INDEX

Index.

Butler, Mrs. John. See Kemble, Fanny
Butler, Mrs. Pierce, 515
Byron, George Gordon, Lord, 182
Byron, Lady, 182
Byron, Moore's Life of, 182

Cadwalader, Thomas, 543-544, 617, 618, 676
Cady, Daniel, letter by, 486-487
Caledonia, The, 322
Calhoun, John C., 198, 268, 374
Campbell, William L., 582
Canada, 259-260, 303, 383
Canajoharie, 340-341
Canning, George, 102, 103, 104-105
Capital punishment, 174-175
Carey, H. C., 269, 330, 359, 365, 372, 379, 573, 574; letter by, 267-269
Carey, Lea & Carey (later Lea & Blanchard), 96, 153, 269, 359, 365, 372, 379, 395, 398, 400, 414, 431, 441, 443, 470, 484, 536, 607; letter from, 129-142
Carisbrooke Castle, 60
Carson River, 713-714
Carter, Mrs. Washington, 623, 624
Censorship, The Italian, 178-179
Cerro Gordo, 581

Chainbearer, The, 479, 552, 559, 561
Chalet, The, 436, 727, 728, 729, 730, 731, 732, 734, 735, 736, 737, 738, 743, 744, 745, 746, 751, 752
Charlemagne, 192, 193
Chauncey, Commodore, 374, 385
Cherry Valley, 17, 340, 341, 342
Chile, 629-630
Chinese novels, 644
Chingachgook, 58
Chodzko, 287-288, 331, 336-337
Chopin, Frederic, 255-256
Christian Year, The, 61
Churubusco, 581
Clark, Charles C., 705-706
Clark, Grosvenor, 571
Clarke, Gaylord, letter to, 590-591
Clarkson, Anne Maria, 647, 657
Clay, Henry, 59, 268, 310, 374, 733; letter by, 98-99; letter to, 97
Clergy, The, 499-500, 527-528, 535-536, 536-537, 551, 552, 553, 561, 604, 693, 694, 695, 696
Clinton, DeWitt, 113, 114; letters by, 97, 98
Closet Hall, 29
Coblenz, 192, 278, 281
Cole, Thomas, 49, 154, 182, 285, 305

Collier, John Allen, letter to, 304-305
Collins & Hannay, 130
Cologne, 191, 192, 246, 273, 278, 280, 282
Colossians, Epistle to the, 739
Columbia, The, 471
Columbus, Christopher, 588
Commercial Advertiser, The, 472, 500-501
Commercial Advocate, The, 298
Concord, The, 424, 426, 427, 428, 429, 433, 434
Conner, Captain David, 484, 543, 544, 574, 575; letter to, 453-455
Constant, Benjamin, 127
Constant, Mme. 265
Constantinople, 263, 264
Constitution, The, 394, 498, 550, 557
Contreras, 576, 581
Cooper, Anne Charlotte Fenimore, 20-21, 41-42, 43, 47, 64, 66, 67, 388, 390, 517, 519, 668, 670, 698, 715
Cooper, Ben, 647, 649-650, 651-652, 655, 657, 657-658, 659, 661, 661-662, 663, 666, 671, 678, 679, 680, 704, 717
Cooper, Mrs. Ben, 657-658, 671, 678
Cooper, Caroline Martha Fenimore, 14, 15, 19, 20, 21, 24, 28, 34, 43, 47, 48, 64, 66, 67, 101, 122, 163, 262, 388, 510, 515, 519, 601, 608, 610, 615, 649, 653, 658, 667, 668, 669,

670, 671, 672, 673, 695; letter by, 420-422; letter to, 599-600
Cooper, Elizabeth Fenimore, 10, 17, 22, 23, 29, 236
Cooper, Fenimore, 47, 51
Cooper, George H., 657
Cooper, George W., 657
Cooper, Gouldsborough, 56, 371, 727, 732, 736, 738, 739
Cooper, Hannah, 17, 335, 645-646
Cooper, Isaac, 12, 13, 14, 77, 86, 235; letter to, 78
Cooper, James Fenimore (1789-1851), at Angevine, 35 ff.; at Fenimore, 9-22; at Heathcote Hill, 23 ff.; birth of, 73, 76, 364; death of, 3, 479, 721-723; in Europe, 4-5, 60-72, 73, 100-324, 328, 334; in New York, 48 ff., 325, 327 ff.; in the Navy, 13-14, 68, 73, 75, 79-81, 490, 668; journals of, 3, 4-5, 725-752; libel suits of, 3, 325, 392-393, 394-395, 396, 414-418, 419, 419-420, 435-436, 450, 451-452, 457, 458-460, 461, 463, 464, 469-470, 470, 471, 472, 473-474, 475-476, 485, 485-487, 490, 492, 493, 494, 499, 537, 538, 539-540, 540-541, 569, 592-593; marriage of, 26-27, 73; literary, political, religious, and social opinions of, 97, 103, 133, 150, 151-153, 166, 169-170, 171, 180-182, 186, 204,

636-637, 671-672; quoted,
721-723. See also *Rural
Hours*
Cooper, Judge W i l l i a m
(father of James Fenimore
Cooper), 13, 14, 17, 18, 76,
88, 274, 335, 343, 363; letters to, 77, 78-79
Cooper, Mrs. William (wife
of the preceding), 12-13, 14,
15, 18, 21, 76, 343, 344, 363
Cooper, William (brother of
James Fenimore Cooper),
14, 19, 27, 52, 60, 83
Cooper, Mrs. William (widow
of the preceding), 643, 674
Cooper, William (nephew of
James Fenimore Cooper),
52, 56, 60, 68, 71, 158, 160,
162, 184, 186, 229, 231,
234; death of, 247, 249
Cooper, William ("Bill"),
369, 378, 426, 453-454; letter by, 711-715
Cooper, William (heir to
Three-Mile Point), 344
Cooperstown, 4, 9-22, 23, 40,
48, 49, 52, 73, 83, 229, 232,
234-236, 275, 313-314, 335,
341, 342-343, 343-344, 358,
366, 378, 413-414, 479, 519,
520, 521, 539, 548-549, 561,
580, 581, 625, 715-716, 721,
727-746, 750-752
Cooperstown, New Jersey, 363,
675
Corinthians, Epistles to the,
735, 736, 737, 738
Cory, Oliver, 233

Courier, The, 509, 510 ff., 567
Courier and Enquirer, The,
244, 457, 458
Cowboys, The, 43, 584
Cowes, 60, 64
Crater, The, 479, 572-573,
574, 588, 733
Crippen, Schuyler, 420; letter
to, 457
Critic, The, 182
Crosby, Enoch, 42, 684, 685
Cruger, Eliza, 639
Cruger, Henry Nicholas, 186-
187, 362, 398, 399, 409, 435,
469, 576, 587, 606-607, 614,
615, 616, 619, 625, 628, 636,
641, 643, 645, 646, 647, 650-
651, 655, 657, 660, 664, 665,
666, 667, 673, 676, 677, 678-
679, 681, 685, 687, 688, 707-
708, 749; letters by, 187-
190, 197-200, 206-226
Cruger, Mrs. Henry Nicholas
(Harriet Douglas), 142, 145,
409, 435, 469, 576, 605, 606-
607, 609, 615, 619, 645, 651,
652, 664, 677, 678-679, 681,
707-708
Cruger, Peter, 688, 689, 691,
693, 749
Curiosities of Literature, Dis-
raeli's, 733
Cyclopædia of Geography, 372

Daily Advertiser, The, 392
Dallas, George M., 529, 531-
532
Damas, Baron de, 102
Damas, Baroness de, 102, 105